The Making of Modern Kosovo

The Making of Modern Kosovo

Reassessing Ibrahim Rugova's Policy of Non-Violence

Jakup Azemi

BLOOMSBURY ACADEMIC

LONDON · NEW YORK · OXFORD · NEW DELHI · SYDNEY

BLOOMSBURY ACADEMIC
Bloomsbury Publishing Plc
50 Bedford Square, London, WC1B 3DP, UK
1385 Broadway, New York, NY 10018, USA
29 Earlsfort Terrace, Dublin 2, Ireland

BLOOMSBURY, BLOOMSBURY ACADEMIC and the Diana logo
are trademarks of Bloomsbury Publishing Plc

First published in Great Britain 2025

Library of Congress Cataloging-in-Publication Data
Names: Azemi, Jakup author
Title: The making of modern Kosovo : reassessing Ibrahim Rugova's
policy of non-violence / Jakup Azemi.
Description: London ; New York : Bloomsbury Academic, 2025. |
Includes bibliographical references and index. | Summary: "Explores how the
independent state of Kosovo was built, not only through the success of the war of
1998-1999, but also through Ibrahim Rugova's decade-long policy Policy of
non-violence, which led to NATO intervention and international support for the
creation of modern independent Kosovo"– Provided by publisher.
Identifiers: LCCN 2024052802 (print) | LCCN 2024052803 (ebook) |
ISBN 9781350460058 hardback | ISBN 9781350460065 paperback |
ISBN 9781350460072 epub | ISBN 9781350460089 ebook
Subjects: LCSH: Kosovo (Republic)–History–Autonomy and independence
movements | Kosovo (Republic)–Politics and government–1980-2008 | Kosovo War,
1998-1999 | Nonviolence–Kosovo (Republic) | Rugova, Ibrahim, 1944-2006
Classification: LCC DR2086 .A94 2025 (print) | LCC DR2086 (ebook) |
DDC 949.719/024–dc23/eng/20250313
LC record available at https://lccn.loc.gov/2024052802
LC ebook record available at https://lccn.loc.gov/2024052803

ISBN: HB: 978-1-3504-6005-8
           PB: 978-1-3504-6006-5
           ePDF: 978-1-3504-6008-9
           eBook: 978-1-3504-6007-2

Typeset by Integra Software Services Pvt. Ltd.
Printed and bound in Great Britain

For product safety related questions contact productsafety@bloomsbury.com

To find out more about our authors and books visit www.bloomsbury.com
and sign up for our newsletters.

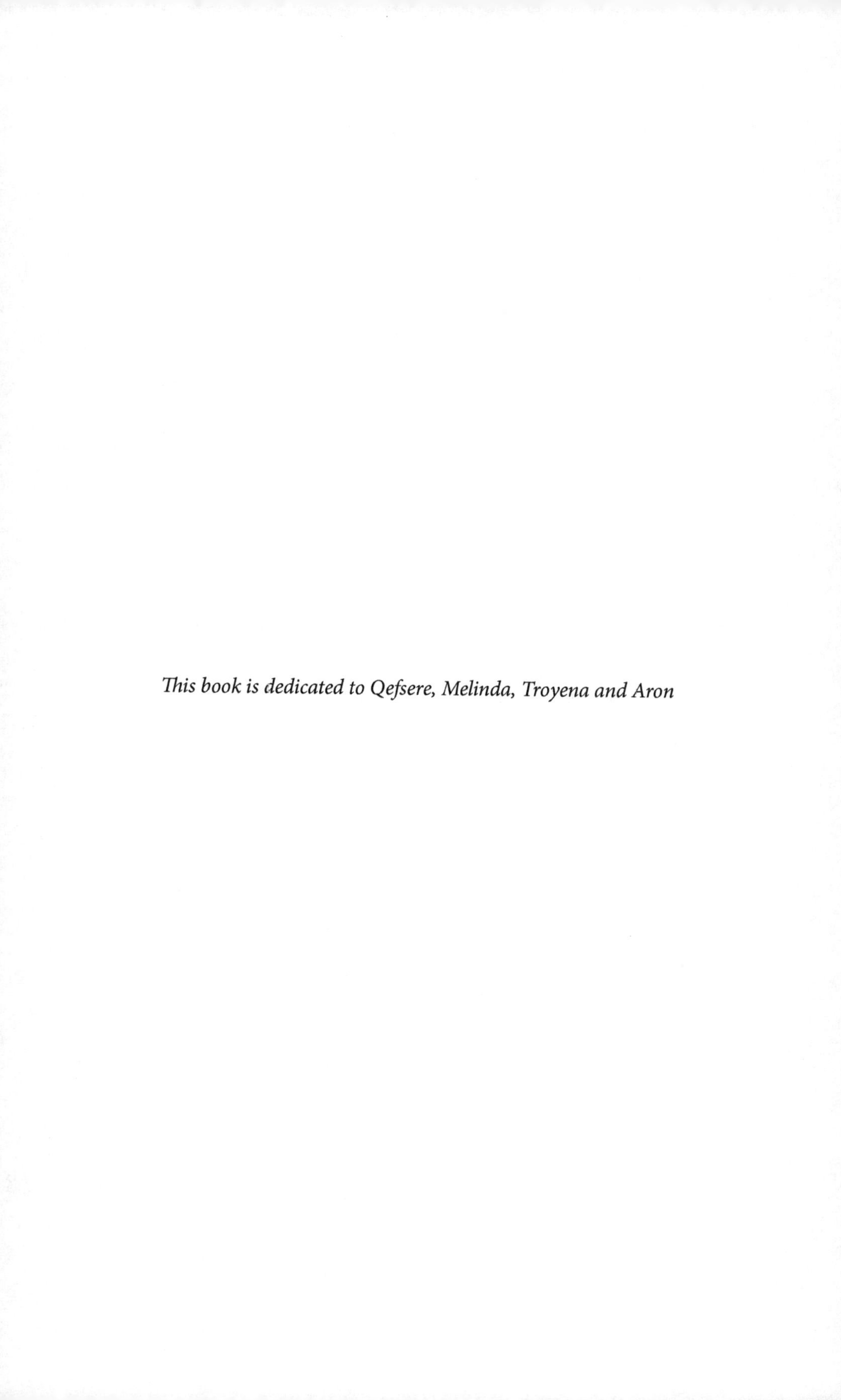

This book is dedicated to Qefsere, Melinda, Troyena and Aron

Contents

Figure

Preface

This book has been developed from my PhD thesis on Ibrahim Rugova's policy of non-violence in Kosovo during the 1990s. While I was completing the final draft of my thesis, and then later giving shape to this book, I relived the events of the late 1980s and early 1990s that gave rise to Rugova's policy of non-violence. I realized that this was about more than just writing a book on how modern Kosovo took shape: it was also about myself and hundreds of thousands of other Kosovo Albanians. Rugova's non-violence not only shaped my intellectual upbringing, it also saved me and hundreds of thousands of, mostly, ethnic Albanians from losing our hopes of living in peace and freedom.

As a first-year law student at the University of Prishtina in 1988–9, I witnessed the Serbian authorities, under the most unprecedented circumstances, gain increasing power in the Socialist Federal Republic of Yugoslavia by dismantling the political autonomy Kosovo had enjoyed since 1974 and implementing discriminatory policies against the Albanian community, Kosovo's majority population. They sought to crush our hopes of continuing our cultural, economic and political development. It was a concerted effort by the Serbs to forcibly incorporate Kosovo into its political system, once and for all. The removal of autonomy sent a clear message to the Kosovo Albanians: accept Serbian rule and/or leave Kosovo. This was deemed legitimate by the Serbs, who for over a century had held the false perception that Kosovo historically belonged to Serbia and should again be part of it. In this discourse, a series of myths were invented, and reinvented, leading to some of the most bizarre claims one could imagine against the Albanians. But Albanians were not prepared to settle for that predicament. The proceeding ten years witnessed the mobilization of a resilient movement of non-violence led by Ibrahim Rugova which was nothing less than monumental. While refusing to fall into the Serbian trap of a violent conflict, Rugova's strategy derailed Serbia's goals. As a student, I participated in many peaceful protests and witnessed years of tumult, while having to vacate university premises and dormitories and become part of a 'parallel-state system'.

Although events in Kosovo were overshadowed by conflicts raging elsewhere in the Former Yugoslavia for most of the 1990s, by 1998–9 Kosovo had moved to the top of the international agenda. The determination to confront aggressive Serbian nationalism went far beyond just Kosovo's Albanian community, as illustrated by the fact that NATO, the world's largest international military alliance, intervened against Milosevic's forces. Creating and maintaining peace in Kosovo was rightly deemed essential not only for the survival of the Albanian population of Kosovo but for stability in the southeastern region of Europe as a whole. It is my firm belief that analysing the origins and strategy of the organic civil resistance movement that engaged in the most formidable political battle Kosovo Albanians have ever waged in their quest for freedom and independence matters; this is what I have endeavoured to do.

Acknowledgements

This book would have not been possible without the help of, and contribution from, various professional people, colleagues, friends and family members whom I should mention here.

The bulk of the material in this book formed part of my PhD thesis, which I completed at University College London, the School of Slavonic and East European Studies. I was privileged to have had the opportunity to do my research there under the supervision of Professor Eric Gordy, who guided me over various hurdles with his professional and imaginative mentorship. I have benefited from various personnel at the school, including Dr Felix Ciuta, Dr Titus Hjelm, Dr Ger Duijzings and Dr Philip Cavendish.

Special credit is reserved for my interviewees, who were participants in Rugova's non-violent movement, various political activists in Kosovo during the 1990s and military men. They include Professor Ali Aliu, Dr Bujar Bukoshi, Dr Edita Tahiri, Dr Milazim Krasniqi, Dr Rexhep Gjergji, Dr Mentor Agani, Dr Alush Gashi, Shaip Latifi, Lirije Kajtazi, Blerim Shala, Hafiz Gagica, Xhafer Shatri, Musa Jupolli, Hydajet Hyseni, Skender Hyseni, the late Ramush Tahiri, Ilaz Ramajli, Dr Sabri Kiçmari, Dr Rifat Haxhiaj, Rrustem Mustafa (Remi), Gani Geci, Ibrahim Kelmendi, Ismet Abdullahu, Ismet Ibishi, Saim Tahiraj and Asdren Idrizaj.

Particular credit is reserved for the late Dr Sami Repishti, Dr Muhamet Hamiti, Dr Skender Zogaj, Anton Kolaj, Professor Nicholas Pano, Dr Kujtim Mani, Dr Aidan Hehir and Dr Nicola Guy. They were available to me on multiple occasions with interviews and various resources, comments, feedback and help as I prepared the manuscript. A very special credit goes to Francis Bennett, who helped me publish this book.

Other contributors whom I would like to acknowledge include Dr Ibrahim Berisha, Dr John Hodgson, Dr Kaltërina Latifi, Dr Blerim Reka, Dr Gëzim Krasniqi, Frank Shkreli, Fehmi Ismaili, Ibush Jonuzi, Ismet Beqiri, Bajram Mjeku and Ibish Neziri.

I am particularly grateful to the director of the City Library of Prishtina, Dr Munish Hyseni, for his assistance with the literature, as well as to Safet Zejnullahu for his sources and contacts.

Finally, my family, my brothers and sisters, and also other relatives and friends who have given me constant moral support and encouragement over the many years I have been writing my thesis and the book deserve special thanks.

Abbreviations

AACL	The Albanian American Civic League
AI	Amnesty International
AK	Alternativa Kosovare (Kosovo Alternative)
AWK	Association of Writers of Kosovo
AWS	Association of Writers of Serbia
BSPK	Bashkimi i Sindikatave të Pavaraura të Kosovës (Independent Trade Union of Kosovo)
CCAPP	Coordinating Council of Albanian Political Parties
CCAPPY	Coordinating Council of Albanian Political Parties in Yugoslavia
CCLCS	Central Committee of League of Communists of Serbia
CCLCY	Central Committee of the League of Communists of Yugoslavia
EPCY	European Peace Conference for Yugoslavia
EU	European Union
FARK	Forcat e Armatosura të Republikës së Kosovës (Defence Forces of the Republic of Kosovo)
FCO	Foreign and Commonwealth Office (UK)
FKB	Fronti i Kuq i Bashkuar (United Red Front)
FRY	Federal Republic of Yugoslavia
FYROM	Former Yugoslav Republic of Macedonia
KDOM	Kosovo Diplomatic Observer Mission
KFOR	Kosovo Force
KKPPSH	Këshilli Koordinues i Partive Politike Shqiptare (Coordinating Council of Albanian Political Parties)

KLA	Kosovo Liberation Army
KMDLNJ	Këshilli për Mbrojtjen e të Drejtave dhe të Lirive të Njeriut (Council for the Defence of Human Rights and Freedoms in Prishtina)
KVM	Kosovo Verification Mission
LBD	Lëvizja e Bashkuar Demokratike (United Democratic Movement)
LCK	League of Communists of Kosovo
LCY	League of Communists of Yugoslavia
LDK	Lidhja Demokratike e Kosovës (Democratic League of Kosovo)
LPK	Lëvizja Popullore e Kosovës (Popular Movement of Kosovo)
LPRK	Lëvizja Popullore për Republikën e Kosovës (Popular Movement for the Republic of Kosovo)
MoD	Ministry of Defence (UK)
NAAC	National Albanian-American Council
NAC	North Atlantic Council
NATO	North Atlantic Treaty Organization
OMLK	Organizata Marksiste Leniniste e Kosovës (Marxist-Leninist Organization of Kosovo)
OSCE	Organization for Security and Co-operation in Europe
PCCLCY	Presidency of the Central Committee of the League of Communists of Yugoslavia
PKMLSHJ	Partia Komuniste Marksiste Leninste e Shqiptarëve në Jugosllavi (Marxist-Leninist Communist Party of Albanians in Yugoslavia)
PPK	Partia Parlamentare e Kosovës (Kosovo Parliamentary Party)
QIK	Qendra e Informimit të Kosovës (Kosovo Information Centre)
SAWP	Socialist Alliance for Working People
SFRY	Socialist Federal Republic of Yugoslavia
SHIK	Shërbimi Informativ Kombëtar (Albanian information service)

SNC	Strategic Non-violent Conflict framework
UJDI	Udruženje za Jugoslavensku Demokratsku Inicijativu (Association for the Yugoslav Democratic Initiative)
UNIKOMB	Uniteti Kombëtar (Party of Albanian National Union)
UNMIK	United Nations Interim Administration Mission in Kosovo
YPA	Yugoslav People's Army

Introduction

When the Republic of Serbia abolished Kosovo's[1] autonomy in 1989, not many people who understood the political realities in the Former Yugoslavia could have anticipated the turn of events in Kosovo. While violence was burgeoning elsewhere in Yugoslavia, Ibrahim Rugova (1944–2006), an ethnic Albanian intellectual, emerged on the political scene in Kosovo and gave the Albanians' political efforts a different direction. Along with a group of Albanian cultural intellectuals mostly centred on the Kosovo Writers' Association (KWA), Rugova formed a political party, the Democratic League of Kosovo (Lidhja Demokratike e Kosovës – LDK), and launched a policy of non-violence vis-à-vis Serbia. This political movement changed the destiny of Kosovo Albanians and Kosovo, while giving a different dynamic to the Kosovo conflict.

Since its incorporation under Serbian and Yugoslav control in 1912–13, when Kosovo was carved out of the Albanian state that was eventually recognized at the 1913 London Conference of Ambassadors,[2] Kosovo Albanians have suffered continuously, owing to the violence and repressive measures inflicted on them by various Yugoslav and Serb governments. It is only their high birth rate and their survival instinct that have enabled Albanians to sustain their ethnic identity in Kosovo. When violent military action fell short of success, a series of detailed memorandums and elaborate blueprints were designed by such Serb intellectuals as the Nobel Prize winner for literature Ivo Andrić (1892–1975), with his blueprint 'Draft on Albania', published in 1939,[3] and political and cultural institutions, including the Serb Academy of Sciences and Arts with their famous 1986 memorandum[4] for 'resolving' the Kosovo issue. These were efforts to ethnically cleanse Albanians from Kosovo, or reduce their presence in the Albanian-inhabited lands in the Former Yugoslavia to an insignificant number that would not pose any threat to Serb control of Kosovo. Among the most transparent of these are the two so-called *elaborates* produced by the Serb scholar and politician Vaso Čubrilović, who, in 1914, as a student had participated in the assassination in Sarajevo of Archduke Ferdinand of Austria-Hungary, an event that sparked the First World War. His first memorandum appeared in 1937, entitled 'The Expulsion of the Albanians',[5] only seven years later, on 3 November 1944, presenting his other blueprint, 'The Minority Problem in the New Yugoslavia: Memorandum'.[6] Čubrilović's principal aim was to expel Albanians and colonize Kosovo with Serbs. In his 1944 memorandum he called for the expulsion of some 40,000 Albanian families, the number suggesting a population of roughly 200,000, but as the historian Noel Malcolm has pointed out, the outbreak of the Second World War prevented this from happening.[7] The re-confirmation of Yugoslav sovereignty over Kosovo after the Second World War placed the Albanians' fate yet again in the hands of Yugoslav and Serb control.

It is believed that the discretional use of ruthless methods against Albanians by the then Yugoslav Interior Minister of Serb Nationality, Alexandar Ranković (1909–83), immediately after the Second World War, was a direct consequence of Čubrilović's blueprints. According to some estimates, during the period 1953–66 alone, while Ranković was in office, around 80,000 Albanians were forced to leave Yugoslavia.[8] Relying on Yugoslav and Serbian sources, a recent publication shows that between 1912 and 1966, at least 55,371 Albanians were killed and 565,392 were forced to emigrate from Kosovo. This means that in just over five decades there were at least 620,763 fewer Albanians in Kosovo as a result of killings and mass expulsions.[9] This is a staggering number, considering that in 1920 the Albanian population in the whole of Yugoslavia counted somewhere between 700,000 and 800,000 (Yugoslav official census sources give a much smaller number – 288,900 Albanians in Kosovo over the same period).[10] The trend of decrease in the Albanian population under violence is further illustrated if we look at this phenomenon from a different angle: the Yugoslav census of 1961, which shows a total number of 646,805 Albanians in Kosovo, but in two decades this number had almost doubled – according to the 1981 Yugoslav census, the Albanian population had risen to 1,226,736.[11] This explains the fact that when the repressive measures and expulsion policies stopped or slowed down, the Albanian population increased dramatically. Only when the Yugoslav leader, of Croatian nationality, Josip Broz Tito removed Ranković from office in 1966 and increased Albanians' rights in the form of substantial autonomy in 1974 did their conditions start to change. Kosovo became a full constituent member of the Yugoslav Federation, along with six other republics and the province of Vojvodina. Evidently, this move had left many Serbs angry, whose hopes for effective control over Kosovo were derailed – at least temporarily.

The death of Tito in 1980 left Yugoslavia with an uncertain future, but it also provided the opportunity for Serb nationalists to map out strategies with a view to establishing their supremacy over the rest of the country. The first destination was Kosovo, whose autonomy was to be reversed; control over Kosovo was to be reinstated and resolved once and for all. A two-fold campaign was launched: first, it involved a publicity and propaganda campaign that aimed at demonizing the Albanians and qualifying them as 'not fit to rule Kosovo; therefore the autonomy they enjoyed had to be removed'. In line with this view, large numbers of Kosovo Albanians were imprisoned and tortured immediately after 1981 following massive protests by Albanians on the streets of Kosovo for their political demands. By the mid-1980s a practice of accusations against and demonization of Albanians had reached hysterical levels; some of these will be elaborated on later in this book. It is this political and propagandistic mobilization that prepared the ground for the removal of Kosovo's autonomy of 1974, an action that was carried out in 1989 by Serbia under the leadership of Slobodan Milošević.

This constitutional and political reversal, largely amid silence from the other republics of Yugoslavia, presented Kosovo Albanians with a very bleak cultural, political and existential future. Just over one and a half million Albanians in a territory of less than 11,000 square kilometres faced an historic dilemma: fight against Serbia, which had the most effective access to the federal institutions of Yugoslavia, including significant control over the Yugoslav People's Army, arguably the fourth most powerful military in Europe, or accept its destiny as prescribed by the Serb regime.

Traditionally, Albanians have never hesitated to fight their oppressors, and there was no reason to wonder how they would respond to this precarious predicament either. For those less informed, it is worth mentioning that before the Ottomans left the Balkans in 1912–13, it was the Albanians who fought them much more than their Balkan neighbours. The British politician and traveller to the Ottoman provinces in the Balkans Aubrey Herbert stated: it was the Albanians and not the Serbs, or Bulgars, or 'Greeks who defeated the Turks',[12] and yet they ended up the worst off, arguably owing to their untimely choice to fight, which was well before their neighbours did.

The intensity of Albanian protests in the streets of Kosovo increased, and the momentum was seemingly rising, while the Serbian authorities eagerly responded with violence. However, an unexpected political turn in Kosovo came about in the form of the policy of non-violence led by the Kosovo Albanian intellectual Ibrahim Rugova, which gave the Kosovo conflict a radically different dynamic. Focusing on almost a decade of Rugova's policy of non-violence, the present book explains how this peaceful discourse took place, and how it successfully guided Kosovo through the turmoil of the Yugoslav wars, and how, in the process, Rugova created a cultural and political environment in Kosovo, where a new political identity for Kosovo took shape and the idea of Kosovo's independence developed. Moreover, the book shows how, building on cultural and historical legacies, Rugova was able to create a movement of resistance by non-violent means, which was a novelty not only for Albanians but for the whole Balkan region. A modest social movement (the Slovenian Peace Movement) was evident in Slovenia during the 1980s, but its effects were marginal[13] and cannot be compared to Rugova's movement.

Furthermore, the book examines and explains the effects of Rugova's parallel state beyond what has become a simple narrative of Rugova's parallel-state system providing social, medical and education needs: the effects of the parallel state were much more than this. It had a profound impact on developing the idea of a state, created a democratic culture and gave cohesion to elite and non-elite perceptions of the idea of Kosovo's independence, which was a crucial factor in pursuing the political battle towards the ultimate objective – precisely, the independence of Kosovo. Subsequently, the book offers an extensive analysis of how Rugova's parallel state launched a successful international diplomatic and information campaign that aimed at internationalizing the conflict of Kosovo. The result of Rugova's policy of non-violence was that he successfully pulled Kosovo out from the marginalization that Serbia had placed it in, established a culture of resistance, created the parallel state and brought international attention to the conflict of Kosovo. The foundations of statehood were thus created by this movement.

Despite Rugova's political campaign, independence for Kosovo was not achieved; this, along with several other factors, spawned the rise of violent actions by the KLA, which led to the decline of Rugova and of his policy of non-violence. The disproportionate response from Yugoslav–Serbian[14] forces escalated the conflict and subsequently triggered an international response. The international community, through the so-called Contact Group, consisting of the United States, the UK, France, Russia, Germany and Italy, spent over a year in diplomatic efforts to reach a political settlement, including the organization of a peace conference at Rambouillet, France, in February 1999.

Therefore, after the failure of the peace conference organized by the Contact Group, the international community, through the North Atlantic Treaty Organization (NATO), intervened in Kosovo with military action, compelling Yugoslav forces to vacate the region and establishing a United Nations (UN) presence there. Almost ten years of a policy of non-violence under Rugova's leadership was then condemned as failure, thus consolidating the widely held perception that violence remained the only model for resolving ethnic conflicts in the Balkan region.[15] During the many years that the policy of non-violence lasted, the main international players unreservedly supported Rugova and his strategy. However, in the competition for power among different groups, these same international players shifted their support in favour of the KLA over the LDK, thus contributing to a further strengthening of the KLA's grip on power. This new constellation of powers enabled the Popular Movement of Kosovo (Lëvizja Popullore e Kosovës – LPK), a Marxist-Leninist and Enverist[16] organization, which controlled the KLA, to exploit the political and institutional vacuum created by the withdrawal of Federal Republic of Yugoslavia (FRY) forces on the one hand and the neutralization of Rugova's parallel-state structures on the other. Thus began a new chapter in the history of Kosovo, which many saw as having started with the KLA's rise to power shortly before, and Rugova and his role in the LDK were forgotten. Necessary co-operation between key international players, including NATO, with the KLA powerholders seemingly placed the two parties on the same page, bestowing on the latter the much-desired legitimacy for their claim that it was the LPK-led KLA[17] that had won the war and set Kosovo on the path to independence. In line with this view, a set of changes, including the renaming of Kosovo's cities and streets, took place,[18] while the mere mention of Rugova's name and that of his party, the LDK, was associated with failure, and at times even represented risk.[19]

Against this background, the international community went on to establish a temporary UN administration over Kosovo, suspending Yugoslav and Serbian control over it, before it sponsored Kosovo's independence in February 2008. The independence of Kosovo, as a political outcome, was thus attributed to the international community and to the military structures of the KLA.

The arguments put forward in this book take an alternative perspective: although the LPK-led KLA escalated the conflict, taking it out of the LDK's control, which eventually led the international community to intervene in Kosovo militarily, it was Ibrahim Rugova, with his strategy of non-violence, who created the state structures and a framework of domestic and international political support that laid the groundwork for the independent state of Kosovo. Moreover, the book provides an analysis surrounding the emergence of the military structures that later came to be known as the KLA, and challenges the dominant view that the KLA and the military option in Kosovo were a non-LDK entity, respectively associated solely with the LPK.

The book therefore sheds light on a significant part of Kosovo's political history and its association with the Yugoslav crisis, which arguably started in Kosovo and may have returned to Kosovo with even greater force.[20] The bulk of the scholarship consulted is dominated by the effects of NATO's intervention in 1999[21] and thereafter, which led to a discussion of Kosovo from the perspective that a military explanation for the Kosovo conflict was more compelling than a political one. Also, much of the literature was focused on the post-1999 period, which was concerned with the UN Interim Administration Mission in Kosovo (UNMIK), and not with local political history prior to the installation of the international administration.[22] Equally, authors who have dealt with Rugova's policy of non-violence, with the exception of Marie François Allain and Xavier Galmiche's *La Question du Kosovo/Ibrahim Rugova*, approach the subject with the assumption that that policy failed or was only marginally successful.[23] There is a more nuanced acknowledgement of Rugova's policy of non-violence by a few Albanian authors, but their approaches remain limited in terms of the scope of the subject, and at times their views take on a hagiographic character.[24] These dominant approaches, therefore, have eclipsed the significance of local political actors, such as the role of Kosovo Albanians and their political organization around the LDK and Rugova's policy of non-violence, spanning almost a decade, a period that forms arguably the most critical part of Kosovo's political history.

Having established the necessity for a different approach to Rugova's policy of non-violence, and the political events that led to the independence of Kosovo, I lay out the case for a specific focus, namely an historical approach with cultural interventions, which includes research from archival sources and oral history by the actors who participated in these events to tell the story in this book. This narrative shows how Rugova was able to create a culture of resistance in which the cultural and political identity of Kosovo took shape. It shows how Rugova masterfully drew on Albanian historical and cultural legacies, and how he gave a different interpretation of these to Kosovo Albanians, as peaceful and democratic, countering stereotypes applied to them by Serbian propaganda as violent and incapable.

The structure of the book

Following on from the above introduction, the rest of the book is structured as follows:

In Chapter 1, I examine the political circumstances that influenced the rise of Ibrahim Rugova in politics and the emergence of the policy of non-violence. I first describe the political environment created in Kosovo as a result of relentless pressure and intrusive policies and publicity against Albanians from Serbian cultural and political institutions following the 1981 Albanian demonstrations that demanded the status of a republic for Kosovo. The failure of the League of Communists of Kosovo (LCK) to respond more vigorously to intrusive Serbian policies, which resulted in the transformation of the conflict from political institutions into cultural clashes, forms a critical part of this chapter. More specifically, the chapter looks at the response of Kosovo writers to Serbian ones, who visibly colluded with the official Serbian political discourse, a confrontation that brought Kosovo writers to the forefront, and eventually taking the national interests into their own hands. This led to the formation of the LDK, with Ibrahim Rugova, then the head of the Association of Writers of Kosovo (AWK). The relevance of this chapter centres on the introduction of Rugova into politics, and how he institutionalized Albanian political demands through peaceful means and averted violent clashes between the Albanian and Yugoslav authorities. Rugova's success in introducing the policy of non-violence to Albanians is explained through the theory of symbolic power as developed by Pierre Bourdieu.

The cultural environment that enabled the emergence of Rugova's policy of non-violence is elaborated in **Chapter 2**. I first examine the challenges to the Albanian cultural and political elites in responding to Yugoslav and Serbian propaganda that portrayed Albanians with a set of negative stereotypes, a discourse in which the political, academic and religious institutions of Serbia colluded. I then examine the Albanian cultural and historical legacies on which Rugova built his non-violence approach, which forms the crux of this chapter. I show here how Rugova was able to build a political movement that incorporated issues related to Albanian identity and culture, and that interpreted Albanian tradition as non-violent and secular, which was in a stark contrast to interpretations by their Serbian–Yugoslav opponents. This new approach also meant that the policy of non-violence was a more successful strategy in achieving political and national goals than violent means – practices that historically had proved ineffective for Albanians. This chapter also examines Rugova's linguistic toolkit, which was inclusive of various audiences, as well as a series of symbols of state he introduced that completed the infrastructure and added to the cohesion of his parallel state. This chapter sets the scene upon which the rest of the book proceeds.

Chapter 3 deals with the development of the parallel state. Here I use the concept of legitimacy as a framework to explain the effectiveness of Rugova's parallel state. I then examine the political dynamics in which the process of the institutional set-up took place under the LDK and Rugova's leadership, using the democratic principles and popular support that the two enjoyed. I argue that the popular support the LDK and the parallel state gained resulted in a delegitimizing of the Serbian presence in Kosovo while instituting their own popular legitimacy in Kosovo. Subsequently, I explain how this popular legitimacy was reaffirmed through elections and a referendum for Kosovo independence with massive participation of the population. A series of functions that the parallel state fulfilled for nearly a decade, including social, health and educational needs, in addition to being an instrument that helped maintain unity among different Albanian political fractions and ideologies, are examined in this chapter.

The chapter concludes that while the parallel state fell short of being a complete state, it was instrumental in creating the conviction among elites and the population alike that the independence of Kosovo was not only possible, but its complete realization was just a matter of time.

Chapter 4 examines how Rugova's policy of non-violence internationalized the conflict of Kosovo. Internationalization here refers to a process characterized by a series of purposeful actions to draw international political and public attention to the status of Kosovo. Kosovo was a small region populated by an Albanian majority, which had suffered from economic backwardness and from the stereotypes that Yugoslav–Serbian propaganda cast upon them. As such, internationalization of the Kosovo conflict, as argued in this chapter, formed one of the key objectives of Rugova's non-violence policy. It derived from the strategic calculation that a diplomatic and information campaign would be the most effective way to get Kosovo onto the international agenda and ensure international help to resolve the Kosovo conflict by non-violent means, while preserving the population. I first enumerate the challenging factors the LDK leadership was faced with, before I examine their strategy to target a series of such players as international media, political actors, intellectuals and activists, as well as the Catholic Church. The chapter concludes that Rugova's parallel state created an exceptionally effective information and diplomatic campaign, which elevated Kosovo from a zone that required improvements in the human rights domain, into an international issue that required specific international attention. Despite remarkable success, it fell short of the goal – bringing in the international community in the form of a protectorate to avoid the violence, and facilitate a political process for a transitional phase before Kosovo would gain independence, as Rugova for years had campaigned to achieve.

Chapter 5 deals with the transformation of the conflict from non-violent to violent. It first outlines the challenges that Rugova's non-violence strategy was faced with, followed by a detailed analysis of the emergence of the guerrilla groups that came to be known as the KLA, a military wing of the Marxist-Leninist groups. The interviews and other primary sources examined showed, however, that it was the structures of Rugova's parallel state that provided military training in the early 1990s and formed the military units, but their use was placed on hold before the LPK took ownership of these groups and formed the KLA. A detailed analysis is provided as to how this process unfolded. When militant actions (such as shootings) by the KLA became more frequent, a disproportionate response from Yugoslav forces followed, a dynamic that left many dead, mostly civilians, forcing the international community to become more directly involved in the conflict. This is when Rugova's policy of non-violence began to lose its influence. When, finally, it had appeared that Rugova's lobbying activities had succeeded, the same lobbyists shifted their support to the KLA. This shift was further consolidated during the international conference for Kosovo organized at Rambouillet, France, in February 1999. For the first time in his political career, Rugova was outnumbered by non-LDK individuals, including independent political representatives of Kosovo, who were now gravitating towards the KLA. In this way, members of the LPK and the KLA seemingly established their supremacy and, when the war ended, after NATO's intervention, acted as though it was they who had freed Kosovo.

Chapter 6 provides an analysis of why it is that Rugova's policy of non-violence in fact led Kosovo to independence, despite the KLA having escalated the conflict. Several factors that sustain this argument are enumerated here. First, I explain how Rugova's political movement transformed the political environment in Kosovo, whereby Albanians could institutionalize their political demands, and the idea of independence was born. In doing this, Rugova's policy led to the creation of Kosovo's parallel state, which gave Albanians' political organization a legitimacy in their political representation in the world. The third argument builds on the internationalization of the Kosovo issue. I argue that before Rugova's political campaign Kosovo was known very marginally by the international community, but it was his political campaign and lobbying activity in the world that changed the perceptions of various political actors, international human rights organizations, media, academics and political analysts reporting on Kosovo, which in turn led to the Kosovo issue being presented as a crisis that required international attention far beyond the human rights domain in which Kosovo was initially considered. However, violence as an internationalization variable, the fourth factor, became a component, and it necessarily accelerated the conflict of Kosovo to the top of the agenda of the international community. Nevertheless, despite the LPK, who eventually came to control the military option in Kosovo, I maintain that it was Rugova's political battle and his parallel-state structures that formed the basis on which the LPK–KLA built and eventually claimed the merits of the victory.

In my last, fifth argument I include a section on Rugova's political legacy.

Chapter 7 ties up the book in the form of a summary of all the chapters.

1

The rise of Ibrahim Rugova and the emergence of his policy of non-violence

Introduction

The principal aim of this chapter is to analyse the circumstances that led to the rise of Ibrahim Rugova in Kosovo politics. The chapter begins with a review of the legacy of the 1981 Kosovo Albanian protests that demanded a republic of Kosovo in Yugoslavia. The protests led the League of Communists of Yugoslavia (LCY) to define them as counter-revolutionary;[1] they were followed with punitive measures that had profound effects on hundreds of protesters and their families. These effects spread into other parts of the population and other sectors in the province. Ultimately, the goal of the LCY, dominated by Serbian discourse, became the opposite of the 1981 protesters' demands – a review of the Kosovo autonomy of 1974. After a long battle with the Yugoslav–Serbian[2] political leadership, the Kosovo political elite lost its power and ability to defend the province's constitutional status. It is these circumstances that led to the emergence of Kosovo's intellectual elite centred around the KWA. The chairman of the KWA, Dr Ibrahim Rugova, stood out, thanks to his critical intellectual approach and his predisposition resolving the problems in Kosovo between Albanians and Serbs by peaceful and democratic means.

However, in 1989, when Serbia recentralized its powers over two provinces, Kosovo and Vojvodina, Kosovo Albanians refused to accept the outcome of their downgraded status. A series of protests and a general strike followed, resulting in many Albanians being killed by the Yugoslav and Serbian security forces. This situation of political breakdown and social unrest resulted in the necessity for a new political force in Kosovo, which was manifested with the formation of the LDK under the leadership of Ibrahim Rugova. The central argument in this chapter is that Ibrahim Rugova and his innovative, non-violence approach, despite a traditional culture of resistance by violent means, appealed to the

Albanian population, which subsequently enabled Rugova to avert a military conflict in Kosovo and wage a political battle instead.

The chapter is organized as follows: first, I elaborate on the legacy of the Kosovo Albanian protests of 1981 and the administrative and political measures taken in response by the LCY. The shift of political debates to the intellectual level forms the second part of the chapter, where I highlight the vastly different views on Kosovo between Serbs and Albanians. In the third part, Serbia's actions in abolishing Kosovo's autonomy and Albanian reactions are analysed. Lastly, I examine the rise of Rugova and the political turn following his principle of non-violence.

The Albanian protests of 1981 as a prologue to the Kosovo crisis

A serious, scholarly approach to Rugova's political campaign would have to begin with a review of the circumstances that prepared the ground for his rise in the political scene in Kosovo. Examining Kosovo's political history of the second part of last century arguably should start with the events of 1981. In March of that year, protests had erupted at the University of Prishtina, motivated by demands for better conditions for students. However, the protests quickly became politicized and spread throughout Kosovo, with demands for a 'Kosovo Republic' with equal status in the Socialist Federal Republic of Yugoslavia (SFRY). However, the LCY defined their demands as 'counter-revolutionary', and heavy repressive measures and imprisonments followed.

The condemnation of the demonstrations was accompanied by a crusade that targeted personnel from both political and intellectual circles, during which a number of key Kosovo Albanian intellectuals were persecuted and arrested, and the rector of the University of Prishtina was fired. On the political level, the circumstances became even worse when the LCY turned to the Kosovo Albanian leadership and accused them of not having waged an effective campaign against 'greater Albanian nationalism and irredentism'.[3] Subsequently, the LCY pursued a punitive policy against the Albanian protesters. This was manifested in a series of arrests, prosecutions, and the imprisonment of intellectuals, workers and students, including minors, for 'nationalist activity' and 'verbal and political crimes'. This resulted in Kosovo Albanians having the highest percentage of political prisoners in the Socialist Federal Republic of Yugoslavia. In its 1985 report, Amnesty International provided statistical figures extracted from

Yugoslav official sources documenting that, of sixty political trials (among others) that involved more than 210 people, most were ethnic Albanians from the province of Kosovo.[4] In its next report, several months later, Amnesty added that 'between the outbreak of nationalist disturbances in the province in 1981 and the end of 1985, 1,200 people had been sentenced for political crimes and a further 6,440 people summarily sentenced for minor political offences'.[5]

The LCY's qualification of the 1981 demonstrations as 'counter-revolutionary' enabled the Yugoslav state to wage an orchestrated campaign in which, according to Muhamedin Kullashi, 'all the institutions of the state were summoned to take part'.[6] This campaign, according to Kullashi, aimed to create 'the production of the Albanian enemy',[7] a process in which the most vital sectors of Albanians' life, such as education, the economy and healthcare (including the birth rate), were attacked.[8]

Judging from the unfolding events and policies of the federal institutions in which Serbia had great influence, the events of 1981 were exploited by the Serbian authorities, who were unhappy with the 1974 constitutional arrangements that had decentralized Serbia's powers over the province of Kosovo and Vojvodina. Jasna Dragović-Soso argues that 'the demonstrations considerably reduced the manoeuvrability of the province's Albanian leadership, while enabling Serbian politicians who had long been unhappy with the constitutionally untenable situation in the republic to demand a revision of the autonomy of the provinces (1974)'.[9] After all, this was not a new enterprise. In 1975, just one year after the constitution had been approved, the president of Serbia had appointed a group of legal experts, aiming 'at recovering and reinforcing Serbia's power over its autonomous provinces'.[10] Two years later, these experts published their analysis in a so-called 'blue book', a top-secret document about the 'malfunction' of relations between Serbia and its provinces. However, this demand was silenced by Tito at the time. Gazmend Zajmi, a constitutional expert, also confirmed this, arguing that 'the expression of this Albanian demand [for a Kosovo republic] was then seized upon as an opportunity – both in Serbia and at the Serbian-dominated federal level – to formulate a political programme which entailed quite the reverse: the abolition of Kosova's autonomy'.[11]

In addition, under LCY pressure, a submissive attitude on the part of the Kosovo leadership[12] to Belgrade's diktat was subsequently established. Among the most influential among them was Azem Vllasi, a young and ambitious Kosovo Albanian politician. Vllasi actively implemented the LCY Central Committee's qualification of the 1981 demonstrations as 'counter-revolutionary', and he had played a crucial role immediately after the events of 1981 by executing the LCY's platform on Kosovo. For his active role in pushing the differentiation[13] process post-1981, he was accused of treachery and vilified by large sections of the Kosovo Albanian population. He was only later to be partly rehabilitated when he turned against Milošević's efforts to change the constitution of Kosovo. This will be discussed later in this chapter. Below I proceed to examine the inclusion of the intellectual community in the debate over Albanians' cultural and political rights in Kosovo.

The shift of the Kosovo debate to the academic level

As stated in the introduction to this book, Serbian intellectual elites had been active for many decades in shaping the views of and guiding Serb policies vis à vis Kosovo. In the mid-1980s their role came to prominence yet again, when they became actively involved in framing the Kosovo issue as an acute problem for Serbia, and arguing that Serbian authority had to be reinstated. It was Dimitrije Bogdanović's publication of *Knjiga o Kosovu* (Book on Kosovo) in 1985 that prominently influenced a framework in which to define the Kosovo question in Serbia in the 1980s. He was a respected scholar of medieval Serbian literature and a member of both the Serbian Academy of Sciences and Arts and of the Committee for the Defence of Freedom of Thought and Expression, as well as having a degree in theology. He was also involved in the Serbian Church's activities in Kosovo.[14] In his book, Bogdanović attacked critical aspects of Kosovo Albanian history and urged 'the government of Serbia to act quickly [in Kosovo] before the problem became "internationalized"'.[15]

A more prominent effort, however, followed with the Serbian Academy of Sciences and Arts' publication of the so-called *Memorandum of 1986*, which stimulated and intensified political discourse in Serbia in relation to Kosovo. Although the *Memorandum* later became 'a guiding document for the policies and public declarations of Slobodan Milosevic'[16] for the whole of Yugoslavia, an unequivocal emphasis was placed on Kosovo. 'The *Memorandum* warned of an impending Serbian genocide in Kosovo if extreme measures were not taken and advocated for the forcible creation of an expanded Serbian state'.[17] The impact of the *Memorandum* on public discourse is described by Jasmina Udovićki and Ivan Torov as follows:

> Phrases such as 'genocide against the Serbs', 'the Serbian Holocaust', 'Serbian Martyrdom', 'the tragedy of Kosovo Serbs', 'the Serbian Exodus' [...] entered the vernacular of politics, and particularly the media, and shaped the framework of many public discussions taking place at the dawn of the war.[18]

The subsequent years saw action at the political and academic levels and intellectual discourse, preparing a scene of irreparable relations between the constitutive elements of Yugoslavia's federation. As far as Kosovo was concerned, the political establishment there had to a large degree taken on a submissive role, following the 1981 demonstrations and the political actions of the LCY.

The intelligentsia in Kosovo, which had only begun to develop following the establishment of Prishtina University in 1968, now found themselves compelled to take responsibility and defend Kosovo. However, this task entailed potential consequences, as events post-1981 had proved.[19] Due to the large-scale repercussions after 1981 and the arrest and differentiation (see note 13) of many young intellectuals and students, a mainly silent intellectual line had become more characteristic of the Albanian intelligentsia. A prominent example of Serbian repercussions were the cases of Ali Hadri, who was removed from his position as director of the Institute of History, and Ukshin Hoti, who was imprisoned for several years.[20] They had both supported the 1981 demand for Kosovo to be a republic within Yugoslavia.

However, there was one segment of the Kosovo intelligentsia that was yet to be tested. These were the writers of Kosovo, and more specifically the AWK. Before 1970, the writers of Kosovo acted under the umbrella of the Association of Writers of Serbia (AWS). However, after Kosovo gained a substantive autonomy and established their own university after 1970, writers within Kosovo established their own association, which was then able to represent Kosovo in congresses and other events on the same level as writers' associations from other republics. The AWK became the main academic entity in Kosovo, being thus a gravitational hub for serious young Kosovo intellectuals. These intellectuals ventured to express their views not only in the spheres of literature, culture and history but also in political affairs.

In 1985, at the Annual Congress of Yugoslav Writers in Novi Sad (18–20 April), we can already find a subtle but compelling expression of disagreement by Ibrahim Rugova regarding the Serbian political discourse that had penetrated the Serbian writers' agenda. In this prominent annual gathering, the reputable Serb writer Miodrag Bulatović had called for a revision of political and cultural systems in Yugoslavia, with a specific focus on Kosovo. In order to justify his claim, Bulatović described the situation of the Serbs of Kosovo in provocative language that contained such terms as a 'genocide' against Kosovo Serbs in Kosovo,[21] a qualification that compelled a reaction from Rugova. Rejecting the language used in presenting the situation in Kosovo and the conditions of the Kosovo Serbs, Rugova had instead called for the freedom of literature from politics and the restrictions imposed upon it. In his paper, Rugova stated:

> How can I live freedom, as an intellectual, when dogmatic and pseudo-intellectual forces are imposed on my assimilation, and my national history, and historical and social reality are aimed to be vanished? [...] In the end, I would like to add, that historical reality proves that societies and cultures that value art had a longer lifespan, and literature thrives in good and just policies both in material and spiritual terms.[22]

Rugova and the Albanians writers experienced a similarly tense atmosphere when they were guests of the 1986 (18–20 October) international gathering of the AWS in Belgrade. There, Rugova denounced Serb writers for their negative presentation of Kosovo. While there had been a hostile reception to Rugova's speech from Serb writers, it is important to mention that Rugova also reported acknowledgements and positive individual comments expressed privately in the halls of the conference: 'for the sake of the reality, it should be mentioned that in private discussions, but not from the speakers who occupied the platform, I received positive acknowledgements concerning the issues I raised in my discussion'.[23] This clearly indicates Rugova's aim not to treat every Serb intellectual in the same way, for he was always in search of those with whom common understanding and compromise could be reached.

However, it was following an invitation from the AWS to a Writers' Association meeting in 1988 between only Serbia and Kosovo that brought the vast underlying differences to the surface and involved a clash between the two entities. As it became clear, the division between Serbia and Kosovo was greater than had hitherto been thought. In this gathering, held at Belgrade University, prominent representatives of both associations met in a two-day conference (26–7 April 1988) to discuss the topic 'The Serbs and the Albanians in Yugoslavia today', and open confrontation surfaced.[24] Although the aim of the meeting was to discuss cultural, historical, linguistic and political issues, the latter fully dominated the debate. Thus, the Kosovo conflict had been transferred from the political to the intellectual level.

In his published memoirs, Jusuf Buxhovi, a participant at the meeting and one of the active members in the formation of the LDK, and a former correspondent in Germany for *Rilindja*,[25] described how the meeting was characterized by fierce debates, arguments and counterarguments.[26] The setting was designed in such a manner that one member from each association was confronted on a panel by one of the opposing side. The AWK delegates were Ibrahim Rugova, Rexhep

Qosja, Besim Bokshi, Ali Aliu, Sabri Hamiti and Jusuf Buxhovi. They were also supported in the background by Hasan Mekuli and Azem Shkreli. On the Serb side, participants included Aleksandar Petrović, Pavle Ivić, Rade Stojanović, Milan Komnenić, Radovan Samardzić and Jovan Deretić. Other members who assisted the Serb speakers were Živorad Stojanović, Petar Sarić, Dušan Bataković and Radosav Zelenović.[27]

According to Buxhovi, the meeting was observed closely by Dobrica Čosićq, who was probably the most influential Serb intellectual at the time, which suggests the prominence of the event in Serbian public life. In 1992, Čosićq also became the president of the remaining FRY, consisting of Serbia and Montenegro.

From the excerpts of the speeches that took place during this gathering, it is evident that the meeting was a serious intellectual confrontation not seen before. On this occasion the Albanian writers presented their views in the most vigorous fashion ever seen and refuted the presentation of the Serb perspective on the Kosovo situation presented by their Serbian colleagues. It is worth examining some of these excerpts to show the intense nature of the confrontation expressed in this meeting. The presentation by Aleksandar Petrov, chairman of the AWS and one of the most outspoken participants, is among the most significant.

As reported by Buxhovi, Petrov's presentation was focused on 'all issues that had been raised since the Political Platform for Kosovo was approved by the Central Committee of the League of Communists of Yugoslavia (CCLCY) on 5 April 1981 when the Kosovo demonstrations of 1981 were to be qualified as "counter-revolutionary"'.[28] Subsequently the platform for 'the Serbs' "historical" rights over Kosovo was relaunched, by condemning directly the Constitution of 1974'.[29] What sets Petrov's discussion apart from any other at the meeting was his presentation of the relationship between Serbs and Albanians as a state of war 'between "Albanian animalism" and the defence of "European civilization" by the Serbs'.[30] The Albanians were accused of many other things, including 'the use of the birth rate and everything else in their war to achieve their aims, whereas the Serbs [were presented] as lonely and anathemized because they had more vital interests with which to preoccupy themselves'.[31]

Rugova was again found at the forefront of the Albanian side, as he had been at the two previous occassions: the 1985 and 1986 Congress of Writers international gathering of the AWS, with a prominent presentation that is worth citing here. Like Petrov, who was chairman of the AWS, Rugova too was now chairman of the AWK. In his speech entitled 'The Negative Strategy', signifying a strategy that his Serb colleagues had adopted vis à vis Kosovo and their Albanian colleagues, Rugova stated:

> Judging by the tense relations among our peoples [Serbs and Albanians] over the last seven years, one could get the impression that enemies are facing each other, but on the basis of our will and the positive history of our peoples, which often is being forgotten, or ignored – we could say that we are sitting here as friends, who have many misconceptions, but aim to contribute to improving this relationship.[32]

In a subtle fashion, Rugova recalled the historical evidence on the relations between Serbs and Albanians as having been misinterpreted, going on to say:

> As far as Serb–Albanian relations are concerned, there are more imposed conflictual issues than real, and that some want to obscure the reality and raise these alleged issues to the level of partial interpretations and even resolve them based on prejudice and from the position of power in the style of the last century, which has continued in the region of the Balkans and then been imitated among other Balkan peoples. Therefore, as writers and intellectuals, we perceive these discussions as an opportunity for an exchange of ideas with good will, and through a process of clarification to express our views, whereas other issues remain for other respective sciences – which require time and scientific impartiality without exercise of power.[33]

Rugova went on to suggest that, as writers, they should remain impartial and resist flirting with the power of the state, saying:

> If we remain in the positions where we belong, which means in *savoir* [knowledge], which is our tool and our power, if we have any power at all, then it would mean that we exist and act accordingly.[34]

He further elaborated his notion of 'negative strategy' by exposing a discourse that was intended to treat Kosovo negatively, whereby an existing reality is nullified and a new one, a 'mythologeme', or conception based on myths, is created.[35]

Rugova asserted that it was on account of this strategy that the Serbian notion of Kosovo was dying, because it was not based on facts and an existential reality but on myths. Throughout his paper, Rugova denounced the Serb discourse in a dispassionate fashion, and further argued:

> During the past seven years some labels have been created that have been used as mechanisms of a hidden 'negative strategy', such as 'Albanian nationalism or irredentism', 'separatism', 'counter-revolution', 'genocide', 'fascism', 'albanophobia', 'albanianism', 'the silence of the Albanian intelligentsia', 'anarchy', 'lawlessness', 'explosion of population', and so on.[36]

After an extensive examination of his concept of 'negative strategy', Rugova outlined a number of points in which he suggested the way forward to improve the situation in Kosovo; 'it was not as bad as presented', he argued, and proposed to replace the 'negative strategy' with a 'positive' one. He proposed that:

1. The situation in Kosovo should be left to be resolved by the nations and nationalities in Kosovo through agreement and not [a solution] imposed from above.
2. The human capacities of all sectors of society in Kosova should be allowed to contribute (for seven years this potential had been blocked).
3. A rehabilitation of prisoners [participants in the 1981 demonstrations]. They should be guaranteed their right to education and work without political prejudice.
4. The situation in Kosova is not as bad as it is portrayed, and it can be improved substantially through democracy and the relaxation of the relationship between the nations. It should not be through repression either but exactly as I demanded two years ago [at the Novi Sad meeting], a demand that unfortunately I have to repeat.[37]

And he went on to conclude:

> All this requires an end to the 'negative strategy', which should be replaced with a 'positive strategy'. This requires more sense, mutual understanding and respect among all peoples in Kosova. This is not impossible. This is our intellectual conviction, to which we are fully committed today and in the future.[38]

Judging from subsequent developments, this event represented a major turning point in relations between Serbs and Albanians. It was the first time that the Albanians had confronted the Serbs in this fashion. A subsequent meeting was scheduled to be held in Prishtina, but it never happened – the Serb writers reportedly did not respond. Clearly, Serb writers and intellectuals had miscalculated the response of their Kosovo counterparts, which apparently produced unintended consequences. In an interview for the Slovenian newspaper *Večer*, in April 1989, Rugova explained this by saying:

> They [the Serb writers] had thought we would support their perspectives. But because it did not happen as they thought, they got upset. They demanded of our politicians [Kosovo Albanian politicians] that they attack us. When the time arrived for their visit, the Committee [Central Committee of Serbia] exerted pressure on the Serbian writers, alleging that the previous meeting was not a dialogue, because we [the Albanian writers] had spoken against them [the Central Committee of Serbia], which should not have happened.[39]

Except in Serbia, where it was overlooked and misrepresented, the event had been followed and reported on extensively by other Yugoslav media, as well as by the international media. For instance, the German newspaper *Süddeutsche Zeitung*, according to Buxhovi,[40] had devoted an entire page to the 'duel' of the writers in Belgrade. 'Albanian writers have said no to the Serb *Memorandum*', it reported.[41]

Since the meeting with the Serb writers, along with Rexhep Qosja, who for many Kosovar Albanians was the most respected intellectual at the time, Rugova had become recognized as one of the most courageous Kosovo intellectuals, who frequently risked going to prison or even losing his life by publicly denouncing Serbian policies in Kosovo. His appearance in the national and international media, such as the *Voice of America, Radio Free Europe* and *Radio France International*, as well as in such international newspapers as *Le Monde* and *Le Figaro*, to name but a couple, enhanced his intellectual prominence.

The crisis frame and the reinvention of the Kosovo myth

The involvement of intellectuals from both sides of the debate on Kosovo confirmed deeply opposed views, but it is also exposed how Serbian intellectuals were in unison with the ongoing political discourse in Serbia. Meanwhile, Serbian aspirations for regaining control over Kosovo had received a massive boost with the rise to power of Slobodan Milošević. Serb cultural and political institutions had for months been evoking the historical event of the Battle of Kosovo of 1389, in which the peoples of the region, led by Prince Llazar, had lost to the Ottoman Turks. By celebrating the 600th anniversary of the Battle of Kosovo, the Serbs wanted to show that they were coming back to regain Kosovo. Milošević became most invested into that event. Having sensed the nationalist sentiments among Serbs during an April 1987 visit to Fushë Kosovë/Kosovo Polje, near Prishtina, where the Battle of Kosovo had supposedly taken place, he spoke to a large number of Serbs, and reportedly Milošević returned to Serbia 'a changed man', as he had 'smelled glory', as a Serbian author observed.[42] Not long after this famous speech, the dynamics of the political scene in Belgrade changed, the nationalist academic community shifting their support to Milošević.[43] From then on, he aggravated the political conditions and ethnic relations in Kosovo and propelled the process towards constitutional change.

The crisis frame – the context in which the crisis was framed – was resurrected by Serb intellectuals, who built on the alleged 'plight' of Kosovo Serbs, and was now being reproduced and pushed forward by Milošević.[44] A tense atmosphere grew throughout Kosovo, but to some extent also spread to other areas of Yugoslavia. To enable constitutional changes that would return Serbia's control over the two provinces, not to mention its position in the Yugoslav Federation, the Central Committee of the League of Communists of Serbia (CCLCS) had launched a campaign against core Kosovo politicians. Key among these politicians was Azem Vllasi, a once-celebrated communist and a key Kosovo politician who had led the 'pacification' of Kosovo in the 1980s and had now ensured the support of a few high-ranking politicians in Kosovo, Kaçusha Jashari, Ekrem Arifi and Remzi Kolgeci, and had also positioned himself well to defend the Kosovo autonomy of 1974. In fact, Vllasi's entire campaign of 'defensive' manoeuvres and the execution of the CCLCY's policies in Kosovo after the events of 1981 were oriented towards defending the Kosovo constitution of 1974. He was able to sense early on the real intentions of Serbia – the revocation of Kosovo autonomy. Now the necessity to defend Kosovo autonomy presented itself, and Vllasi had nowhere to go but to stand up and be counted. Milošević, the leader of the League of Communists of Serbia at the time, had become a powerful politician in Serbia and Yugoslavia. He had played a key role in placing the issue of constitutional change on Serbia's political agenda and was prepared to remove any obstacle to achieve his goals.

The Serbian determination for constitutional change came as a result of various factions within Serbian politics and the academic community that were unhappy with the decentralization of Serbian powers over the two provinces of Kosovo and Vojvodina, which had been ensured by the constitution of 1974. The two provinces had gained a status following the constitution of 1974 that ensured their representation in the federal level of the SFRY and consequently had weakened Serbian control. The constitutional change that would ensure Serbia gained control over the two provinces included the removal of article 47, which required the consent of the provincial assemblies in order for Serbia to implement any constitutional change in relation to the provinces. In addition, Serbia would require the removal of the constitutional courts of the provinces, and other aspects that ensured control of security.

After a series of street protests by supporters of the Serbian leader, Slobodan Milošević, in the so-called 'anti-bureaucratic revolution' that ran from 1988 to 1989 in Serbia, Montenegro, Vojvodina and Kosovo, in November 1988 Vllasi, Jashari and Arifi were toppled, owing to their unwillingness to accept the constitutional amendments curbing Kosovo's autonomy. Following their replacement by appointees loyal to Slobodan Milošević, a series of public protests by the local population of Kosovo in support of Vllasi, Jashari and Arifi followed. Their support was perceived by the population as a defence of the autonomy of Kosovo and triggered a massive campaign involving over 1,000 Trepça miners (the largest mine in Kosovo) who went on hunger strike from 20 to 28 February 1989. They demanded the resignation of the three political officials imposed by Milošević and the reinstatement of Vllasi, Jashari and Arifi. Within a short period, the hunger strike received support from almost the entire Albanian population, which was evidenced by protests throughout Kosovo.

Despite overwhelming opposition from all segments of society, the Kosovo institutions could not sustain pressure from Serbia. The Yugoslav authorities declared a state of emergency in Kosovo and sent over 15,000 armed troops to the province, and on 23 March 1989, while literally under siege by tanks and the police, the Kosovo Parliament voted in the constitutional changes.[45] Five days later, on 28 March, the Serbian Assembly declared Serbia an 'entire state',[46] having recentralized the two provinces, Kosovo and Vojvodina, within its constitution. A succession of measures followed, such as the abolition of all aspects of Kosovo autonomy within the judiciary, and the police and provincial administration were brought under the direct control of Belgrade. Many Albanians were killed, and by the beginning of April 1989, 200 Albanian intellectuals of all profiles had been arrested, kept isolated and tortured in the most inhumane conditions, and confined to prisons in Serbia. An atmosphere of fear and insecurity had spread across Kosovo that targeted all those who disagreed with Belgrade's policies in Kosovo. In these critical months, Rugova was among the very few Albanian intellectuals and politicians who had the courage to denounce the Serb discourse against Kosovo. The Slovenian newspaper *Večer* printed an interview with Rugova in April 1989. Its opening paragraph, which includes an eloquent description of the political climate, states:

> It seems Dr Ibrahim Rugova is still the only Albanian in Kosovo who dares to speak as he thinks. I fear that soon he won't do that, either. They will force him to be silent through the process of 'differentiation', which has already started. In the process of brainwashing, whether you want it or not, the Albanian brain has to start to think like the Serb brain.[47]

The accuracy of the Slovenian journalist's account of the political climate in Kosovo during the period of late 1988 into 1989 was confirmed when Rugova, along with 215 Kosovo intellectuals, on 15 February 1989, signed a petition that was sent to the Parliament of Serbia, the presidency of Yugoslavia, the presidency of the CCLCY, presidencies of Republics, and of Kosovo and Vojvodina. The petition expressed the Albanian intellectual position regarding the change to

Kosovo's constitution; the petition was ignored, and instead arrests were made of many of its signatories. However, Rugova was adamant about his right to express his views, irrespective of the risk that posed. 'They may change my head, but not my thoughts', Rugova said in this interview.[48]

Indeed, the presence of military and police forces in Kosovo was in synchrony with the dynamics of the constitutional changes, which demonstrated the determination of Serbia's government to resolve the Kosovo 'problem' with all means available, including the use of military force. In other words, the intention of the Serbian government seemed to have been to place firm control over Kosovo to effectively neutralize any future Albanian legal and political capacity that could challenge Serbian control. Shkëlzen Maliqi, a Kosovar Albanian political analyst and author, highlighted this succinctly:

> Serbia's militarization of Kosovo is the doing of the Serbian regime, which does not conceal that its ultimate goal is not only the annexation, but also change in the ethnic structure, of Kosovo. This is indicated by the belief in Serbia that Kosovo is its land and that Serbs are entitled to use all means to re-establish a Serbian majority there.[49]

The concentration of police and military forces in Kosovo, therefore, seems to fit the view of Maliqi, who went on to say:

> As per Maliqi's indication above, the concentration of police and military forces in Kosovo, seemed to fit with an imminent Serbian scenario to provoke conflict with the Albanian population, which would justify its drastic actions against the Albanian population in Kosovo.

In line with this sequence of developments was the announcement in 1989 by the Serbian authorities and the Orthodox Church of the commemoration of the 600th anniversary of the 1389 Battle of Kosovo in Gazimestan–Kosovo, which the Serbs and others, including Albanians, had lost against the Ottomans. The celebration of the Battle of Kosovo in Kosovo itself, with a contingent of hundreds of thousands of Serbs from all over Serbia, and at a time when Kosovo had just lost its autonomy, was perceived as a clear and open provocation to the Albanians. Rugova himself had raised concerns about the danger this 'provocation' posed. In an interview with the German magazine *Der Spiegel*, on 26 June 1989, he stated:

> My impression is that there are forces in Yugoslavia that want terrorist actions in Kosovo. If there is gunfire, here in Kosovo, then that will justify increased repression against Albanians.[50]

The conversation between the journalist and Rugova in the following quotation reveals the alarming circumstances present at this time even more vividly: 'The Albanians have shot [in the past] against the Serbs. Are they prepared for a civil war?' was the question from the journalist. 'People no longer see any alternative', Rugova responded.[51]

The Albanian response

Although the Kosovo Albanian population was significantly outnumbered by the Serbs and had far less access to power and technological resources, it was almost impossible to foresee an Albanian settlement under the conditions created following the constitutional changes in Kosovo of 1989. The 1974 constitution had allowed Kosovo Albanians a short period of freedom and relative prosperity that they had never enjoyed before. In other words, they had tasted relative freedom; therefore, the ahistorical constitutional changes went drastically against their aspirations for more freedom and destroyed their ambition to upgrade their political status to that of a republic. However, they had some countereffects, as they gave ammunition to the Marxist-Leninists and Enverists to wage a reinvigorated campaign against Serbia. Despite the severe punitive measures that the Yugoslav authorities had inflicted on these groups after 1981, they had not been rooted out completely. They had migrated predominantly to Western Europe, reorganized around different organizations and launched their campaign from abroad under a common designation – *Ilegalja*.[52]

Initially, these activists were dispersed among several organizations. However, in February 1982, several fragmented strands of *Ilegalja*, including the Marxist-oriented group Organizata Marksiste Leniniste e Kosovës (OMLK – the Marxist-Leninist Organization of Kosovo) and two other major Enverist groups, Partia Komuniste Marksiste Leninste e Shqiptarëve në Jugosllavi (PKMLSHJ – the Marxist-Leninist Communist Party of Albanians in Yugoslavia) and Fronti i Kuq i Bashkuar (FKB – the United Red Front), had formed what became known as Lëvizja Popullore për Republikën e Kosovës (LPRK – the Popular Movement for the Republic of Kosovo).[53] Hockenos argues that the Kosovar exiles' strategy was twofold: to produce propaganda material for distribution within Kosovo (and the other Albanian-inhabited parts of Yugoslavia) and to court the ranks of the Albanian guest workers who had flooded Western Europe since the 1960s.[54] Throughout the 1980s, *Ilegalja* kept their activities alive and remained 'on standby' to react once conditions allowed them to launch their actions and fulfil those aspirations of theirs that had been cut short in 1981. The atmosphere after the constitutional changes of 1989 left fertile ground for them to revive their agendas and respond more firmly to Serbia's policy in Kosovo.

The prospects for violence seemed more plausible once some of the veteran leaders of the 1981 demonstrations were freed, having served their Yugoslav prison sentences, and they had enjoyed a reputation for standing up to the Serbian regime. Therefore, they had the potential to radicalize other segments of society. However, the LDK and Rugova used their strategy of welcoming all those who were interested in waging their political battle for Kosovo, which resulted in many of them joining the LDK. It was a well-thought-out political act by the LDK to hold this potential contingent under control while providing some space for their political agitation by sharing power. However, their aspirations grew larger: they intended to gradually strengthen their presence in the LDK and eventually worked towards their ambition of 'occupation from within',[55] whereby they could dictate events in Kosovo accordingly.

Another factor that may have added to the possibility of an escalation in the Kosovo conflict was related to underlying traditions within Albanian culture. Aubrey Herbert, who had interacted with the Albanians and campaigned for their political interests since 1900 or so, describes three main Albanian characteristics in their struggle for freedom:

> 1. The Albanians are the oldest Balkan race; 2. They form a solid block, differing in language and custom from their neighbours; 3. Throughout history they have continuously struggled for freedom. No conqueror has ever done more than hold them temporarily. They have never been absorbed or subjugated.[56]

Shkëlzen Maliqi adds to this line of cultural description: 'Albanians' self-understanding and self-esteem are based on their upholding the values of the honour of the highlander and the so-called ethics of "untarnished face", assuming vehemence, bravery, indomitability, readiness to sacrifice oneself for national freedom and ideals, etc.'[57]

Above all, however, despite a short-lived period of prosperity between 1974 and 1981, underdevelopment in Kosovo was the most salient factor that motivated Albanians not to comply with the political reality created through the recentralization of Kosovo by the Serbian government following the 1989 constitutional changes. Referring to historical factors since 1945, when Kosovo was reincorporated within Yugoslavia and Serbia, it remained the most underdeveloped region. Much of Kosovo's economy was based on agriculture, but owing to the collectivization process, the rural economy fell behind during the late 1940s and early 1950s. While around 85 per cent of the province's active population was unemployed, agricultural industry remained largely primitive until very late.[58] Industry, in general, was progressing very slowly, mostly due to a federal policy that, from 1944 to 1957, discriminated against Kosovo in the distribution of investment funds.[59] By 1958, it had affected Kosovo's industry, which had only forty-nine industrial enterprises, in comparison with Slovenia's 465.

The population density of Kosovo was the highest in Yugoslavia (in 1975, Kosovo had 133 inhabitants per square kilometres, cf. eighty-four inhabitants per square kilometres for Yugoslavia as a whole), which was an additional problem. In 1979, Kosovo accounted for 7.8 per cent of Yugoslavia's population (22 million), yet its share of the total social product of the country was considerably below that proportion – only 2.1 per cent. Slovenia, with only a slightly higher population percentage (8 per cent), accounted for 16.5 per cent of the country's social product, or about eight times that of Kosovo.[60] While the birth rate in Kosovo was the highest in Yugoslavia, in terms of education, rates of illiteracy were very high. According to a survey carried out in 1948, 74 per cent of all Kosovo Albanians over the age of ten were illiterate. There were slightly more than 300 Albanian schoolteachers employed in 1945.[61] By the end of the 1970s, official Yugoslav sources admitted that pupils of Albanian nationality were markedly underrepresented in high schools.[62]

The standard of living in Kosovo was low – far below average for the whole country. According to the 1981 census, only 178,000 people were employed, with 67,000 of the 1.5 million inhabitants registered as unemployed.[63] Little progress was made between 1981 and 1989, when the last official census in Yugoslavia was held, despite political unrest and instability. It is worth bearing in mind that the protests started by students in 1981 were due to poor conditions in the University of Prishtina dormitories.

The persistence of underdeveloped sectors such as the economy, agriculture, education and industry in Kosovo during the 1980s represented sufficient motivation for triggering a violent response against the Serbian presence there. The sensitivity of the situation at the time was described by Maliqi, who asserted that 'until the end of 1989, i.e. the greatest depression caused by the forcible annexation of Kosovo, the prevalent feeling among Albanians was one of revenge: they waited for a moment of maximum mobilization to start a massive armed uprising'.[64] He went on to say that 'some political agitators, who subsequently had an important role in the formation of political parties, believed that an uprising was inevitable, irrespective of casualties. "We will lose 50,000 or

100,000 people but we will finally be free'", they would argue.[65] The cumulative factors outlined above represented a serious risk of a violent response against the Serbian presence in Kosovo prior to the emergence of Rugova's policy of non-violence, to which I now turn.

The political turn – the formation of the LDK and the policy of non-violence

Before I further explore the political background and the context that created the conditions for political organization in Kosovo, I will first provide some theoretical background that will help explain the emergence of Rugova as an influential political leader in Kosovo. More specifically, in order to explain the success he enjoyed in his campaign and the support he gathered within a short period of time, and mostly sustained throughout his political career, I will turn to the theory of symbolic capital as developed by the French intellectual Pierre Bourdieu. In his 1991 book *Language and Symbolic Power*,[66] Bourdieu elaborates on the role of language and its relation to power and politics. He pays particular attention to the (official) language, which not only has the role of communication but is also a medium of power through which agents pursue their own interests and display their authority (their 'delegated authority'). Thus, an agent to whom this power is delegated has the authority – the 'symbolic capital' (i.e. prestige, honour, the right to be listened to, etc.) – as a crucial source of influence. Depending on the recognized power that an agent receives from a group within a particular field, these agents are then able to structure their perception of the social world.

When one looks at Ibrahim Rugova's political strategy, it is evident that he extensively used language skills and the symbolic power delegated to him by the Albanian population of Kosovo. He earned this while he occupied a significant position in the cultural field, where he was a well-known literary critic, author and journalist, and was also known for having done postgraduate work under the supervision of the French poststructuralist Roland Barthes in Paris. Prior to his election as the chairman of the LDK, Rugova was also chairman of the KWA, remaining in that position even after he entered politics. Symbolic capital is the most available power an individual may have in stateless societies where there are relatively few institutions and few mechanisms through which power is exercised. The case of Rugova in Kosovo is an exemplary one and warrants closer attention.

The formalization of political pluralism and the transition to democracy in Yugoslavia provided the opportunity for an alternative political organization of Kosovo Albanians. As a result, several entities, associations and political parties were announced. The foundation of the LDK was among these early initiatives. According to Ibrahim Berisha, one of the founding members of the LDK,[67] who in 2012 published some excerpts from his diary, the idea for the formation of some form of cultural association to represent Kosovo Albanian interests was conceived by a group of writers and journalists. These included Xhemajl Mustafa (who was later assassinated), Mehmet Kraja, Milazim Krasniqi and other intellectuals during one of their regular meetings with Ibrahim Rugova, who was at the epicentre of these debates.[68] Berisha, who was himself a member of the KWA, revealed that two days before one of these meetings, on 17 July 1989, having met the US ambassador to Yugoslavia, Warren Zimmerman, Rugova admitted that 'there was positive pressure from Zimmerman for finding some form of "articulation" of Albanian standpoints and demands'.[69] In subsequent months, the idea was crystallized, and in December 1989, on the premises of the KWA, the LDK was established, with Ibrahim Rugova as its chairman.

There have been rumours and speculations as to why Rugova was elected instead of Rexhep Qosja, who was considered by many 'the father of the Albanian nation' during those years. Qosja was Rugova's senior, and he was also a writer and a critic of literary history, and (in 1974) the author of a well-received novel, *Vdekja më Vjen prej Syve të tillë* (Death Comes from Those Eyes), in which he criticized the Yugoslav regime's policies in Kosovo. According to Buxhovi, who had become one of the most active members once the idea for the formation of a party was communicated to him, Qosja had even refused to join the group of the founding members, reportedly having asked to sign the LDK foundational document on condition that some names were removed from it beforehand, a condition that was not accepted.[70] The individuals that Qosja wanted removed from the list, were Ibrahim Rugova and Fehmi Agani, according to Ibrahim Berisha.[71]

From the outset of its formation, the LDK aimed to apply an inclusive approach and develop a powerful network of branches and sub-branches not only throughout Kosovo but also among the Kosovo Albanian diaspora in Europe and the United States. Albanians in southern Serbia, the Presheva Valley, in the Republic of North Macedonia, in Montenegro and elsewhere in Yugoslavia also formed political parties on the LDK model and developed close ties with the LDK in Kosovo. This approach was manifested alongside another novelty – the mobilization of women into Kosovo politics. In March 1990, the LDK formed the Women's Forum of the Democratic League of

Kosovo (Forumi i Gruas të Lidhjes Demokratike të Kosovës), which within several months gathered 80,000 women, according to a report from Luljeta Pula-Beqiri, the first chair of the forum.[72] Although this massive participation of women in the non-violence movement was driven primarily by reasons of national interest, as Mujiko Chao argues, 'the nonviolent civil resistance process gave women the opportunity to participate in the public sphere',[73] a role they had enjoyed only symbolically during the communist system. This is testified to by Lirije Kajtazi, a young female activist from the early 1990s, who passionately campaigned in the LDK from day one. Reflecting on the 1990s, Kajtazi argues that 'it is the tradition that the LDK created during the 1990s that helped the institutionalization of women's rights in all public sectors in post-conflict Kosovo, including roles in government institutions, Parliament and the presidency of Kosovo'.[74]

Clearly, the LDK aimed at and succeeded in establishing a collective Albanian front in Yugoslavia that would enable all resources to be mobilized, managed and preserved against external influence (i.e. Belgrade). This was particularly important, since it was not clear until after 1990 how the political destiny of Yugoslavia would evolve, and it was critically important that Albanians spoke with one voice. Therefore, the political course that Albanians in Yugoslavia would pursue depended significantly on how events in Yugoslavia unfolded.

Furthermore, the strategic decision to apply a policy of non-violence was dictated by the reality of the limited power Kosovo possessed vis-à-vis Serbia. This implied that the choice of a strategy of non-violence was a calculated approach that concluded that a violent conflict with a disproportionately more powerful opponent, Serbia, arguably in command of the fourth-largest military power in Europe, could not be won but might instead lead to long-term consequences, including a potentially significantly reduced Kosovo population. Historically, as briefly mentioned in the introduction to this book, Albanian strategies of violent confrontation with Serbia had ended without success owing to the large difference in power and access to international support.

This conscious assessment by Rugova of the circumstances and relationships between powers was observed from the early days of the LDK's existence, but were also discernible in the debates between the AWK and the AWS when Rugova had been looking for compromise and mutual understanding.[75] His positioning for non-violence was then reiterated through his personal interviews, public statements and party press releases.[76] Ultimately, there were two fundamental goals that Rugova aimed to achieve with the strategy of non-violence: the first was to save the Albanian population while avoiding a direct clash with a significantly mightier Serbia; and the second, to internationalize the Kosovo conflict as a means of getting the international community involved in resolving it.

It is worth addressing, however, the views of some scholars who have attributed the emergence of the policy of non-violence to events, starting with the miners' general strike and some other activities organized by leaders of mainly left-wing political parties and associations established at the time.[77] But a closer look at these events leads to different conclusions. Indeed, the political landscape in Kosovo was eventually enriched by 1990 by a number of new political parties and associations that became active in various forms. First among the parties that were established in the early days was the Kosovo branch of the Association for a Yugoslav Democratic Initiative (Udruženje za Jugoslavensku Demokratsku Inicijativu – UJDI) at an all-Yugoslavia level, led in Kosovo by Shkëlzen Maliqi and Veton Surroi, but it was a rather belated multi-ethnic effort to save Yugoslavia. Since the UJDI did not attract any significant support in Kosovo, Maliqi and Surroi soon founded their own political parties and non-governmental organizations, such as the Social Democratic Party and the Youth Parliament (later transformed into the Kosovo Parliamentary Party, Partia Parlamentare e Kosovës – PPK), but neither of these was largely successful. They did not enjoy popularity like Rugova's, for instance, but their projects also suffered owing to their communist legacy – both leaders were sons of communist functionaries, which was not perceived as a positive factor by Albanians.

All these groups and parties later transformed into what was a loose term – Alternativa Kosovare (AK – Kosovo Alternative) – with the LDK as the dominant force.[78] A number of activities took place in these early days of political pluralism in Kosovo motivated and organized by the leaders of these associations and political parties. The latter included Isuf Berisha, Shkëlzen Mailiqi and Veton Surroi, with the last particularly known for having initiated the petition 'For Democracy against Violence', a campaign that gathered some 400,000 signatures expressing opposition to the violence of the Serb regime. However, for these actions to be successful, some form of LDK support was critical. For example, AK plus the LDK organized a mass protest, namely the Quiet Burial of Violence, a 'procession' in which an estimated 100,000 participated.

While these activities and forms of protest should be acknowledged, I contend that the policy of non-violence as a methodical and formal approach was only applied and recognized as a part of Rugova's statements and the LDK campaign after December 1989. The above-mentioned political parties, organizations and protests, including the general strike of 1989, were a result of merely ad hoc activities without a long-term strategy or clear political aims. There was no concept of a parallel-state system or a policy of non-violence prior to the concept advocated by Rugova and the LDK. Through a novel movement, Rugova and the LDK offered a peaceful, yet promising, strategy that attracted massive support and an expansion of the LDK's membership, which reached around 700,000[79] within several weeks – a staggering number for a region with a population of fewer than 2 million.

Another attempt to explain the rapid rise in LDK membership at this time is offered by Besnik Pula, who associates it with the abandonment en masse of Albanian members of the Socialist Alliance for Working People (SAWP), the Yugoslav regime's official front organization, who then joined the LDK.[80] Indisputably, the transformation of the SAWP had an impact on the rising LDK membership; however, I argue that the main reason for such an allegiance of Kosovo Albanians, including the SAWP membership shifting their allegiance to the LDK, was due to the fact that they all found the LDK and Rugova a credible, national political force. Therefore, it was not the SAWP who mobilized the LDK but the other way around. Most importantly, this credibility was owed especially to Rugova's agency and his symbolic capital. As explained earlier in this chapter, Rugova had become known through his bold public statements and vision, and was eventually recognized as the most credible voice for Kosovo Albanian interests, and thus joining the LDK was seen as a logical act.

There are two factors that sustain this argument. First, as we saw earlier, there were other political parties in Kosovo established at approximately the same time as the LDK was, or, in the case of the UJDI, even earlier. But these leaders' ideals were not entirely aligned with those of most of the Albanian population. Besides, the loyalty of the electorate does not remain static in the political process, and in that respect LDK support might have shifted to other entities had they provided any credibility in their programmes or clear perspectives for resolving Kosovo's problems. However, as Maliqi, who was himself among the first to appear on Kosovo's political scene, admits, 'this massive Albanian allegiance with the newly formed LDK was a confirmation of a refusal of Serb policies. It is on this basis that the LDK was formed, but it also reflected a substantial personal vote for Ibrahim Rugova.'[81]

Second, not long after the death of Ibrahim Rugova, the LDK's support shrank significantly from the number-one undisputed party during Rugova's tenure to one with support that barely reached 30 per cent, and there has been a gradual decrease since then. There have been three successive LDK leaders since (at the time of writing), and they have both suffered electoral losses according to post-2006 successive elections in Kosovo. The next chapter will examine more closely the unique characteristics, such as the cultural component, rhetoric and the symbols that Rugova introduced into his non-violence campaign, that made his policy appealing to Albanians, as well as to the international community.

Conclusion

This chapter began with a survey of the developments and the legacy of the 1981 Kosovo Albanian demonstrations for republican status for Kosovo within Yugoslavia. The demonstrations, it was argued, were used by Serbia as a pretext for a new political discourse in order to set a new agenda with the aim of regaining its constitutional and political control over both Kosovo and Vojvodina. The clash between Serbia and Kosovo over the political, cultural and ethnic conditions in Kosovo created a fierce debate in both Serbian and Kosovo intellectual elites revolving around the two respective writers' associations, which transferred the conflict from the political terrain into the cultural and intellectual spheres as well.

It is these debates that brought Ibrahim Rugova – a Kosovo Albanian literature critic and author, who, in a clear and objective argumentative fashion, disputed the discourse pursued by Serbian political and academic institutions and called for a reasonable, peaceful and pragmatic resolution of Kosovo problems – to the fore. However, when the Serbian authorities succeeded in changing Kosovo's political and constitutional arrangements, which led to a worsening of the situation in Kosovo, Rugova stepped up in defence of Kosovo Albanians' rights. He became the chairman of the LDK, a political party that in a short period of time gathered a staggering amount of support – more than one-third of the entire population joined. The popularity and symbolic capital that Rugova enjoyed, it was argued, ensured massive support among ethnic Albanians and subsequently enabled him to design a rather unconventional political strategy, namely the policy of non-violence, which he institutionalized as a pragmatic policy in response to Serbia's belligerent approach.

2

Non-violence and Albanian culture

Practice against violence corresponds somehow with our character, a tradition of endurance vis à vis all foreign dominations [...] We have found our way through our active resistance based on non-violence and solidarity. We have now succeeded in tapping into this feature of the Albanian spirit.

Ibrahim Rugova, *Qështja e Kosovës*, 134.

Introduction

In the previous chapter I explained the political circumstances in the period following 1981 and the unfolding of events that led to the 1989 constitutional changes and the removal of Kosovo's autonomy. These events, it was argued, triggered the Kosovo Albanian protests, which subsequently stimulated the organization of the Albanian intellectual elite around the KWA and, most prominently, led to Ibrahim Rugova leading the denunciations of Serbia's policies and practices in Kosovo. These events created the preconditions for Rugova's arrival in politics as the chair of the LDK, established in 1989, which led to a campaign of non-violence.

The chapter will analyse why and how Ibrahim Rugova's policy of non-violence became so attractive for the population of Kosovo and the international community. With this objective set, I will examine the cultural knowledge and resources on which Rugova drew and used to amplify the policy of non-violence and to generate wider local and international support. More specifically, it will be argued here that the policy of non-violence was supplemented by a cultural dimension, which placed an emphasis on an inherent Albanian non-violent cultural legacy, as opposed to the radical, violent and backward stereotypes that Serbian propaganda had ascribed to Albanians, while presenting the Serbs' own political and cultural interests in Kosovo, which were based largely on myth and policies that legitimized radical and violent means.

This novel approach was founded on rediscovering and reinterpreting Albanian cultural elements, which, besides attracting internal support, were highly successful in refuting Serbian interpretations of the Albanians and Kosovo, around which Serbian claims over Kosovo revolved. This chapter will analyse in detail the rhetorical modes Rugova used in addressing the population of Kosovo and the symbols he developed and used in the function of his political vision. The chapter will analyse a series of such variables as culture, language and symbols in order to understand how these became salient factors within Rugova's strategy of non-violence, which subsequently enabled the LDK to set its long-term political goals for the resolution of the Kosovo conflict, and hence the Albanian issue.[1]

I first analyse the Serbian political and cultural challenges that the Albanian political elite was faced with. I then move on to analyse the policy of non-violence and Albanian culture, which sets the background for examining the reaffirmation of Albanian culture, with language, symbols and a series of cultural reinventions by Rugova forming the fourth and fifth sections, before I end with the conclusion.

Cultural and political challenges facing the Albanian elite

Before delving into a more detailed analysis, I will begin first with a summary of how regional interpretations of political and cultural realities have shaped political discourse in the Balkans, with specific focus on Serbian discourse in relation to Kosovo. For a very long time, the Balkan region has been imagined and portrayed through images of violence and a series of negative stereotypes, a phenomenon that Maria Todorova has brilliantly unravelled in her book *Imagining the Balkans*.[2] As the section below will show, the Albanians in general, but more specifically Kosovo Albanians, suffered even more as a result of the Serbian regime's long-term political projects that employed propaganda to paint a specific image of Albanians.

As argued in the previous chapter, both Serbian academic and government institutions were able to communicate a specific version of the political history of Kosovo over a sustained period, supplemented by a series of stereotypes to describe Albanians with.[3] These shaped the Serbian public's perception of Kosovo as one of specific 'historical importance' but also one that exported this perception of importance for external consumption. This was achieved through the addition of violent stereotypes to Albanian culture and by adding more negative religious stereotypes that presented Albanian affiliation to Islam as an Islamic extension with the potential danger of establishing Islamic fundamentalism in this part of Europe,[4] while presenting the Christian Serbs as victims. This conceptual lens that sought to present Albanian identity in religious terms extended to other (Eastern Orthodox) neighbouring nations, who perceived Albanian identity not only in ethno-linguistic but also in religious terms, labelling them as a 'Muslim' nation or 'Muslim fundamentalists', a process that placed the secular character of Albanian identity under pressure.[5]

The Serbian discourse in presenting the Albanians with negative image and stereotypes as being inferior and incapable of building a nation state, in order to justify official policies towards Kosovo, has been intermittently active over a long period,[6] and whenever these conceptual frameworks appeared in the Serbian public domain they were predictive of potential upcoming practical policies on the ground.[7] However, for practical purposes, this section is focused primarily on the period post-1981 and the events therein, which had an immediate effect on Kosovo. It should be made clear at the outset that a major factor enabling this Serbian discourse was the reality of uneven access to power in Yugoslavia's federal institutions, which were monopolized and utilized effectively by the Serbian authorities. For example, following the massive Albanian protests of 1981, the LCY, under the influence of Serbian Communists, was forced to push onto the agenda of federal institutions the Albanian protests and classify them as counter-revolutionary, a condemnation that had severe consequences for the Albanians and the status of the province.

Despite the hard-line approach taken by the federal institutions under the influence of the Serbian political leadership following the 1981 Albanian protests, it was the Serbian nationalist intelligentsia that, in the mid-1980s, rose against the official Serbian discourse, for alleged insufficient protection of Kosovo Serbs, and took the role of a *de facto* opposition as Jasna Dragović-Sošo observed.[8] The key, common element for Serb intellectuals dominated by the nationalists was their misrepresentation of the treatment of the Serb population in Kosovo under Albanian dominated self-rule, which provided them with the 'justification' to put forward the demand 'to reduce the province's self-rule despite Albanian demographic preponderance in the province'.[9]

Next, a fusion of ideas from the academic and religious elites was brought forward. With its traditional role as the 'guardian of Serbian identity', the first institution to mobilize in the 'defence' of Kosovo in the 1980s was the Serbian Orthodox Church, Sošo argues.[10] Having undergone a 'silent' period during communist rule, the Serbian Orthodox Church found the subject of Kosovo appealing and used the 'plight' of the Kosovo Serbs as a cause for revival, thereby fulfilling its traditional role as the guardian of Serbian identity.[11] The attention that the Serbian Orthodox Church placed on Kosovo was due partly to a host of medieval Orthodox cultural and religious sites, such as the monastery of Deçan/Dečani, the monastery of Graçanica/Gračanica and Gazimestan's memorial to the 1389 Battle of Kosovo, the latter having passed into Serbian national mythology, despite the historical fact that the Ottomans destroyed the remains of the Serbian empire.[12] It is worth adding, though, that the Serb narrative that presented the Orthodox cultural legacy in Kosovo as exclusively of Serb heritage has been challenged by recent historiography. For instance, an academic from the Institute of the History of Kosovo, in a well-researched study, has argued that during the Serb conquest of Kosovo between 1321 and 1371 the Serbs, in fact, adapted and rebuilt many Albanian Catholic churches, which now are considered Orthodox and as belonging to the Serbs.[13] Moreover, the five most important of these Orthodox sites, among them the monastery of Deçan/Dečani, the monastery of Graçanicë/ Gračanica and the patriarchy of Peja/Peć, were in fact built on existing Albanian Catholic and Orthodox churches erected long before the Serbs' conquest of Kosovo.[14]

As early as in 1982, in two instances, several priests and prominent bishops, including Atanasije Jevtić, Amfilohije Radović and Irinej Bulović, who eventually became the most radical proponents within the Serbian Church, demanded that the church break its silence and publicly appealed for the 'protection of the Serbian population and their sacred monuments in Kosovo'.[15] The language used by the three bishops began to cement the sentiments related to the Ottoman period and attempted to implicate Kosovo Albanians as a Turkish–Ottoman extension in order to sway public opinion more effectively on the side of their political agenda regarding Kosovo. Their letter portrayed the emigration of Serbs from Kosovo as simply 'the last stage of "the policy from the Bosphorus" aimed at wiping out "the last remnants of the cross and the last pockets of resistance of the Serbian people in Kosovo", whose executioners were Muslim Albanians',[16] thus disregarding economic factors as the main reason for the emigration of Serbs. In the early 1980s, a figure of 200,000 Serbs who allegedly had been 'expelled' from Kosovo was circulated via 'Serb propaganda' (in Howard Clark's words), a figure that was later doubled.[17] Albanian scholars such as Professor Fehmi Agani denied that there was violence involved (violent pressure to emigrate) on the part of Kosovo Albanians, or that there had been such a large number of Serbs and Montenegrins who emigrated from Kosovo, because according to the census of 1948, there were fewer than 200,000 Serbs and Montenegrins living there. He stated:

> From all the sources I possess, it turns out that there was no violence. I don't exclude violent deviations and excesses, of course. […] How could it be possible that from 1968 to 1981 200,000 emigrated while we still have just over 200,000 today?[18]

There is also further evidence against the argument that pressure and violence from the Albanians were relevant factors in Serb and Montenegrin emigration. For example, according to a survey published by Petrović and Blogojević, official reports on the reasons given for emigration from Kosovo by the 14,921 Serbs who left in the period 1983–7 show that in 95 per cent of all cases emigrants had cited either economic or family reasons, and only in eleven individual cases (less than 0.1 per cent) was Albanian pressure given as the main cause of emigration.[19] In 1988, the Croatian author Branko Horvat published an in-depth book called *Kosovsko Pitanje* (The Kosovo Issue), in which he found that the main reasons for the emigration of not only Serbs and Montenegrins but also Albanians were related to the economic underdevelopment of Kosovo.[20]

A close symbiosis of religion and academic discourse is noted with the already cited prominent Serb author Dimitrije Bogdanović (see the previous chapter) with the publication of his *Knjiga o Kosovu* (A Book about Kosovo). Bogdanović was a respected scholar of medieval Serbian literature and a member of both the Serbian Academy of Sciences and Arts and the Committee for the Defence of Freedom of Thought and Expression, who also had a degree in theology, as well being involved in the Serbian Church's activities in Kosovo. In his polemical book, Bogdanović contended that 'Kosovo is a Serbian land' and accused the Albanian population of trying to create an 'ethnically pure' province, criticizing the Albanian claim of an Illyrian ancestry as not only historically unjustified but 'an essentially racist thesis'.[21] The significance on which Bogdanović's book rests is that, as Dragović-Soso argues, its version of history provided the framework for the definition of the Kosovo question in the 1980s.[22] The theoretical narrative that the Serb intelligentsia shaped subsequently translated into the political realm with direct effects on the real-life activities of Kosovo Serbs: countless incidents involving the Serb population and clergymen levelling accusations against Kosovo Albanians were reported to have occurred in Kosovo, albeit they were not substantiated, aimed at legitimizing this intellectual and political discourse, and frequently led to absurd claims.[23]

Along with the above, Serbian intellectual discourse utilized already existing religious stereotypes about 'Muslim' Albanians as an extension of Turkey and the Ottomans, and, by reaching out to other Eastern Orthodox nations in the region, such as the Greeks, Bulgarians, Montenegrins and Macedonians, aspired thus to mobilize an alliance similar to that of 1912.[24] The objective was also to win sympathy and create a perception of Kosovo and the 'Muslim' Albanian population there for Western powers, in which the Serbs were the ones engaged in preventing this 'Islamic belt'. Maliqi (1996) sums up this discourse as follows:

> Over the last decade, Serbian propaganda, especially that produced for Western consumption, has persistently claimed that the conflict in Kosovo is based not only on ethnic or national but also on religious intolerance of the (Muslim) Albanians towards the (Christian Orthodox) Serbs. As a matter of fact, the Albanians are said to be waging a Jihad, a Muslim Holy War, against the Serbs. Their alleged aim is to Islamize the area and to expand the Muslim faith further north into the heart of the Balkans.[25]

The importance of this view is that the conflict over Kosovo was presented with arguments that had a basic correspondence to other forms of anti-Islamic rhetoric that were gaining currency globally in this period. Samuel Huntington's famous 1993 article 'The Clash of Civilizations?' (in *Foreign Affairs*) had become one of the most cited sources at the time. In this article Huntington had placed the Albanians, and hence Kosovo, on the fault line where all three major civilizations coincided: Western Christianity, Eastern Orthodox Christianity and Islam.[26]

The above summary contains the crux of the philosophy of Serbian discourse in interpreting their political ambitions over Kosovo and the presentation of the Albanian population there, a narrative against which the LDK and Rugova had to compete. The section below will show how Rugova's non-violence movement responded to these interpretations, and how elements of Albanian culture were utilized in deploying the strategy of non-violence.

Non-violence and Albanian culture

As already mentioned elsewhere in this book, owing to their access to power and Yugoslav federal institutions, Serbian political and academic institutions were in a much better place to portray a specific image of Albanian national identity and culture. A great challenge, therefore, for the Albanian political leadership was to invent a political movement that incorporated issues related to Albanian identity and culture that interpreted Albanian tradition as non-violent and secular, in stark contrast to the interpretation of their opponents.

Efforts to refute the Serb interpretation regarding Albanians were seen from the outset in the non-violence movement. This required a degree of organization, which in the given circumstances was exceptionally difficult to achieve and required self-discipline and self-organization, for which Rugova himself appealed, saying: 'In this moment our organization also requires an internal reformation, which is not easy to achieve, even in developed societies and states, let alone in our circumstances.'[27] Towards that end, non-violence was evidently seen as a strategy and a tool to achieve these goals. Although Rugova was frequently compared to Gandhi, a close examination of his statements and of the political activity of the LDK's senior leadership leads one to understand that Rugova's strategy of non-violence was an indigenous movement, and that there had been no reference to previous theories of non-violence. It was a strategy that was dictated by the circumstances, and through a process it became enriched with a repertoire that relied on historical and cultural experiences. The LDK senior political activist and intellectual Ali Aliu stated: 'We did not rely on any concept of non-violence or methodology that we would have followed, and we did not study those theories. But after our membership increased massively, and we had the destiny of 80 or 90 per cent of the population on our shoulders, we acted as we saw fit.'[28] If anything, Rugova liked to associate his policy with Albanian traditions and Christian values, most frequently invoking the sacrifice of Mother Teresa, which will be examined in more detail later in this chapter.

Albanian intellectuals sought to refer to Albanian cultural legacies, with Rugova himself most responsible for a fusion of non-violence and the Albanian cultural tradition. He describes the symbiosis of Albanian culture and non-violence as follows:

> Practice against violence corresponds somehow with our character, a tradition of endurance regarding all foreign domination. These virtues have been preserved since Lekë Dukagjini,[29] the Albanian prince of the fifteenth century. We have 'found our way' through our active resistance based on non-violence and solidarity. We have now succeeded in tapping into this feature of the Albanian spirit.[30]

The *Kanun* represented for Albanians a form of 'common law', which preserved the national tribal tradition but also rejected Ottoman Sharia law, as well as the rest of the Balkan nations that sought to establish formal laws over the Albanians.

Kanun culture promulgated a tradition that required the resolution of problems by means of the model of dialogue called *pleqërimi*,[31] a form of council that consisted of men, a model that to some degree may have been adopted within the LDK and in the Coordinating Council of the Albanian Political Parties (CCAPP).

To some degree, Rugova also noted elements of a strategy of non-violence during the cultural events he himself experienced in Kosovo in the 1970s and would later use as a foundation for his strategy of non-violence. He evoked the traditional annual literary festival Shtjefën Gjeçovi,[32] organized by the AWK in the city of Prizren during the 1970s, which was attended by thousands, including participants from various villages, who came to listen to Albanian writers and poets from all the Albanian territories.

Although these events had a cultural character, Rugova found in them an environment where the seeds of resistance could be cultivated. He states: 'The mobilization of Albanian intellectuals during those years had a cultural rather than political character. But it is the cultural events during those years that have somewhat contributed towards preparing our present (political) resistance.' He then adds: 'They helped me to understand the profoundness, the heart of Kosova, that has the patience, skilfulness, humbleness and, above all, tolerance of everything.'[33] It may not be coincidental that the massive campaign of the early 1990s for the eradication of blood feuds was so successful mostly because it was led by such cultural intellectuals as Anton Çetta, to whom Rugova was very close and whom he supported. If the blood feud had its roots in the *Kanun*, it was precisely in the *Kanun* that the power of conciliation was to be found, which in turn served as a basis on which non-violence could be built.

It was precisely this integration of the Albanian cultural legacy into the political movement that sought to reflect an image of Albanians as resilient, peaceful and non-violent, with a predisposition to democracy that would be perceived as closer to that of Europeans, and therefore Western cultural and political values. To ensure that this tone was formally instituted, a great many debates were held in the process of the formation and naming of the LDK. Buxhovi states that, in that process of forming the LDK, in all versions of LDK preambles and statutes closeness and attachment to 'the West' was paramount, and this was situated as one of the central components of the LDK's political strategy.[34]

Prominently, though, Rugova became synonymous with this symbiosis, pursuing a specific line of cultural representations of Kosovo and the Albanians with the objective of inventing a new Albanian framework that would appeal to an increasingly nationalistic audience within the Albanian population, yet one that was more moderate and more advanced than Serb nationalist perspectives, such that it would be acceptable to his targeted local and international audiences. In this context, it could be argued that Rugova's non-violence approach and his specific form of political ideology integrated quite uniquely both civic and ethnic nationalisms. When he addressed various cultural entities in Kosovo, with a particular emphasis on the Serbs, he appeared to promote a civic form of nationalism that adhered to liberal values of freedom, tolerance, equality and individual rights.[35] One of his frequent utterances when addressing the Serb population in Kosovo was that 'Serbs would enjoy all their national rights, including their right to be a constituent nation of the [future] state of Kosovo [...] and their [Serbs'] traditions would be protected'.[36] However, in order to realize his project, that of creating an independent state of Kosovo, he thought that the Albanians had the responsibility to drive the process forward, since they were the dominant population in Kosovo. In doing this, he subtly shifted to a moderate language that was related to ethnic nationalism, which, however, was not enforced with exclusivism, as it was in Serbia and elsewhere in the Balkan region.

This successful integration of political and cultural components into his political paradigm helped him face the challenges his political movement was confronted with. First, as argued earlier, the Balkan region in general had been suffering from a surplus of 'imagined' stereotypes, sometimes generated by others, and other times self-designated and reproduced from within; but, in general, the region was viewed through the same lens of negative images and stereotypes. Second, in the case of Kosovo Albanians' being significantly underdeveloped in comparison with their neighbouring nations, but also being the recipients of negative images and stereotypes from those same neighbouring 'Orthodox' nations, the situation was even more precarious. Describing the economic disproportionalities with other entities in the former Yugoslavia, in his study on Kosovo Michel Roux qualified it as the 'Third World within Europe, "the veritable périphérie de la périphérie"'.[37]

Notwithstanding the challenges, however, as the analysis of the remainder of this chapter will show, the policy of non-violence was remarkably successful in presenting Kosovo through a different lens. In particular, Rugova was instrumental in integrating these cultural and political components for his audience. In doing so, he cultivated a subtle and moderate language, yet his jargon possessed an abundance of ethno-nationalist content that remained consistent throughout his political campaign. In doing this, he was successful in competing with other nationalist figures not only among the Albanians within Kosovo but also within Albania, as well as in the territories inhabited by Albanians in the former Yugoslavia. The unique element of his narrative was that he developed nationalist ideas that already existed but pushed them using non-violent and non-militant discourse. In fact, it can be argued that he cultivated Albanian nationalism to the extent that most Albanian radical nationalists could not compete with Rugova. In respect to the historiography on Albanian identity and culture, whose autochthony had been challenged by the Serbs, Rugova developed a line of arguments that relied, according to him, on scientific evidence, arguing:

> Today, we could say that it is a recognized fact in the fields of archaeology, literacy and ethnology that proves the territorial belonging of Albanians to Southern Illyria, that is Albania, Kosova – the Ancient Dardania and Macedonia that survived the history of the Illyrian Peninsula in today's southeastern Europe.[38]

At times, to make his arguments about the ancestry of Albanians in the Balkans more resounding, Rugova stated: 'the Albanians are an ancient nation, whose origins can be traced back to the Bible'.[39]

Rugova's framework included creating and building friendships and allies, particularly with Europe and the United States, that marked a departure from a 'myth' present among some Albanians that emanated from their perception that, because large numbers of them belonged to Islam, they were treated differently by the Western powers. This perception held that 'the West' (Europe) had overlooked the national and political interests of the Albanians, having left them under Yugoslav sovereignty.[40] Disappointment with the European influence on the destiny of Albanians in the Balkans led to a common view, espoused by the famous Albanian author and priest Gjergj Fishta in his epic poem *Lahuta e Malcis* (Highland Lute),[41] in which he describes Europe derogatively as a 'whore' for her alleged conspiracy against the Albanians. Fishta's epic was largely celebrated by Albanians in both Albania and Kosovo, and his narrative was frequently cited and praised.

In contrast to this view, while addressing Europe's 'mistakes' in the past, particularly in regard to the decisions taken in 1912–13 by the Great Powers that resulted in official recognition of the annexation of Kosovo by Serbia and its affiliation to Yugoslavia, and its reintegration to Yugoslavia again post-1945, Rugova adopted a new discourse, one that generated hope that the 'new' Europe offered. He asserted:

But now Europe has introduced a new organizational concept – that of a reduction in the significance of borders. It acts according to the logic of not dealing with past mistakes merely for the sake of admitting the mistakes, but in order to understand them, and work towards the new concept that rectifies them. All Albanians should fight for integration in Europe, without border differences.[42]

This diplomatic paradigm, and unique ability and strategy in cultivating amicable relations, in particular with the United States and Europe, was described by his close literary colleague and political ally Sabri Hamiti as follows: '[Rugova], more than anybody else, managed to prove to the world not only that Kosova is geographically, but historically and culturally, part of Europe, but also that it will be part of Europe politically as it moves towards European integration.'[43] Hamiti goes on to depict other of Rugova's characteristic qualities that demonstrate his significant role in integrating Albanian cultural elements into the policy of non-violence, saying: 'Ibrahim Rugova was tolerant, patient, and brave. He possessed Naim's [Frashëri's][44] devotion, [Gjergj] Fishta's revolutionary fervour, with both qualities attained in [Pjetër] Bogdani, with whom he became so identified both in life and in his intellectual work.'[45] It is not by accident, therefore, that there were so many cultural components incorporated into the policy of non-violence.

The cultural environment as a stimulus to the formation of personality

Before going into greater detail on the corpus of Rugova's cultural and rhetorical turn, I will briefly examine his upbringing and the impact of cultural and environmental factors on his intellectual formation. Having grown up in a typical, traditional environment in the Rugova region (his surname carrying this geographical toponym of where his family originated), Rugova had picked up elements of Albanian traditional culture and *Kanun*, which he later reproduced in a modern form, both in literature and politics. The education system was slower to reach Albanians compared with neighbouring nations, and therefore oral narratives and cultural memory remained among their unique characteristics, revolving around local and national heroes 'who had sacrificed their lives for the sake of nation' under the Ottomans and Serbs.

These narratives transmitted from previous generations left a mark on Rugova's memory, he himself asserted.[46] At the same time, relying on modern historiography, he was a leading Albanian intellectual who had successfully challenged the unilateral interpretation of Serbian historiography. In particular, in issues of an historical and political character, such as the 1389 Battle of Kosovo that Serb historiography, particularly over the previous several decades, had presented as a Serb-only battle, Rugova asserted that there existed enough historical evidence of Hungarian, Croat, Bosnian and (of course) Albanian participation in the battle fighting on the side of the Serb prince, Lazar.[47] After all, in 1389 the Albanians were still Christian, and they too fought against the Ottomans and Islamization. In an interview for the German magazine *Der Spiegel*, Rugova asserted that the Serb myth of the Battle of Kosovo was created in the nineteenth century, after the establishment of the Serbian state.[48] Rugova's argument is validated by Anna Di Lellio's anthropological study *The Battle of Kosovo 1389*, in which she introduced a new perspective, showing how the same narratives have been used and interpreted in different ways among different groups (Serbs and Albanians in this case). She argues that there was a parallel myth among Kosovo Albanians about the Battle of Kosovo, alongside the Serbian battle myth, albeit not politicized and not on the same scale as the Serbian historiography. The epic songs examined by Di Lellio portray the alleged Serb hero who killed the Sultan not as Miloš Obilić but Milosh Kopiliq, an Albanian, born in a hamlet in rural Drenica – Kosovo. 'In truth, no historical evidence confirms Kopiliq's Albanian origin, but no evidence confirms Obilić's Serbian origin either', Di Lellio concludes.[49]

Rugova's predisposition in establishing the uninterrupted continuity of an Albanian ethnic presence in the region, but also establishing an affiliation with Christian values, hence, those of Western European civilization, led him to the study of an impressive medieval Albanian Catholic archbishop and author, Pjetër Bogdani (1620–89).[50]

Bogdani was born in a village near Prizren, Kosovo, and was known for his campaign against the Turks in Kosovo and Northern Albania. Following the coalition of Austria and the Vatican against the Turks in 1683, Bogdani left Kosovo, but after the publication of his manuscript he returned. He led the Albanian resistance against the Turks but also assembled an army of 6,000 Albanians to assist Piccolomini's forces, which headed to Prizren only to be defeated by a combination of the Turks and cholera, which had plagued the area.[51] Because of the activity of Bogdani and his brother, Gjon, the Bogdani family was subjected to torture. Moreover, after his death, the Turks exhumed Bogdani's body and fed it to the dogs in the centre of the market in Prishtina.[52] Studying Bogdani's monumental manuscript *Cuneus Prophetarum* (1675), a vast treatise on theology, published in both Italian and Albanian, Rugova depicted a complex and erudite figure, who in this volume had considered problems of the philosophy of nature, astronomy, ethno-psychological and historical issues, literary theory, poetry and so on.

Rugova also travels the same historical trajectory in most of his other published work, most notably in the volume *Kahe e premisa të kritikës letrare shqiptare* (1986), which covers the period 1504–1983. It would appear that working on this voluminous publication enabled Rugova to learn and create a national vision, a line of research through national symbols such as the medieval Albanian hero Gjergj Kastrioti Skënderbeg or more recent historical figures such as Gonxhe Bojaxhiu (alias Mother Teresa).[53] As the section below demonstrates, Rugova extensively exploited the publicity of Mother Teresa as an ethnic Albanian and a reputable, humanitarian nun.

However, it is the publication of his last volume of essays in literary criticism, *Refuzimi Estetik* (Aesthetic Refusal, 1987), in which Rugova subtly reveals his intellectual position regarding the Serb pressure on Kosovo Albanians that was exerted on multiple levels during the middle of 1980s. The book begins with an essay that resembles a political treatise more than a literary essay per se. It reads:

> To reject means to refuse, to refuse something that is imposed on you, and that is a personal standpoint, but a collective decision as well. The most effective rejection is the one that relies on conviction and conviction based on argument.[54]

Analysing the role of intellectuals within their societies when faced with external threats, Rugova contextualized his own position in response to challenges to the Albanian 'essence'. Quoting Jean-Paul Sartre, he reminds the reader of two types of intellectual: accidental intellectuals ('intellectuels par accident') and essential intellectuals ('intellectuels par essence').[55] In the former category are placed those intellectuals who at a particular moment decide to take on more responsibilities of a social nature, whereas the latter category of intellectuals consists of those who are naturally engaged in the social and human fields. Writers fall into the latter category. It would appear Rugova met the criteria of both types of intellectual, as subsequent developments proved. He argued, 'There is a lesser risk, or no risk at all, of aesthetic rejections when performed in greater nations, but an aesthetic rejection is more difficult to be performed in smaller nations, where there is an appetite among greater nations for dominating smaller ones'.[56] However, Rugova argued that at the time an aesthetic rejection was a legitimate action against external encroachments.[57] Referring to Rugova's transition from the field of literature to political action, Sabri Hamiti depicts Rugova's statement on the role of intellectuals found in those circumstances: 'there is no escape, therefore, for the author (intellectual) but "a move from a meditative individual to a militant one"'.[58]

The above analysis shows how such intellectuals as Rugova trod carefully in situations where their national and cultural identity was threatened, which drove them to embark on political projects; in Rugova's case, non-violence as a substitute for an aesthetic rejection. The publication of *Refuzimi Estetik* may be considered in retrospect an announcement by Rugova that he was about to take up a more responsible role in Kosovo. This argument is reinforced when one considers that Rugova's additional literary work was focused on a series of Kosovo Albanian authors, many of whom were members of the AWK and others who eventually lined up in one way or another to support the policy of non-violence. It is safe to argue, therefore, that the seeds of Rugova's political action and of non-violence are found in his *Refuzimi Estetik*.

Reaffirming Albanian culture

Drawing on Albanian cultural traditions, Rugova saw the relationship between religion and national culture as complementary rather than competitive, and successfully realized this view by establishing a close relationship with the relevant Albanian Christian intellectuals and clergy. This opportunity then helped him supplement his 'political turn', relying on rediscovered cultural values represented by a series of Albanian Christian intellectuals, a discourse that was embraced by most of the Albanian population. As this new cultural and political climate was gaining cohesion, a number of Catholic Albanian intellectuals were trusted senior positions in the LDK, such as Anton Kolaj, Kolë Berisha and many others, whereas the academic Mark Krasniqi, who was the leader of the Christian Democratic Party, remained a close ally to Rugova and the LDK's efforts to build the state of Kosovo throughout the whole period of their political activity. Amid this rediscovery and appreciation of cultural values, and the intellectuals who gave weight to it, was the distinguished cultural intellectual Professor Anton Çetta, who led the action for the reconciliation of blood feuds in Kosovo during the 1990s. Rugova was often seen with Professor Çetta, and undoubtedly his non-violence movement capitalized also on the peaceful environment created by the blood-feuds reconciliation campaign.

Another Catholic Albanian intellectual who became a popular figure in Kosovo during Rugova's tenure was Monsignor Don Lushi Gjergji, a young scholar at the time of his first encounter with Rugova, who had published a monograph about Mother Teresa. In his article 'Filozofia dhe politika sipas Dr Ibrahim Rugovës' (The Philosophy and Politics of Dr Ibrahim Rugova), Gjergji recollects some important details:

> I met Rugova in 1981 at the writers' meeting in Brezovica and offered him my first monograph for Mother Teresa and a copy of the New Testament translated by Dom Simon Filipaj, published by Drita (a Kosovar Catholic community journal). He was very happy with the New Testament and added: 'This is a small miracle, which can help rejuvenate our cultural and biblical tradition. The four books that mark our four pillars: the Bible, the catechism or our true education, your dissertation, perhaps unique for Albanian women, but more specifically what I like most is your monograph on Mother Teresa [...] I will read them as soon as possible, then we will meet and discuss them together [...] From today you are a member of the Kosovo Writers' Association, because we need people like you and the type of literature you provide [...] I thank you from the bottom of my heart.'[59]

Gjergji further states:

> He amazed me with his assessment, saying: 'Our Catholic Church has offered an extraordinary contribution to our language, tradition, culture, and the issue of our ethnic nationality. I think we should meet again and co-operate.'[60]

Rugova eventually developed a close relationship with Gjergji and Archbishop Nik Prela. Both became very active in establishing Rugova's contacts with the Holy See and, along with the rest of the Albanian Catholic community, dedicated themselves to supporting the non-violence movement. The humanitarian society 'Mother Teresa', established by Gjergji in May 1990, was placed almost exclusively at the service of Rugova's non-violence movement, and it co-operated closely with the LDK and the parallel state.

As stated earlier in this chapter, Rugova placed a particular emphasis on the much-celebrated figure of Mother Teresa. By invoking her name, he intended not only to appreciate the virtues and the humanitarian contribution of Mother Teresa in the world but also to extend his affection for and the affiliation of his political project with Christian values and the Western world. Eventually, Rugova was to play a key role in initiating the building of the first cathedral in Kosovo, devoting it to Teresa and in fact naming it 'the Mother Theresa Cathedral' on 23 August 2005, when the foundation stone was laid. It is important to quote some excerpts from the statement he made during the inauguration ceremony in front of a large presence from the international community, accredited diplomats and missionaries in Kosovo at the time, including the US ambassador, Philip Goldberg:

> This Temple will reflect the peace, love, compassion and solidarity of the figure of Mother Teresa. This Temple begins today, in the year of Mother Teresa's beatification, of the Albanian Mother, the world's Mother [...] The erection of this Temple means that Kosova is a country of peace, and its people are peaceful.[61]

By instituting the Albanian connection with Mother Teresa, Rugova then tried to establish the similarly peaceful struggle of Kosovo Albanians by reminding those present of his policy of non-violence and the parallel state of Kosovo by saying:

> Kosova has a peaceful tradition. For more than ten years, inspired by Mother Teresa, Kosova has built a peaceful resistance and a peaceful movement for freedom and independence, and its state, that was defended by Kosovars and our friends, the USA and the European Union and NATO.[62]

Conscious of the moral credibility and power of influence on public opinion of the Western world, his specific target was the Holy See: Pope John Paul II, who had died in early 2005, had received Rugova in audience a number of times. Capitalizing on the presence of an Albanian Catholic community in Kosovo, and their relations with the Vatican, but also recollecting a more distant historical past when, in the fifteenth century, the Albanian hero Gjergj Kastrioti Skënderbeg had earned for his military resistance against the Ottomans the papal commendation of *Atleta Christianitatis* (Athlete of Christendom),[63] Rugova sought to extend this historical legacy with the Holy See. A cohesive relationship was eventually built with the Holy See and the Community of St Egidio, which became a frequent destination for Rugova over many years, the latter community mediating in the agreement between Milošević and Rugova on the issue of education in Kosovo.[64] Rugova began to be seen as a promoter of a reinvigorated Christianity in Kosovo, 90 per cent of whose population was estimated to consist of Muslim Albanians. It is important to mention that most Kosovars were extraordinarily receptive to this discourse, with no reported incidents or any form of animosity, confirming the cultural tolerance that traditionally existed.

It must be acknowledged, therefore, that the Holy See did indeed respond to Rugova's calls through various expressions of concern over many years. A publication released by the Holy See in 2002 showed that in the period between 8 March 1998 and 30 July 1999 alone, there had been nearly ninety interventions by Pope John Paul II and press releases issued by the Holy See.[65] In the midst of the military campaign, when the Yugoslav president, Milošević, held Rugova and his family under house arrest for weeks, and forced him to visit in Belgrade, it was the Community of St Egidio that was most active, along with the Italian government and pressure from other Western powers on Milošević, in ensuring the release of Rugova, who was then received in audience by the pope. He was then able to relaunch his diplomatic campaign for Kosovo.

To sum up, it should be emphasized that Rugova understood the relationship between religions in a different way from the stereotypical interpretations, and therefore he reinforced and further cultivated good relations with the Catholic community in Kosovo with a perspective that led to a significant cultural legacy. He acknowledged and built on the tradition that several Albanian historical figures before him had done, such as Bogdani, Buzuku, Fishta and Mother Teresa. These figures had contributed to Albanian culture and identity and were of Christian belief, individuals who, having exploited their connection with the Catholic centres of Europe, primarily in Italy, had been educated and were hence able to promote Albanian identity and culture in Europe. Rugova sensed that their ideas would fit into his project of rebuilding the Albanian identity, and for that matter the Kosovo Albanian national identity, with a subtle injection of Christian cultural values, alongside the majority of Muslim Albanians. Although traditionally known for their religious tolerance, given the fact that Albanians adopted all three religions, Islam, Orthodox Christianity and Catholicism, there had never been such a cohesive national unity than in the period of Rugova's years of non-violence. Rugova was uniquely successful in reinvigorating this cultural legacy and marrying it to political pragmatism.

Language discourse and symbols

A major feature of Rugova's success was the mode used to communicate his ideas to various audiences, both local and external, who did not necessarily share the same interests in Kosovo. Therefore, analysing Rugova's political campaign from a cultural approach benefits from an examination of one of its most salient aspects, which is the linguistic toolkit or discourse employed by Rugova, as well as a set of symbols he designed and implemented during his political campaign. As stated earlier in this book, Rugova is recognized for employing a short, concise, meaningful and yet repetitive lexicon. Through this, he intended to convey the message to all parties concerned: the Albanian population of Kosovo and the Serbs, in addition to the international community. His fundamental aim was to construct a new image and hence a new political reality in Kosovo, a reality that was sensible and acceptable to most of the relevant stakeholders. He did this by advocating a peaceful and democratic resolution of arguably one of the most protracted conflicts in the whole Balkan region, which would ultimately take into consideration the democratic and national interests of all parties – but, given the demographics, the Kosovo Albanians would be the biggest beneficiaries.

A critical goal of Rugova's campaign was to inculcate a belief among the Albanian population in Kosovo that the non-violence approach was the best in the given circumstances, and that in the end it would be successful. Towards that end, Rugova intelligently exploited his extensive knowledge of Albanian culture and tradition, understanding its strengths and weaknesses, and utilizing it in the function of successful communication with the Albanian population. Critically, he was able to reinterpret universally known symbols by giving them a different meaning.

While to a large degree Rugova's linguistic lexicon originated from the fact that it was framed by having subscribed to a philosophy of non-violence, the unique characteristic of his account was the utilization of pragmatic and inclusive language. Initially Rugova and the LDK leadership, in addition to the Coordination Council of Albanian Political Parties in Kosovo, were cautious about asserting a clear position on the future of Kosovo's political status. A somewhat elusive position around the famous slogan 'Liri – Pavarësi Demokraci' (Freedom – Democracy – Independence) was frequently uttered without a clear emphasis on the future political status of Kosovo. As circumstances relating to the future of Yugoslavia dictated, the paradigm that Rugova became known for, regarding his vision for the future of Kosovo, was the idea of an independent Kosovo, which was underpinned by means of a repetitive recitation of his slogan: 'We are for an independent Kosova, open towards Serbia and Albania, with all guarantees for the Serbs in Kosova and with an international presence for a transitional period.'[66]

This slogan served two fundamental purposes, internal as well as external. Internally, his aim was to influence the perception among both Serbs and Albanians about their future, whereby both peoples would feel secure. The first part of the slogan, 'for an independent Kosovo', satisfied the immediate interests of Kosovo Albanians, whereas the second part, 'open towards Serbia and Albania', reinforced the emphasis on the Serbs' safety and their future, but also bolstered the views of those who saw their political fate as being closer to that of their respective countries. In this context, Rugova demanded the demilitarization of Kosovo, while retaining a police force, and being without a visa regime, whereas in political terms he envisaged Kosovo as a pluralist, democratic country in which the Serbs would be treated as a nation, not an ethnic minority, where the tradition of both Serbs and Albanians would be preserved.[67] For external purposes, on the other hand, his slogan was aimed at international audiences, where his moderate and non-exclusivist approach would attract better understanding and sympathy from international actors.

Rugova's linguistic discourse also included a cautious approach to the release of his statements, so that there should be no room for misinterpretation by radical elements within Kosovo, or any tone that could provoke the Belgrade regime or contradict Rugova's own publicly declared non-violent intentions to resolve the Kosovo conflict through democratic and peaceful means. This slogan was articulated on a regular basis, most notably during his media conferences in Kosovo, but also during his diplomatic visits and interviews with foreign media.

When the disintegration of Yugoslavia became an irreversible process, the LDK leadership and the Coordination Council of Albanian Political Parties in Yugoslavia assessed the circumstances and developed a strategic proposal for the future of Kosovo within Yugoslavia. The proposal included three outcomes, based on three scenarios: (1) If the internal and external borders of Yugoslavia did not change, then there would be a Republic of Kosovo within Yugoslavia; (2) If the external borders did not change but the internal borders did, then there would be a demand for a republic of all Albanian people within Yugoslavia; (3) If the external borders changed, then the Albanian people in Yugoslavia would declare their will through a plebiscite, thus creating an all-Albanian state in the Balkans comprising all the Albanian territories in Yugoslavia joined with Albania itself.[68]

Since the internal borders resulting from the dissolution of the SFRY did not change, the first option became the pragmatic strategic choice. To those who advocated more adventurous options, such as the unification of all Albanians in one state, Rugova answered in an intelligent and appeasing fashion by saying:

> It is very normal and natural that the Albanians, as all other nations, should be united and live in one state. But in this idea, we must be wise. Unification by force and violence will not be tolerated by Europe. Neither the academies [the Kosovo and Albanians' respective academies of the sciences and arts], nor university institutions, nor think tanks have treated this matter adequately yet. The issue of unification should be a matter of scholarship.[69]

In this manner, Rugova threw open this ambitious nationalist project to the academic community of both Albania and Kosovo, an idea that did not enjoy any significant support anyway, but was being used for the political consumption of the LDK and Rugova's opponents.[70]

Rugova's slogans, or paradigms, were crafted in a careful and calculated fashion after having considered two fundamental aims: one was to preserve the Albanian population,[71] which he saw as indispensable for the existence of Kosovo (otherwise there would be no point in having an independent state); and the other, by maintaining a peaceful environment, that is, without open military conflict, was to enable the LDK and Rugova to engage in an active process of internationalizing the Kosovo conflict (see Chapter 4) and build a parallel state. The goal, of course, was to get the international community to impose a 'non-military' solution in a preserved Kosovo. Rugova's lexicon was, therefore, carefully selected and deployed within that framework.

The symbols

A distinct element of Rugova's cultural approach became evident through the personal style and symbols he designed and utilized in the pursuance of his political goals. He came across as a master of symbols that carried specific meanings – a talent that he may have enhanced further during his research in Paris. During 1976–7 he spent one year under the supervision of the French poststructuralist Roland Barthes at the École Pratique des Hautes Études, where he studied Barthes' work extensively and closely followed great debates between other French intellectuals, such as André Glucksmann, Bernard-Henri Lévy and others. This was a stay that afforded Rugova great experience and the opportunity to create the basis for his future relationship with French intellectuals and France itself. This was the period of Rugova's 'infection' by democracy, as he confessed in a lecture at the University of Paris on 17 December 1996, when he was awarded the title of honorary doctor, a lecture he dedicated to Roland Barthes.[72] The influence of poststructuralism and other philosophical doctrines may arguably have helped Rugova to develop and functionalize their ideas and use them in the pursuit of his political project in Kosovo. In an interview with Marie-Françoise Allain and Xavier Galmiche, he states:

> During my studies, under the influence of Barthes, I meditated a lot on the relationship between power – knowledge – and the functioning of the state, the relationship between intellectual structure and society: it is here, I thought, where we may find the existence of a movement for freedom. I was completely apolitical, although I used to read about the theory of power.[73]

It is right to argue, therefore, that his short stay in France may have been instrumental in his intellectual transformation and brought Rugova closer to politics.

But he cultivated his own unique style, characterized by physical fragility and long hair, but most specifically by a silk scarf that he wore throughout the year (except August) and that was believed to have carried a specific symbolism. It is perhaps some of these attributes that led the French author Marie-Françoise Allain to characterize Rugova as 'le frêle colosse du Kosovo'[74] (the fragile colossus of Kosovo). There have been rumours and myths about the reasons Rugova wore his scarf, one dominant explanation suggesting its association with a traditional scarf worn by men in the Rugova region (where he came from), signifying birth, life and death. Whether or not this association is a myth, it clearly added to his characteristic style and his predisposition to influence a first-time impression on, and intention to build a positive relationship with, the people he met.

In addition to his characteristic style, Rugova also had a reputation as an individual who liked to offer presents. He became particularly known for presenting crystal stones from Kosovo mines as a gesture to honour international visitors, but also to remind them that Kosovo mines were of great economic potential. It is hard to find one international visitor, ranging from politicians, diplomats, journalists and businessmen to authors in the fields of culture, art and history, who, having met Rugova, returned empty-handed from Kosovo. Giving crystal stones away to so many visitors was also accompanied by a description of their origins, which he provided passionately, along with the rich symbolism these mineral crystals represented – indicating, for example, that the conflict over Kosovo was not so much on account of cultural or even political reasons, as Serbia emphasized, but rather economic reasons.

Such was Rugova's commitment to honouring international statesmen, particularly those whose activities were perceived as a contribution towards a better understanding of the Kosovo issue, that he eventually institutionalized a series of presidential decrees derived from his 'constitutional powers' and delivered various awards. During his presidential reign, he introduced several accolades, including the 'Golden Medal of the Prizren League' and the 'Golden Medal of Freedom'. He decorated: fourteen US statesmen, including congressmen and senators, from President Ronald Reagan and President Bill Clinton, to Senator Bob Dole and congressman Tom Lantos, the latter two being great lobbyists in favour of Kosovo Albanians; six UK personalities, including Queen Elizabeth II and former Prime Minister Tony Blair; five French; six German; four Italian; three Spanish; four Austrian; two Swedish; two Swiss; Pope John Paul II;

and also Kofi Annan of the United Nations.[75] To reaffirm the significance of the Prizren League, first organized in the city of Prizren in Kosovo in 1878, which was the first serious Albanian effort towards independence from Turkey, Rugova dedicated the Golden Medal of the Prizren League, mostly to those involved in the field of culture.

Of perhaps equal prominent significance is the invention of several symbols related directly to the existence of a 'parallel state' in Kosovo, or rather to a strategy for making the existence of such a state, established during Rugova's political campaign, a fait accompli. Following the 1991 referendum for the independence of Kosovo, and the first parliamentary elections, which laid the foundations of a parallel state, Rugova himself designed the flag of Dardania, which signifies the historical trajectory from ancient Dardania (of the second and first centuries BC) to contemporary Kosovo.[76] Unveiling it in front of the media, Rugova described the flag and its symbolism, including its dimensions, as follows:

> The deep-blue background of the flag represents peace, with the stamp of Kosova in the middle [...] The stamp contains the black eagle, the national symbol of all Albanians, which was used by Gjergj Kastrioti Skënderbeg (1405–1458). Its origins dates from Alexander the Great. Gjergj Kastrioti was called Skënderbeg after Alexander the Great, both having a common origin, which is why he [Skënderbeg] adopted his symbol.[77]

Every detail of the flag of Dardania was described, and a meaning ascribed to it, including the red background symbolizing strength and the helmet symbolizing the character of the 'kingdom' of Dardania. There were also two stars on the helmet, symbolizing the movement of the sun and of life, symbols originating in Albanian antiquity. The black and red field symbolizes the Skënderbeg flag.[78]

To add more meaning to the flag, it also comprised another Albanian folkloric element: a white banner with the name of Dardania written across it, symbolizing the white national costume and the white skullcap (*plisi*) that, according to Rugova, was used in the flag of the Roman emperor Justinian, who came from Kosova, Dardania. 'Dardania', according to this interpretation, has an Albanian etymology in *dardhë* (pear), and means *vend i dardhave* (land of pears).[79] At the top of the flag stands a six-pointed star (the star of David), which Rugova claimed was also used by Skënderbeg.[80] Rugova began to use the flag of Dardania in 1992, and it became part of his 'presidential' protocol, as well as LDK posters, until the new flag was introduced by the United Nations and adopted

Figure 1 Rugova interpreting his self-designed national flag in 2001.

by the Kosovo Parliament with the declaration of Kosovo's independence on 17 February 2008.

Conscious that the potential independence of Kosovo would necessarily require specific symbols of statehood, Rugova thought it was imperative that the political establishment of Kosovo should design these components sooner or later. However, as in many other instances in his political career, he was quicker and able to exhibit his vision by laying out his intentions in a masterly way and even pre-structure any potential debate on the issue. The new flag as a national symbol of Kosovo, which would substitute the much adored two-headed eagle with the red-and-black background of the Albanian national flag, was designed in such a fashion that it could resist critics successfully. There was no sustained criticism against Rugova for allegedly having 'betrayed the national interest and undermined the Albanian national flag', since *Dardania*'s flag contained even more profoundly Albanian national elements than the existing one. It is hard to find anything more complex than the flag of Dardania, containing as it does so many Albanian cultural elements, which Rugova interpreted zealously. The flag was readily accepted by the majority, and feeble criticism came only from his usual opponents, or those who did not want two Albanian states in the Balkans.[81] The flag of Dardania was also denounced by elements close to the former KLA, who preferred the Albanian flag and an eventual unification of Kosovo with Albania.

To complete the 'elements of statehood', at least on a symbolic level, the composition of the Kosovo national anthem represented the culmination of Rugova's inventory of state symbols. Adopting an old Albanian song that was sung by Kosovo men during 1908–10, Rugova launched Kosovo's anthem.[82] 'It is an honourable text that contains artistic and musical elements that in due time may be modified in some respects. It reminds me of Beethoven's Ninth Symphony',[83] Rugova explained in an interview for the Kosovo newspaper *Bota Sot* in November 2002.

The text reads:

Kur ka ra kushtrimi n' Kosovë

Kur ka ra kushtrimi n' Kosovë
Kur ka ra kushtrimi n' Kosovë

Janë bashku' qytete, katunde
Dhe bjeshkët me malësorë
Janë bashku' qytete, katunde
Dhe bjeshkët me malësorë

Mirë luftojkan Pejë e Gjakovë
Mirë luftojkan Pejë e Gjakovë
Mirë luftojkan Prizreni, Prishtina e Llapi me Rugovë
Mirë luftojkan Prizreni, Prishtina e Llapi me Rugovë

Ç' na u mbushë kjo tokë me dëshmorë
Ç' na u mbushë kjo tokë me dëshmorë

Të na rrnojë e jona Kosovë, të na rroj o përgjithmonë
Të na rrnojë e jona Kosovë, të na rroj o përgjithmonë.

In English translation:

When Kosova was called to war
When Kosova was called to war
When Kosova was called to war
Town and country

And the men of the Highlands
Joined together

Peja and Gjakova fight so bravely
Peja and Gjakova fight so bravely
Prizren, Prishtina, Llap and Rugova[84]
Prizren, Prishtina, Llap and Rugova
All fight so bravely

Our earth is filled with martyrs
Our earth is filled with martyrs

May our Kosova live forever!
May our Kosova live forever!

With the selection of this old song for the national anthem of Kosovo, Rugova demonstrated yet again his affinity for reaffirming cultural tradition and giving it a new interpretation based on pragmatic choices. There were not many old Albanian songs that found general acceptance among the entire population of Kosovo, and certainly no other example demonstrated Albanian regional and cultural unity like *Kur ka ra kushtrimi n' Kosovë*. The largest regions in Kosovo, Llapi and Rugova, one bordering Albania and the other Serbia, are cited in this song. But so as to complete the geography of Kosovo, and preserve its prominence, the song also celebrates the participation of the biggest towns, such as Prishtina, Peja and Gjakova. Refuting this proposal would only have put Rugova's critics on the defensive, since the song enjoyed great popularity and represented a well-chosen cultural representation. Indeed *Kur ka ra kushtrimi n' Kosovë* is now the national anthem of Kosovo.

Other cultural reinventions

Rugova's ability to reaffirm cultural traditions and resurface them in the public domain with a new contextual meaning was remarkable. Besides the symbolic elements discussed above, his inventive predisposition included attention to some of the deepest cultural traditions, which most local audiences had long ceased to attend to, even though they were part of the cultural repertoire. In his interviews with the French authors cited above, which was published in book form in 1994, Rugova talked about a traditional popular sport that was practised by Albanian men. Even though the sport was practised in a rather primitive fashion, in a remarkable way Rugova draws comparisions between this cultural hobby and the famous sport of golf, which enjoys popularity in many parts of the world.[85] 'We played games like other kids, but we had some traditional games, one of which resembled golf but was a bit more primitive, and another that used small stones. These are very old games', he concluded.[86]

The harvest supper

In a similar fashion, Rugova reintroduced to local practice the so-called *Darka e Lamës* (the harvest supper), a traditional Albanian ceremony, which was practised at the end of the autumn season when agricultural crops were harvested. At one of the solemn events connected to *Darka e Lamës*, to which representatives of all the international organizations present in Kosovo were invited, Rugova interpreted this tradition as an Albanian ritual that dated back to the fifth century BC and that was celebrated annually by the Ilyrians. The tradition was passed down the generations and was celebrated around 23 October among Albanian families with a prayer, which Rugova cited as follows:

Thank you God – Falemi nderit o Zot
For the goods you gave us – Për të mirat që na i fale
In our land, Kosovë – Në tokën tonë Kosovë
Ancient Dardania – Dardaninë antike
In this year – Në këtë mot
We pray to you God – Të lutemi o Zot
To give us more – Të na falësh të mira
Even more – Edhe më shumë
In our land of Kosova – Në tokën tonë Kosovë
Ancient Dardania – Dardaninë antike
Next year – Në tjetrin mot
O God – O Zot[87]

Concluding the prayer, Rugova announced that, since 2002, he had decreed *Darka e Lamës* a national holiday of thanksgiving, which would be celebrated in every family and become a bank holiday in Kosovo. The dinner Rugova provided for his local and international guests was dominated by food products grown in Kosovo – the message, among others, was to stimulate more production by Kosovo farmers.[88]

It is difficult to think of any aspect of traditional culture that escaped Rugova's attention and that he did not reintroduce to the public while at the same time giving it a modern interpretation and making it serve his political vision.

Conclusion

In this chapter I examined a cultural paradigm in which Rugova utilized the manifestation of his policy of non-violence. First, a cultural framework invoked by Serbian literature and propaganda and ascribed to the Albanians, which was utilized by Serbian governments in relation to Kosovo and the Albanians, was illustrated. I then examined Rugova's approach, which was focused not only on refuting the Serb discourse but also on inventing a framework that was more moderate, that promoted Albanian culture as non-violent and that also appealed to his supporters and to the international community.

The chapter further examined Rugova's personal upbringing and intellectual education, which was regarded as crucial to his success in understanding Albanian tradition and turning it into a modern project – the policy of non-violence. The chapter demonstrated Rugova's conviction that the policy of non-violence was deeply ingrained in the Albanian cultural legacy, but that legacy had to be tapped into by its cultural and political elites.

A critical aspect of this chapter formed Rugova's linguistic strategy in communicating with Albanian supporters and the international community. His linguistic paradigms, it was argued, helped construct his new vision, which portrayed the Albanian population as peaceful, but also contained a lexicon that included democratic principles, peace and dialogue.

Finally, I examined a series of symbols that Rugova designed, such as the flag, the national emblem and the hymn of Kosovo, to complete the infrastructure of the state of Kosovo and add to its cohesion. While navigating through a cultural and historical journey, through his public dialogues and statements, Rugova tried to inject a sense of compatibility of Albanian cultural fragments with Western culture and political institutions.

The institutional set-up:
The parallel state of Kosovo

Introduction

This chapter deals with the political dynamics in Kosovo that led to the institutional arrangement that came to be known as the parallel state. I have used the concept of legitimacy to explain the effectiveness of Rugova's political organization in challenging the presence of the Serbian state in Kosovo. More specifically, the chapter looks at how Rugova's policy of non-violence challenged Serbian control over Kosovo from a legitimacy point of view, while demonstrating the viability of his parallel state. Following a summary of the criteria that define the concept of legitimacy according to David Beetham, I explain the challenging political circumstances created as a result of the control that Serbia established over Kosovo with the constitutional changes of March 1989. I then move on to examine how Rugova's non-violence approach institutionalized political life in Kosovo through his party, the LDK, and changed the political environment there, leading to the declaration of Kosovo's independence. This section also looks at how a number of key political acts, of which Rugova's LDK was the driving force, delegitimized Serbian control of Kosovo, while at the same time helped to legitimize Rugova's parallel state.

In the third section, I look at the functions that the parallel state fulfilled, key among them being the social, health and parallel education spheres, the latter being both a product and a constitutive factor of the parallel state. I then look at the effects of the parallel state in managing the internal political challenges that stemmed from diverse political ideologies and the competition for power. Next, the effects of the CCAPP are discussed, with particular focus on its function in the management of sharing decision-making between the political parties and managing internal factions within Kosovo. Finally I look at how the organization of elections in Kosovo was managed, and how they added to the functionality of the parallel state and its legitimacy, before the chapter conclusion.

Kosovo's parallel state and the battle for legitimacy

On 28 March 1989, the Serbian Republican Assembly ratified the Serbian constitutional changes, giving Serbia full control over Kosovo. This followed a controversial act of consent obtained by the Kosovo Provincial Assembly to the constitutional changes on 23 March.[1] However, the vast majority of the population refused to accept Serbia's authority to govern Kosovo. The Albanian population and the political and intellectual elites challenged this authority, on the basis that Serbia had bullied the Kosovo Parliament into adopting the constitutional changes of 1989 against the will of people and therefore had no legitimacy in Kosovo. Legitimacy is a critical quality necessary for the exercise of authority and power by one subject (state) over a population in a specific territory. Legitimacy is usually a derivative of power, which is a problematic concept, and my aim here is not to delve into an exhaustive theorization of the two concepts any further than is necessary for this chapter. I rely on David Beetham' s concept of legitimacy, which, he suggests, embodies three distinct elements or levels. Power, he argues, can be said to be legitimate insofar as: 'i) it conforms to established rules; ii) the rules can be justified by reference to beliefs shared by both dominant and subordinate; and iii) [that] there is evidence of consent by the subordinate to the particular power relation'.[2]

To elaborate on these further, in the first instance power can be said to be legitimate if it is acquired and exercised according to established rules, which may be unwritten, informal conventions or formalized in legal codes or judgements. If power is acquired in contravention of the rules, then it is qualified as illegitimate.[3] But legal validity is not sufficient to secure legitimacy, since the rules through which power is acquired and exercised require justification, which is the second level according to Beetham.

> To be justified, power has to be derived from a valid source of authority (this is particularly true of political power); the rules must provide that those who come to hold power have the qualities appropriate to its exercise; and the structure of power must be seen to serve a recognisably general interest, rather than simply the interests of the powerful.[4]

And the third level of legitimacy implies that there is a 'demonstrable expression of consent on the part of the subordinate to the particular power relation in which they are involved, through actions which provide evidence of consent'.[5] Actions such as concluding agreements with a superior, swearing allegiances or taking part in an election are particularly important in providing legitimacy.[6] In other words, the public actions of the subordinate and the expression of consent represent the source of legitimacy, not the propaganda or public relation campaigns' 'legitimations' generated by the powerful themselves, Beetham argues.[7] If public expression of consent by the subordinate contributes to legitimacy, then the withdrawal or refusal of consent will be the same token detract from it. Actions such as non-co-operation, passive resistance, disobedience and militant opposition on the part of those qualified to give consent will have eroded legitimacy, and the larger the numbers involved, the greater this erosion will be, and then the opposite (or negative) of legitimacy can be called delegitimation.[8] Beetham concludes that for power to be legitimate, all three of the conditions outlined above are required.

Viewed from Beetham's legitimacy criteria, it can be argued that the power of Serbia's authority established over Kosovo with the constitutional changes of 1989 was illegitimate. Various forms of pressure available to the Serbian regime were applied in order to impose its political will over the majority of Kosovo's population, despite large-scale protests throughout the province, which resulted in tens of Kosovo Albanians being murdered. Moreover, as explained above, even the legal validity of the constitutional changes can be questioned on the basis that the pressure from the Serbian and Yugoslav authorities on the political institutions of Kosovo was relentless. Soon after, Serbia adopted its own constitutional changes, which authorized Serbia to extend governance over the province;[9] Serbia thereby declared its legal authority over the province, and, in order to add more effectiveness to this strategy, it embarked on a series of actions, including a policy for the de-Albanization of Kosovo.[10] This included a sequence of political and non-political activities aimed at directly hitting the most vital aspects of life in Kosovo, including security, the economy, health and education, and so on.

According to the late Nekibe Kelmendi, a senior lawyer in Kosovo, and a high-ranking LDK official at the time, the Serbian Parliament adopted a total of thirty-two discriminatory laws, and 470 decrees or special measures were issued by the Serb authorities between 1990 and 1992, as well as two programmes: 'the Orwellian *Programme for Peace, Liberty, Equality, Democracy and Prosperity*

(PPLEDP) of March 1990, and the *Development Programme to Stop Emigration and for the Return of Serbs and Montenegrins* of July 1992'.[11] At the federal level, Kosovo's status had been effectively abolished, meaning that Kosovo eventually ceased to be represented in the federal institutions, and hence was not able to participate in the ongoing negotiations for the restructuring of a potential new federation or confederation of Yugoslavia. All these acts followed directly from the legal changes that left the future of the province and its majority Albanian population under Serbian control seem very grim. This tacitly meant that the Albanians had either to comply with the Serbian regime or leave Kosovo.[12] A third possible alternative was hard to envisage in these political circumstances. However, that perception was soon to be changed. Rugova's policy of non-violence provided hopes for an alternative.

Non-violence and the transformation of the political environment

While the Serbian state's immediate objectives following the constitutional changes were to dismantle the autonomy of Kosovo and establish effective control, the new Kosovo Albanian political elite's immediate goal was to preserve the lives of the population through the policy of non-violence. The repressive measures that were instituted against the Albanians over such a prolonged period, and the constitutional changes that curtailed the rights of the Albanian majority, became a unifying factor among the Albanian population of Kosovo,[13] a unity upon which the LDK and Rugova's strategy of non-violence built. The section below will show how the LDK transformed the political environment in Kosovo, which influenced the anchoring of public consent to the LDK and to Rugova's parallel state.

Having grown into a party with a membership of several hundred thousand in a territory with a population of fewer than 2 million, the LDK now commanded a popular legitimate authority to speak on behalf of Kosovo Albanians. Although the Serbian authorities now controlled the province with the classic elements of power – large contingents of police and military, and an administrative apparatus – it lacked consent from the majority of the population. Therefore, the competition that emanated from Albanians' political organization opened the lid on the battle for Kosovo legitimacy.

The LDK's strategy was twofold. First, it promoted a policy of non-confrontation with Serbian/Yugoslav forces as the safest strategy to preserve the population, as well as to keep some control of the political situation. Rugova was instrumental in wielding popular support favourable to the LDK and drew on Albanian cultural foundations (see Chapter 3). As some argued, 'it [the LDK] pursued a nationalist agenda no less straightforward than its militant-minded rivals, whom foreign journalists referred to as "nationalists",[14] although it was very moderate in terms of the methods used and strategy chosen, a fact that appealed to most Albanians. The other component of Rugova's strategy was concerned with attracting the attention of the international community. Rugova in particular was known for making a series of public statements and pleas for the attention of the international community, which was seen by him as a necessary intervening factor to ensure his policy was successful.

All these factors rapidly raised the LDK's prominence, and, in that respect, the expectations of the Albanian population were raised as well. The LDK was now able to channel Albanian political interests by filling the vacuum left by the collapse of the Albanian communist leadership. However, to be able to deal with the external challenges that the Serbian regime posed, it was critical for the LDK to operate within the system without antagonizing the Serbian authorities. Towards that end, the LDK applied a sensible approach by including all existing political parties and cultural identities, except the Serb population, which refused to participate with the Albanian parties, but which had been participating in the execution of Serbian government policies in Kosovo.

Furthermore, preserving internal Albanian unity was an equally challenging factor, particularly when considering that unity had to be attained in the absence of the Albanians' own institutions. However, this was accomplished thanks to Rugova, who saw unity as a critical factor for the success of his policy of non-violence. Rugova was renowned for his skills in preserving relations within the LDK and between the LDK and the rest of the Albanian population. This included refraining from criticism of the former communist leaders, who had in fact frequently been subjected to criticism for their communist legacy, and of those loyal to Serbia and even of relentless critics, such as Qosja and Demaçi, who constantly attacked him and his policy of non-violence. Commenting on this issue, Edita Tahiri, a senior figure in the LDK, who was foreign minister for the parallel state, said:

> Rugova had a special capacity for maintaining unity. His capacity to unite ensured the movement's success. Because unity was the number one tool for success! So Rugova was not confrontational – he would ignore his critics and small divisions; instead, he focused on the big picture.[15]

One of the most fundamental achievements in those early days was the ability of Rugova and the LDK to establish lines of communication with the deputies of the Kosovo Parliament elected after the constitutional changes in Kosovo in March 1989. The formation of the LDK coincided with this newly elected Parliament, which was convened for the first time in December 1989. Paradoxically, the deputies of this Kosovo legislature had been 'hand-picked' by the Serbian authorities to ensure that their constitutional changes would be implemented in Kosovo swiftly and without obstruction. However, these deputies were quickly exposed to a rapidly changing public and cultural environment that was taking shape in Kosovo. The LDK's membership rose quickly, and it thus became a driving force that generated hope and enthusiasm among the Albanian population, and to some degree it also tapped into the sentiments of the Albanians with a form of populism, notwithstanding its pacifism, which further influenced the change in mindset among the Albanian population. In this changing environment, the mood of the Kosovo parliamentarians changed too. Milazim Krasniqi, Rugova's secretary as chairman of the KWA, and one of the founding members of the LDK, argued:

> The rapid expansion of the LDK led it [the LDK] to be perceived as a major psychological factor in the mind of the Albanian population in Kosovo. Our populist approach that we operated from the beginning imposed the LDK as a factor that had to be taken in consideration seriously. This significantly influenced the behaviour of both Kosovo politicians and the deputies. Under pressure from the LDK's populism, they began to change their political standpoints and gradually became closer to our populist concepts. Certainly, our individual, informal meetings and discussions with Kosovo deputies had a significant effect as well. I myself have had such experiences with at least one of the deputies, and I know others have had the same experiences as well.[16]

Explaining the influence of the LDK in changing the political environment in Kosovo, one of these deputies, who was also a vice-chairman of this legislature, Ilaz Ramajli, stated that the LDK might even have influenced the formation of some other political parties, in order to make political pluralism seem diverse and functional in the parallel system.[17]

The mass protests that initially emerged spontaneously were now institutionalized through the LDK's political activism, and through its non-violent response to the violent Serbian regime. This new discourse in resolving the Kosovo conflict by non-violent means required peaceful relations among the Albanians themselves. In this context, therefore, the strategy of non-violence had a facilitating character for a new atmosphere, in which a wave of blood-feud[18] reconciliation throughout Kosovo took place. During an unprecedented campaign that lasted from February 1990 to May 1992, there had been 2,952 blood-feud reconciliations and other offences, in which an estimated 1.7 million or more people participated.[19] The reconciliation campaign was, arguably, one of the most important factors in this period, which contributed to creating a climate of solidarity and further homogenization. The LDK and its strategy of non-violence undoubtedly capitalized on this atmosphere; Rugova himself was very close to the leading figure of the campaign, Professor Anton çetta, and the two were seen often in public together.

As the Serbian grip on the institutions of the province was seemingly being consolidated, the activity of the Kosovo leadership and their generation of political ideas intensified. Thus, we saw the LDK leadership launch the idea for some form of institutional declaration that would empower it with the formal legitimacy to represent Kosovo. In an interview for the literary magazine *Fjala* on 15 May 1990, Rugova announced that the LDK would be bringing out a constitutional declaration that would legitimize the LDK as Kosovo's representative in the Yugoslav Federation, and indicated that he and the LDK would be engaged in the ongoing debates over the future of Yugoslavia with Kosovo's participation as an independent unit.[20]

Furthermore, Rugova's statement on the declaration of independence found support among members of Kosovo's Academy of Sciences and Arts, the highest academic institution in Kosovo, consisting of important intellectuals, which similarly issued a declaration of support for independence.[21] This semi-covert yet co-ordinated (informal) strategy was then endorsed by an ad hoc forum, namely the Këshilli Koordinues i Partive Politike Shqiptare (KKPPSH – Coordinating Council of Albanian Political Parties), established on 1 July 1990, which consisted of existing political parties and a number of NGO representatives and intellectuals.[22] The Coordinating Council issued a long statement that included a paragraph urging the Kosovo Parliament, which was due to meet the following day, to raise the status of Kosovo as equal to that of other members of the Yugoslav Federation.[23]

The deputy, and later chairman, of Parliament, Ilaz Ramajli, who was one of the most proactive deputies of the provincial assembly during this legislature, recalled:

> There was no strict co-ordination between Parliament and the political parties, but if you look at the sequence of events, before the declaration of 2 July 1990, the Academy of Arts of Kosovo had issued a statement in which it gave some orientations for the demands of the Kosovo population, which was directed to Parliament. On 1 July 1990, the Council issued a statement that demanded Parliament issue a declaration on the status of Kosovo.[24]

This silent but intense activity on the part of certain members of the LDK, including Rugova himself, with the provincial institutions in the days prior to the declaration of independence on 2 July 1990 is also confirmed by Jusuf Zejnullahu, the first minister of the provincial government between 1989 and 1991. In an interview he stated that Rugova had more than once discussed with him issues concerning security and the plans for the declaration of independence and the constitution of Kosovo.[25] Also, on 1 July, the Coordinating Council issued a statement in which it urged Parliament to issue a declaration on the status of Kosovo. Ilaz Ramajli confirms that 'most of the principles of the Coordinating Council were incorporated into the declaration of independence issued a day later'.[26] On 2 July 1990, the Kosovo Parliament declared Kosovo's independence.

The formal act, which curiously followed only sixteen months after the previous parliament had voted in constitutional amendments in favour of Serbia, marks the origins of the parallel state of Kosovo. The act was received with great enthusiasm among the population and the whole Albanian political spectrum. Milazim Krasniqi reported that 'in the premises of the KWA, where the LDK's official seat was located, more precisely in Rugova's office, we celebrated the declaration of independence with whisky'.[27] On the same day, Rugova invited the chairs of all twenty-two LDK branches in Kosovo to publicly endorse the declaration of independence, emphasizing that the LDK and all political parties in Kosovo would have to act according to the national will as stipulated by Parliament's declaration.[28]

This shows how the LDK, with a political programme aimed at implementation through a strategy of non-violence, along with a form of moderate populism in addition to intelligent political manoeuvrings, had been able to realize a different cultural and political climate in Kosovo and ensure unequivocal support from the intelligentsia, which was also a significant factor. This movement produced a changed political reality, which was eventually confirmed by the declaration of independence. In addition, this new political climate and the declaration of independence also demonstrated three fundamental aspects to challenging Serbian legitimacy over Kosovo: one, that there was no conformity of the majority to (Serbian) established rules; second, that there were no shared beliefs among the dominant Serbian regime and the majority of the population; and third, that legitimacy had shifted in favour of Kosovo's parallel state.

The conclusive part that shapes the withdrawal of legitimacy from the Serbian authorities and conferred legitimacy on the parallel state was reached with the approval of Kosovo's constitution in September 1990. Although Serbia suspended the Kosovo Parliament soon after it declared independence on 2 July, the latter continued its activity despite the risks and complications arising from the arrest warrants issued by the Serbian authorities. A Constitutional Commission consisting of prominent legal experts was formed to prepare the constitution on Parliament's behalf. In the absence of the parliamentary chairman, Djordje Božović, who was of Serbian nationality, Ilaz Ramajli took on his role, and the majority of deputies proceeded with their parliamentary duties.[29] The parliamentary hearing was held in the small town of Kaçanik, the LDK branch there having ensured the logistics and security.[30] Kaçanik is a remote valley with an historical reputation for fierce Albanian resistance to foreign domination. Due to its unique geography and proximity to the border with the Republic of North Macedonia, Kaçanik was considered a suitable place for such an event and provided a safe route in case the meeting was interrupted by the Serbian authorities. On 7 September 1990, Parliament approved the constitution. The meeting lasted only a short time, but it conducted business according to its legal requirements. With a majority consisting of over two-thirds of the total of 111 deputies, Parliament declared the Republic of Kosovo's constitution. In its first article it read:

> The Republic of Kosovo is a democratic state of the Albanian nation and members of other nations and minorities of its citizens; Serbs, Muslims, Montenegrins, Croats, Turks, Roma and other minorities, who live in Kosovo.[31]

Along with the announcement of the constitution, Parliament also approved several other rulings, including the Electoral Act, and an act that regulated political pluralism in Kosovo.[32] In this way, Parliament managed to set a legal process in motion – the parallel state. Most of the deputies who participated at these two events, the 2 July declaration of independence and the 7 September act of declaration of the constitution, were forced to leave the country, the majority of them moving to Slovenia. Some of these deputies lobbied from within Slovenian institutions, but they also maintained their contacts with political figures in Kosovo such as Rugova and Agani. During their stay there, Parliament held several meetings and made a number of decisions. These included a formal decision to remove from office the chairman, Djordje Božović, and replace him with his deputy, Ilaz Ramajli, who, along with a few other deputies such as Halit Muharremi, played a vital role in bringing in the most relevant legislation to help create the legal infrastructure for the parallel state.[33]

With these two legal acts, suddenly, within a matter of months, the LDK had been able to transform the political environment and enthusiasm of the Albanian population from the chaotic state in which they had found themselves after the constitutional changes forced on them by Serbia. The popular support that it enjoyed gave the LDK a legitimate responsibility, which it used intelligently in semi-covert co-operation with Parliament and the government of Kosovo. It comes as no surprise, therefore, that the declaration of Kosovo's independence was incorporated into the LDK's programme, which Rugova and the LDK doggedly pursued throughout their campaign of non-violence.

Social, health and education challenges and the parallel state

Although social protection is not broadly recognized by scholars as a subject linked to legitimacy, such authors as Babken Babajanian have argued for a correlation between social protection and state legitimacy.[34] In this section, it will be shown how the Serbian government's failure in its duty of care for all citizens was replaced by the responsibilities of the parallel state.

From the outset of its formation, the LDK established branches throughout Kosovo's municipalities, with sub-branches in villages. Within a short time the LDK's political organization covered every corner of Kosovo. Besides their political role and ability to pass on information,[35] these structures also functioned as agents of social and medical care. This became particularly pertinent when the Serbian authorities intensified their repressive methods and adopted new administrative measures – the so-called 'emergency measures'. These stipulated that all employees had to accept the authority of Serbia, and new heads of enterprises and companies, hospitals, schools etc. were put in post, which subsequently resulted in around 15,000 Albanian workers losing their jobs. In protest against this, on 3 September 1990 the Independent Trade Union of Kosovo (Bashkimi i Sindikatave të Pavaraura të Kosovës – BSPK) called a general strike throughout Kosovo, which, despite its aims, resulted in a further 5,000 workers who participated in the strike losing their jobs.[36] In this way poverty began to loom, and that required intervention.

One of the positive developments in the dynamics of the politics of Yugoslavia in the early 1990s was the introduction of the market economy throughout the country. This was implemented rapidly in Kosovo by the Albanians, who had high unemployment as a result of en masse dismissals. Many Kosovo Albanians embarked on private initiatives, a number of these being in the medical sector, which subsequently contributed greatly towards providing a health service for a very notional fee. But these initiatives only helped a small number of families. Most of the population was medically and socially unprotected.

Therefore, the LDK's initial social activity called for aid, which found major support from the humanitarian organization Mother Teresa, formed in May 1990 by a group of young intellectuals supported by Zef Gashi, from 1998 to 2016 archbishop of Bar (Montenegro), in response to the emergence of severe social and health needs. Mother Teresa worked closely with LDK activists, and in many instances humanitarian actions were even undertaken by LDK volunteers. Skender Zogaj, the chairman of the LDK in Fushë, Kosovë (Kosovo Polje in the Serbian language), the first LDK branch outside Prishtina, states:

> We had many people there, including those who did not want to be visible in the political organization but were LDK supporters. So they were able to execute the LDK's programme on the ground. We used to send them the lists of people in emergency need, and Mother Teresa personnel would come to us (to me, for example) and bring us the distribution lists.[37]

The effects of addressing these emergent social and medical needs were characterized by a uniquely spiritual dimension in the form of solidarity during the years of the parallel state. How widespread and deep this solidarity had penetrated into the psyche of the population is illustrated by an example that Ibrahim Berisha, one of the LDK's founders, provides. On the twenty-fifth anniversary of the foundation of the humanitarian organization Mother Teresa in Kosovo, which was celebrated in September 2015, Berisha recalled:

> At one of the food delivery locations, Kodra e Trimave in Prishtina, the head of a family, who had food for two more days, refused to collect the last remaining food, allowing his neighbour, who had nothing left, to feed his family.[38]

The social funds initially came from individual donations, predominantly from the diaspora. Skender Zogaj explained: 'For example, in 1991, I, as leader of the LDK's branch in Fushë Kosovë, received aid from a businessman in Norway (Fatmir Zymberi) in the amount of 10,000 German Marks. We distributed this fund to fifty families, each receiving 200 German Marks.'[39] Eventually, the LDK institutionalized these forms of donation by creating its own social programme, the so-called Commission for Aid, which operated throughout Kosovo in LDK branches and sub-branches, distributing aid to every corner – including the most remote parts – of Kosovo. The main financial source eventually became the prominent '3 per cent fund', which the parallel government of Prime Minister Bujar Bukoshi founded in exile. This government fund fulfilled some basic social needs, but most importantly, it financed the education sector, the expenses of the parallel institutions and the maintenance of the LDK's offices and so on. In this way, Kosovar Albanian society to a large degree became self-sustaining, and it consolidated popular belief in the self-government institutions of the parallel state.

The parallel state and education

One of the most successful achievements of Rugova's parallel state was establishing and maintaining an independent education system in Kosovo, at all levels of education. Parallel education was both a product and a constitutive aspect of the parallel state. To a large degree, they seem to be mutually constitutive. Education in the Albanian language in Kosovo had a short history, dating from well after the end of the Second World War, and it was perceived as one of the main Albanian victories during the Yugoslav regime. Education had thus become a symbol of national consciousness and a source of cultural and political survival. Since Kosovar Albanian society was generally young, and education included a significant portion of the population, ranging from primary school pupils to university students, having control over this sector gave the LDK and the parallel state great impetus.

It may not be a coincidence, therefore, that education throughout Kosovo, in particular secondary education, was hit by a massive and 'mysterious' poison epidemic in March 1990, with up to 7,600 children poisoned, mostly girls between the ages of 15 and 19. Curiously, the poisonings occurred shortly after the Serbian authorities had accepted demands from the local Serbian community that their children not attend their classes at the same time as their Albanian peers, except for morning sessions.[40] The Serbian authorities not only denied the poisoning occurred but also said the Albanians' claim was false, while the Serbian press 'diagnosed' the Albanians as suffering from nationalism; therefore, the appropriate therapy advocated was 'action by the relevant state and judicial organs', rather than by 'ointments and liquids'.[41] Despite these denials and counter-accusations, there was no doubt among Albanians that these acts were committed by the Serbian secret service and military. Their claim has been corroborated by testimonies from Kosovo Albanian doctors and by some international observers and international laboratory analysis.[42]

The 'emergency measures' and other legal provisions introduced by the Serbian authorities during 1989–90, which aimed to implement a unified Serbian education system that included Kosovo, added more strain and instability to Albanian education. Most importantly, in August 1990, a short time before the new academic year, the Serbian authorities required that all educational institutions in Kosovo introduce Serbian curricula,[43] which was a radical setback for education in Albanian.

However, this was universally refused by Kosovo teachers, parents and children, and in addition the Council for Education in Kosovo (Pleqësia e Arsimit të Kosovës), on 24 August 1990, approved the Plans and Education Programmes for Primary and Secondary Schools according to the existing curricula.[44] At this meeting, the council adamantly defied Serbian encroachment on the autonomy of Albanian education and issued a statement in which they articulated several points. Key among them were support for the declaration of independence and refusal of the 'emergency measures', for education to continue according to Kosovo's existing legal provisions and in harmony with the declaration of independence, and for only Kosovo educational institutions to be recognized as legitimate.[45]

These point-blank refusals of the Serbian measures and curricula led the Serbian authorities to physically prevent Albanian children and students from entering their buildings, and they subsequently terminated financial support for all levels of education in Kosovo. In response, Albanian political leaders and the education authorities reacted by organizing education in private buildings. 'In the summer of 1991, I and professor Agani from the LDK and two representatives from the trade unions, as well as two others from the institute of education, in total six of us, met to discuss the issue and decided to begin education in private buildings', says Rexhep Gjergji.[46] Again, financial support for education started with individual donors, who mostly sent money directly to LDK activists, who then disbursed them,[47] but such an enterprise required substantial funds and logistics, and could only be sustained with the support of parallel institutions. As the parallel government was being consolidated, Bukoshi's government extended its financial responsibility to supporting education.

As can be seen, the declaration of independence had a profound effect on the education authorities – not only in defying the Serbian authorities by not implementing Serbian legislation in Kosovo Albanian education but also in generating the mobilization of all sections of the Albanian population. In turn, the necessity of maintaining educational autonomy required the LDK and parallel institutions to intervene with both human and financial resources. The significance of parallel education, therefore, lies not only in the fact that it enabled the continuation of education in Albanian but also in the fact that it served as a mechanism that played a large part in the materialization of the parallel state at the most important levels. In this way, the LDK achieved a fundamental success: it tied parallel education, and hence the whole parallel state, to the LDK. This meant that teachers, university lecturers, pupils, students and their parents, which constituted the largest portion of the Albanian population in Kosovo, were tied to the LDK and Rugova's non-violence movement. In the process, schools and universities became significant agents of the Kosovo parallel state and of the non-violence movement.

Managing internal political factions through the parallel state

Building the parallel state became a long-term political goal through which Serbia's control was meant to be delegitimized and eroded. At the same time, the parallel state became an instrument that maintained internal cohesion. The LDK and Rugova himself would frequently remind their supporters that the choice of non-violence was a long-term and difficult process, but it was the safest route towards the realization of their national goals. He stated:

> We are driven by pacifism, in a long-term, non-violent resistance, by withholding our people from resisting and restraining them. It is clear we are not talking about a few days, but years, and in a situation when every individual might have gone out and resorted to violence it was necessary to open avenues through which Albanian demands might be articulated.[48]

The influence of Rugova in cultivating the internal political dynamics of Kosovo and the LDK's long-term strategy in maintaining the discourse of non-violence paradoxically meant that he also held some soft form of monopoly over several political and cultural entities.[49]

As discussed in Chapter 1, Kosovo's internal politics were not so coherent as they may have been perceived as being by both the local population and international observers. Kosovo was characterized by different political ideologies and different views on ultimate political goals, and proposals for radically different methods with which to confront Serbia. While Rugova and the founders of the LDK had a peaceful strategy implemented in the LDK mission statement from the outset, the party also housed a significant number of former Marxist-Leninist groups, or, as one LDK founding member characterized them, 'national communists'.[50] Some of these groups were also proponents of the idea that Kosovo should join Albania, an option seen as unviable by most. However, the LDK embraced their adherence for two main reasons. First, it was Rugova's deliberate strategy to incorporate the Marxist-Leninist radicals within the LDK so as to have them in a position where they could be controlled, and second, it was a general aspiration of the LDK leadership to include this persecuted group in order to expand the LDK's inclusiveness and political representation.[51]

However, there remained several political parties led by high-profile politicians and intellectuals. One such party was Uniteti Kombëtar – UNIKOMB (the Party of Albanian National Union) – founded by Ukshin Hoti. Hoti and his successor, Halil Alidemaj, were close allies of the Marxist-Leninists who operated within the LDK but agitated for unification with Albania.[52]

The other group consisted of autonomists and converted democrats who were dispersed both within the LDK and throughout several minor political parties around such influential figures as Shkëlzen Maliqi, Veton Surroi and Luljeta Pula-Beqiri. These also included prominent individuals engaged in various aspects of civil society, such as Adem Demaçi, or such influential intellectuals as Rexhep Qosja, who, for a considerable time, remained as an 'independent intellectual'.[53] But the national communists, to use Mehmet Kraja's term, proved to be a very difficult faction to manage, particularly owing to their ever-increasing number and militancy within the LDK. Their role became more ominous when they 'formed a silent and undeclared coalition with the autonomists', according to Kraja.[54] After having served prison terms for their organization of and participation in the 1981 demonstrations, these contingents adhered to the LDK and paradoxically joined with the same group of autonomists/communists and/or their political exponents who had convicted them in the first place, and formed an influential faction within the LDK. Moreover, several months after the LDK was formed, the LPRK (since 1993 the LPK), their real party of ideals, launched a slogan, published in their party's newsletter *Pararoja* in 1990, namely 'Occupying [the LDK] from Within'.[55]

This ploy became acutely visible during the first LDK party elections in the spring of 1991. During an organized, grassroots campaign, the Marxist-Leninists and national communists had succeeded in recruiting a large number of delegates to the General Council, where they planned to overthrow Rugova by a majority vote. They gained over 60 per cent of the seats, according to Kraja; however, they realized in the process that overthrowing Rugova was impossible, so they changed strategy. Their next objective became the selection of as many as possible from their ranks to the leadership group alongside Rugova, while at the same time several of the LDK's founders were not elected.[56] Senior LDK members such as Rexhep Gjergji and Milazim Krasniqi confirm this synchronized campaign by Marxist-Leninists/national communists. Commenting on this episode, Krasniqi stated:

> The most prominent and outspoken Marxist-Leninists, including Demaçi, who
> had been offered the platform as a guest, attacked us, the founders of the LDK
> and Rugova's allies. I was subjected to harsh criticism and almost intolerable
> statements. At some point, when they seemingly failed to achieve their main
> objective, they gathered in the middle of the conference hall in order to plan
> their next move.[57]

Although the Marxist-Leninist campaign proved successful, at this stage they
fell short of gaining the dominant power in the LDK. Nonetheless, the LDK was
perceived only as a temporary, pragmatic accommodation by these contingents.
Thus, along with other aforementioned groups, they strove to change the
LDK's profile and turn it into a movement that suited their political ideology.
Their efforts to dominate the LDK continued throughout the party's second
elections in 1994. Their conspiracy to gain full control of the LDK included
another important factor: the prime minister in exile, Bujar Bukoshi. Bukoshi
had grown in influence, partly owing to his control of government funds,
which, according to Edita Tahiri, 'had given him a perception of power, and
eventually he thought he should become the main leader'.[58] In this ambitious
goal he found shared interests with the Marxist-Leninists within the LDK.
This synergy enabled the Marxist-Leninists to conduct an effective campaign
for the second elections to the LDK General Council in August 1994, which
resulted in the LDK's founders being outnumbered and several senior figures
failing to get re-elected. The Marxist-Leninists' (LPRK/LPK) campaign had
been conducted acrimoniously against the founders of the LDK, and Rugova's
close allies were accused of being Serbian spies. Rexhep Gjergji reports that
'the core LDK founders were denounced as Serbian spies, and calls were made
by Marxist-Leninists that individuals [Rugova's close allies] such as Professor
Fehmi Agani, Edita Tahiri, Rexhep Gjergji, Skender Blakaj, Naip Zeka, et al.,
should not be voted in'.[59]

The plot almost succeeded. The election of headquarters personnel had resulted
in domination by the Marxist-Leninists, which prompted the resignations of
Fehmi Agani, one of Rugova's right-hand men, and of Edita Tahiri. According
to Gjergji, their resignations aimed to expose the Marxist-Leninists within the
LDK as a branch of the LPK (an illegal organization).[60] Realizing that he was
going to be surrounded by Marxist-Leninists, and also caught by surprise at
this outcome, Rugova reconvened the General Council convention, at which
the resignations were discussed and a more balanced leadership was restored,
including the return of Agani and Tahiri.[61]

Eventually the elections were concluded successfully, and Rugova issued a statement with a subtext that was meant to neutralize these different factions and interests, saying among other things:

> It is a reconfirmed responsibility for us to realize our programmatic goals, the people's declaration of an independent and neutral Kosova, to organize our life better, to institutionalize it, to develop our contacts with the world, and I say it again, that in this difficult situation we must preserve our tolerance among ourselves, our trust between us, our freedom among us. Perhaps you may think I am repeating myself about these things, but repetition always enhances our strength and wisdom.[62]

Therefore, despite increased polarization within the LDK, its political party character and non-violent political orientation were maintained, which, it can be argued, was due mostly to Rugova's undisputedly charismatic leadership authority. He accommodated both groups by choosing two vice-chairmen: Professor Fehmi Agani, his right-hand man and a senior LDK founder, and Hydajet Hyseni, from the Marxist-Leninists group.

However, the Marxist-Leninists inside the LDK were not the only grouping that challenged Rugova's movement. The LDK's rapid growth and dominance brought together a number of representatives from smaller political parties, intellectuals and leaders of civil society in a campaign against the LDK, accusing it of monopolizing the political arena and of inflexible nationalism, and saying it should be placed under a superior authority consisting of selected intellectuals and political experts.[63] This brings me to Rexhep Qosja and Adem Demaçi, who were perhaps the most relentless critics of Rugova's policy. Qosja, one of the most respected nationalist writers among Albanians in Kosovo and beyond, constantly challenged Rugova's discourse of non-violence from behind the veil of an 'independent intellectual'[64] or via various intellectual associations. However, it is difficult to formulate a solid political or intellectual framework through which Qosja articulated his opposition to Rugova bar a simple disagreement with his non-violence approach. He called Rugova's non-violent resistance 'condescending towards and denigratory of Albanian dignity',[65] and yet he was unable to articulate any alternative political strategy for confronting Serbia. It is thought that his animosity originated from the days when he was the director of the main cultural institution of Kosovo, the Albanian Institute (Instituti Albanologjik), where it was reported that Rugova had not been treated fairly by Qosja. Rugova's spectacular rise as an intellectual and politician, who so rapidly garnered widespread support through his policy of non-violence, seemed to have overshadowed Qosja's reputation as the 'father of the nation' that he had until then enjoyed. An initiative in the form of the Albanian Democratic Forum (Forumi Demokratik Shqiptar – FDSH), formed on 1 July 1990, was largely perceived as the invention of Rexhep Qosja. Mehmet Kraja, a well-informed LDK insider, argued that the Forum was initiated by those political forces and intellectuals who insisted on diminishing the LDK's 'monopoly' of power but were also against Rugova being the only powerful leader.[66] Nonetheless, Rugova had reluctantly attended a well-prepared Forum meeting, which had a visibly overwhelming representation of these exponents. In a short inaugural meeting, the Forum issued a political statement summing up the political situation at the time, including a statement in which it urged the Kosovo Parliament, which was due to meet the following day, to raise the status of Kosovo to equality with that of other members of the SFRY.[67]

However, the ultimate goal of the Forum protagonists, according to Kraja, was to force the LDK to concede power in favour of a supra-political entity (the Forum), in the name of a 'superior' national interest, where decision-making would take place through majority voting (on issues of national interest) among the party leaders that had participated in Kosovo's political campaign, rather than through a consensus.[68] However, despite this 'conspiracy', the Forum did not survive beyond its first gathering – there are no records that it ever convened again after 1 July, nor was it able to deliver any political results. Its activity was reduced to a body that was mostly concerned with academic publications.[69] Eventually, Qosja formed his own political party in 1998 called the United Democratic Movement (Lëvizja e Bashkuar Demokratike – LBD) along with a number of former Marxist-Leninist activists who had defected from the LDK, such as Hydajet Hyseni, in order to bolster opposition to the LDK and Rugova. However, even then, he enjoyed very little popular support, and after the conflict his party was disbanded.

Adem Demaçi (1936–2018) was in many ways not dissimilar to Qosja. He was the most prominent Kosovo Albanian political prisoner, having spent twenty-eight years in Yugoslav prisons. For this reason, he was frequently called the Balkans' Mandela and received the Sakharov Prize for Freedom of Thought from the European Parliament. He enjoyed widespread respect among Albanians for his stoicism and for his fight for Albanian rights. When he was released from prison, Rugova offered him a role in the LDK, which Demaçi refused. Instead, he became a human rights activist, among other roles, and a relentless critic of Rugova's policy of non-violence. Like Qosja, Demaçi failed to articulate a solid alternative, although he appealed for a 'strategy of non-violence, and not a pacifist and "cowardly" one [referring to Rugova's approach], but a powerful and liberationist policy'.[70] However, it is not quite clear what he meant by this slogan, since he never undertook a political initiative to realize his ideas. At times he put forward controversial proposals, such as an idea for a Kosovo confederation with the two remaining entities of the former Yugoslavia, Serbia and Montenegro, which he called Balkania. But this idea failed, because it did not enjoy any support.[71] In 1996, he replaced Bajram Kosumi, a former Marxist-Leninist prisoner, as the leader of the Parliamentary Party of Kosova, but soon left the organization. When the Kosovo crisis descended into military confrontation, Demaçi became the political representative of the KLA in Kosovo. Therefore, when analysing Demaçi's shuttling from one entity to another, and from one idea to another, one gets the impression that, just as it was with Qosja, much of Demaçi's criticism of Rugova stemmed from antagonistic reasons, as a result of his diminished recognition by the Albanian population of Kosovo, who had embraced Rugova's ideas.

Rugova and the LDK successfully neutralized these efforts, refusing to concede power to smaller parties and preferring instead to operate within the pluralist political system that they promoted. In a quite elegant fashion, and by means of a moderate political slogan, Rugova responded: 'Well, we live in a time of political pluralism, therefore all forms and political activities that are in favour of Kosova are welcome.'[72]

Therefore, under pressure to manage these internal political factions, the LDK transformed itself and became an 'institutionalist' party.[73] By rejecting the trap of entering into tribal cultural forms of congregating and decision-making, which would also have held the LDK hostage to smaller parties and authoritative intellectuals in the name of 'national interests', the LDK changed the culture within which politics was conducted. In the process, it also transformed itself. Through this process of transformation more creative methods of managing political differences and reaching common decisions were discovered – an entity in the form of the CCAPP, or KKPPSH, to which I now turn.

The CCAPP/Y as an instrument for internal political management

The formation of the Coordinating Council of Albanian Political Parties (CCAPP) came to fruition as a result of several factors, but most importantly it was formed for the purpose of sharing power between the Albanian political parties and decision-making regarding issues of central national interest. Initially, it was named the Coordinating Council of Political Parties in Kosovo (Këshilli Koordinues i Partive Politike – KKPP) in the late summer of 1990. The council consisted of a representative from each of the six existing political parties, except the LDK, which was represented by two members, Rugova and Professor Fehmi Agani, and the third de facto LDK representative was Professor Ali Aliu, who hosted some of the council meetings.[74] The formation of the council appeared a pragmatic choice that would facilitate decision-making by consensus. Rugova himself stated: 'We take decisions together; decide the organization of referendums, elections, creating the government and for all other issues that are vital for our national existence. But every party preserves their independence.'[75] However, this does not conceal the fact that Rugova and the LDK had ensured they would retain decision-making power through consensus, which was critical for avoiding decisions that could potentially go against the LDK's ultimate goals and its strategy of non-violence.

With the situation in Yugoslavia heading towards disintegration in July 1991, the council expanded by incorporating four other political parties that represented Albanians outside Kosovo. Two of these, Partia për Propsepritet Demokratik and Partia Demokratike Popullore, represented Albanians in Macedonia, whereas Lidhja Demokratike në Mal të Zi and Partia për Veprim Demokratik represented Albanians in Montenegro and Serbia respectively – the Presheva Valley. All three major parties in each of these countries were considered to be LDK satellite parties, which were organized in a similar pattern to the LDK. The council was now called the Coordinating Council of Albanian Political Parties in Yugoslavia (CCAPPY). Again, Rugova was confirmed as the chairman of this expanded body.[76]

However, the origins of the CCAPPY are associated with an important event. In January 1991, the former Croatian president Franjo Tudjman facilitated a meeting of a number of Albanian representatives from most of the Albanian parties in Kosovo, and the Albanian parties in Serbia, Montenegro and the Republic of Macedonia, including influential former Kosovo Albanian communist politicians and military experts. Gathered at a tourist resort near Zagreb, Stubićke Toplice, the meeting was sponsored by Tudjman but made use of some Albanians in Croatia as his mouthpiece, such as the Croatia-based Albanian military expert Tomë Berisha.[77] The essential idea of this meeting was to stimulate Albanians to join Croatia in the military conflict against Serbia by opening the so-called 'Southern Front'.[78] Harsh debates are reported to have taken place at this meeting with Berisha and former Kosovo communist leader Mahmut Bakalli, who, after the events of 1981, had resigned from his role as president of the LCK and left politics. Despite having endured criticism and at times offensive language, including accusations of state treason, Rugova had insisted on continuing by political means, non-violent resistance and the internationalization of the Kosovo issue. He firmly refused to budge, saying, 'We will not declare a military confrontation because we do not possess the resources, nor do we have the international support, particularly the support of the United States.'[79] Eventually, the agenda failed to materialize, although efforts continued for some time, only to fade away later.

Otherwise, the role of the council was to co-ordinate actions and build the political platform and strategy, as well as arrive at common decisions, including on Albanian affairs in the other republics within the Former Yugoslavia, in which case the CCAPPY would be activated. Realizing political pluralism through the CCAPP in Kosovo alone became a fruitful form of maintaining unity and managing political differences among political parties. Nonetheless, the LDK was still able to implement its own strategy and control political developments. Skender Zogaj, a senior activist in the LDK at the time, argued, 'most of the decisions were taken by the LDK leadership anyway; they were only sent to the Council for approval in order to give it some publicity'.[80] The most important function attributed to the CCAPPY was the so-called 'statement of the three options'. Despite having declared independence and adopted a constitution, during the early period of 1990 and 1991 the Kosovo leadership was not able clearly to define their options regarding whether to orientate political activity towards staying in the Yugoslav federation, which was seemingly failing, or to move towards pursuing an independent route. As discussed earlier, different opposition groups proposed different approaches, none of which were more suitable, given the circumstances at the time, while Kosovo's destiny depended largely on conditions dictated by developments in the rest of Yugoslavia. Under these circumstances, on 11 October 1991 the CCAPPY issued a political declaration known as the aforementioned 'statement of the three options', which stipulated that Albanians would adopt an option that was appropriate, depending on the circumstances. The statement read as follows:

1. If the internal, as well as external, borders of Yugoslavia do not change, then the Republic of Kosovo should exist as an independent and sovereign state, with the right to join an association of sovereign states in Yugoslavia. Other parts inhabited by Albanians in Macedonia, Montenegro and Serbia will have enjoyed the status of people constituting the (respective) state, as well as all other rights deriving from that status.

2. Should the external borders of Yugoslavia not change, but the internal borders between the republics change, then there will be a demand for a Republic of Albanians in Yugoslavia, created on ethnic and other principles. that is available to Serbs, Slovenes and other peoples of Yugoslavia.

3. If the external borders of Yugoslavia do change, then the Albanian people in Yugoslavia, with a general declaration through a plebiscite, will decide to join Albania, thus creating an integral ethnic state of Albanians in the Balkans.[81]

The flexibility and pragmatism shown in the three political options satisfied all Albanian interests represented in the council, but it was also intended as a message regarding the ongoing discussions for a possible reconstruction of Yugoslavia. Whereas six Yugoslav republican leaders were conducting roundtable negotiations for a future reconstruction, the Kosovo leadership strove to create its parallel institutions. Following the fall of communism, a plebiscite declaration had become political practice in various regions, and Kosovo Albanians decided to exercise this democratic expression too. Thus, the CCAPP announced the organization of a referendum in which the Kosovo population would be consulted about its political future. To that end, Parliament elected a commission to prepare and organize the referendum, which conducted its tasks in co-operation with the CCAPP's representatives.

The referendum was subsequently held on 26 and 27 September 1991, in 1,500 electoral polling stations and 450 electoral units, and 914,802 people voted out of 1,051,357 eligible voters (87.01 per cent). Of this number, 99.87 per cent voted in favour of Kosovo being a sovereign and independent republic.[82] The referendum was covered extensively by many local and international media outlets, which to a large degree lent the referendum more legitimacy.

The formation of the council and the perceived success of the acts of declaration for independence, the constitution and the referendum encouraged the Albanian political elite and members of Parliament to proceed with other political acts. In a move to legitimize its forthcoming actions, Parliament adopted some constitutional changes, which also reflected changes in the Yugoslav political landscape. These changes related to Kosovo's political status within the constitution of the SFRY, and therefore Parliament adopted the term 'the Republic of Kosovo' (Republika e Kosovës) in those parts that reflected the new political and constitutional context of SFRY. Also, these changes allowed Parliament to legislate on issues that the CCAPPY required to execute its political strategy.[83]

While proceeding with a peaceful campaign, the LDK and Rugova were careful, however, not to press ahead with political actions that went beyond what Serbia might have perceived as a threat to its sovereignty over Kosovo. Having achieved its immediate goals by formally downgrading Kosovo's political status and effectively occupying the province, Serbia had imposed a certain impasse on Kosovo Albanians, which resulted in what Raphael Pouyé called a 'co-operative conflict'.[84] This resulted in a certain degree of flexibility on Serbia's part towards Albanian political actions in order to avoid international condemnation, which had been increasing as a result of the information campaign of the policy of non-violence and the work of international observers. Institutions such as Human Rights Watch, Helsinki Watch[85] and Amnesty International, as well as US congressmen and senators, and European Union (EU) Parliament members were among the visitors to Kosovo between 1989 and 1992. Arguably, the parallel state became a compromising factor for both. For Serbia, which effectively held a monopoly on violence, the Albanian declaration of independence, the constitution and the referendum were 'clandestine' actions that had no political or legal significance. For the Kosovo Albanians, on the other hand, these acts represented a basic legal and political infrastructure upon which a gradual realization of the Kosovo state was to be accomplished.

In this context, therefore, the formation of the government was perceived as a step that could have swung the balance in favour of the Albanians but that might have forced Serbian forces to intervene. With that in mind, after a series of meetings the CCAPP agreed to form the Provisional Coalition Government of the Republic of Kosovo and endorsed the LDK candidate Bujar Bukoshi to form a government that would conduct its business abroad.[86] In order to compensate for the absence of a government, parallel covert ministries with unidentified ministers were formed to function in Kosovo that mirrored those of the government in exile.[87]

So, with the act of the formation of a government, the CCAPP facilitated the formation of the parallel-state institutions and eroded further Serbian legitimacy over Kosovo, but it also sent a message to Kosovo Albanians that the Kosovo leadership was establishing the 'state of Kosovo'. Although the CCAPPY had earlier approved three options, the course leading to an independent Kosovo had been considered the most pragmatic one, which Rugova and the LDK firmly embraced at an early stage. During an LDK general council meeting following the first LDK convention in the May of 1991, Rugova indicated his preference for pursuing this course, and he advised LDK political activists to pass on this message to LDK supporters at all grassroot levels. He argued that the LDK's peaceful approach was well received in Europe – and as for those who did not agree with this position, they were free to move to other political parties that were being formed in Kosovo.[88]

(De-)legitimation through elections

At the beginning of this chapter, I summed up Beetham's three levels of legitimacy. In the third level of his concept, he suggested that legitimacy implied 'demonstrable expression of consent on the part of the subordinate to the particular power relation in which they are involved, through actions which provide evidence of consent'.[89] Taking part in elections is one of those actions that contribute to legitimacy.[90] Furthermore, Beetham argued, if public consent is a requirement for legitimacy, by the same token, legitimacy can be withdrawn. 'Actions ranging from non-co-operation and passive resistance to open disobedience and militant opposition on the part of those qualified to give consent will in different measure erode legitimacy, and the larger the numbers involved, the greater this erosion will be. At this level, the opposite or negative of legitimacy can be called *delegitimation*.'[91]

Delegitimizing Serbian control of Kosovo was a strategic goal of Rugova's policy of non-violence. Since the declaration of independence, the Kosovo leadership had called for the boycott of elections organized by the Serbian authorities in Kosovo. At first, those authorities tried to compensate for the lack of Albanian participation through 'loyal' Albanians, but in time even these 'loyal' Albanians were hard to recruit. The Albanian electorate responded massively to the LDK's calls to boycott the Serbian elections in Kosovo in December 1990, as well as the census of 1991, despite pressure from the international community and from moderate Serbian political parties, who tried to lure Albanians into participating in Serbian elections in an effort to build a front that would oust Milošević from power.[92] However, the Albanian leadership in Kosovo consistently maintained the policy of boycotting Serbian elections at all levels. Even an alternative effort represented in Serbia by Milan Panić, an independent Serbian-American businessman and politician, failed to convince the Albanian leadership to participate in the 1993 Yugoslav elections. Political activists such as Veton Surroi and Shkëlzen Maliqi were isolated voices in the efforts to change the LDK and Rugova's stance on this matter.[93] The Albanian leadership's refusal reinforced the popular conviction that Kosovo had nothing to do with Serbia any more. Any participation in Serbian or Yugoslav elections was deemed as legitimizing the Serbian occupation, something Rugova and the LDK were not prepared to risk.

In the parallel state of Kosovo, therefore, withdrawal of consent was performed at all levels. Following a reverse strategy, Rugova's parallel state was consolidating its own legitimacy. As the Parliament accomplished its core tasks: declared the independence, approved the constitution and the referendum for independence, the CCAPP now moved to organize elections. Thus, in May 1992 the first general election, as well as an election for the president of Kosovo, was held. Serbia too had announced its elections for 31 May 1992, which brought to a head the concerns of the Kosovo leadership over the issue of legitimacy. Thus, in a letter that Professor Agani sent on behalf of the CCAPP to the chairman of the Kosovo Parliament, Ilaz Ramajli, on 1 May 1992, he clarified the council's position that the elections in Kosovo had to be organized at least one week before those in Serbia.[94]

The Kosovo Parliament swiftly organized the elections, in which twenty-two political parties and independent candidates competed, including ethnic minority parties, but none Serbian. Although they were held in an atmosphere of fear and intimidation, which included some incidents such as one involving Rugova himself,[95] generally the Yugoslav authorities tolerated the elections, which were observed by a large number of local and international media. As was expected, Rugova was confirmed undisputed leader, becoming thus formally the president of Kosovo. His party, the LDK, which was leading the non-violence movement, won 96 out of 130 deputies in Parliament. In this composition, fourteen seats were reserved for the Serb minority, although they did not participate in the elections; nor were they expected to participate in the parallel-state institutions at that stage.

The elections were considered very successful and of great historical significance, as they completed the formal infrastructure of the parallel state, but they also consolidated Rugova's non-violence approach. The general elections represented a classic component that demonstrated the legitimacy of the parallel state. Internationally, Rugova's role was formally reaffirmed. He received massive recognition from world leaders, such as from the German foreign minister at the time, Klaus Kinkel, who merits being quoted here:

> On the occasion of your election as the leading representative of the Albanian nation in Kosovo, I cordially congratulate you. With these elections, the Albanian nation in Kosovo has given itself a clearly legitimized representation for the negotiations on the political future of Kosovo in the framework of the EC Conference on Yugoslavia.[96]

From the United States, Senator Bob Dole, who had recently lost the US presidential race to Bill Clinton, affectionately greeted Rugova, saying, 'I am glad that at least one of us became president.'[97] Furthermore, on 26 June 1992, sixteen US congressmen, including Eliot Engel and Susan Molinari, sent a letter to Rugova congratulating him on his election as president. The letter, among other things, said:

> We watched the Kosovar elections of May 24 with great concern and anticipation: concern that the Belgrade regime would attempt to forcefully stop the balloting, and anticipation that Kosovars would take another critical step towards independence and unfettered democracy … we wish to congratulate you on your nearly unanimous election to the Presidency and wish you all the best for the difficult tasks that you now face.[98]

The above-mentioned letters and endorsements demonstrate that the elections in Kosovo had been monitored and observed by major international actors, and that they also endorsed Rugova's policy and the institutional organization.

One of the effects of the elections was that their successful outcome helped the Albanian leadership in shaping perceptions among the Kosovo population that things were moving closer to their ultimate break from Serbian control, although the Serbs held firmly on to the means of power, through the police and the military. The parallel state had delegitimized the Serbian government to the extent that it did not even find any people to create a government or fulfil its administrative duties in Kosovo. The late Ramush Tahiri, a Demo Christian party representative at the CCAPP and a covert minster in Kosovo during the parallel state, recalled:

> The Serb state could not find people to create a government – can you imagine!? So, we delegitimized them completely, we took them out of the system and maintained it ourselves. They say parallel state! Parallel state versus who? We did not accept their state, we provided our own organization.[99]

Tahiri's statement shows how deeply the political leadership themselves were invested in building up the Kosovo (parallel) state and how much they believed in their project. Similarly, the senior LDK figure Edita Tahiri confirmed that the leadership was fully engaged in the parallel state and believed in their endeavour:

> We were determined on independence. First, if you wish to achieve something, you want to have a dream, you must believe in your dream, so we believed in our dream. That was very important, and we converted that dream into a vision, into a strategy, into resilience. You know we were being killed every day, but we remained resilient.[100]

Conclusion

In this chapter, I examined the process through which the institutional organization and the creation of the parallel state of Kosovo took place. Using the concept of legitimacy, I analysed the political challenges that the Albanian political elite was faced with as a result of the Serbian control over Kosovo that was established following the constitutional changes of 1989. The chapter argued that Rugova, through the policy of non-violence and his party, the LDK, was remarkably successful on several fronts. First, I showed how the non-violence approach transformed the political environment by pulling the Albanian protest movement from off the streets and into institutionalizing their political demands, whereby a political battle could be waged. Second, I showed how the LDK facilitated the still-existing provincial institutions' joining the LDK's political objectives and created the parallel state of Kosovo through the declaration of Kosovo's independence, constitution and confirmation of independence via a referendum. By refusing to co-operate with Serbian-controlled institutions, it was argued, the Albanians delegitimized Serbian control of Kosovo, while the parallel state of Rugova built its own legitimacy. The third section of this chapter addressed health, social and education needs, which formed the next major success of the parallel institutions. In this section, the ability of the Kosovo Albanian political elite to organize the life of the population under the most unfavourable circumstances was demonstrated. In the fourth section, I showed how the parallel state also fulfilled the role of an instrument for managing internal factions and political dynamics within the Albanian political landscape in Kosovo through the formation of the CCAPPY, which gave smaller political parties the opportunity to participate in decision-making on major political issues.

Lastly, while it orchestrated the withdrawal of consent from Serbian legitimacy by advocating a complete boycott of Serbian elections, the Kosovo leadership organized its own general elections and those for the president of Kosovo, creating its own legitimacy and thus completing the parallel state. These acts in turn gave rise to a perception of success and conviction among political elites and the general population that the independence of Kosovo was not only possible but just a matter of time. The fact remained, however, that the parallel state fell short of achieving complete statehood. The international community was not prepared to recognize the independence of Kosovo, while the Serbian authorities held legal jurisdiction and control via its monopoly on violence.

4

The internationalization of the Kosovo conflict

Introduction

When the Kosovo crisis emerged with the revoking of autonomy in 1989, Kosovo had a very low international profile. News media, human rights activists and political actors treated it as a region that required improvements in human rights but not one with any high political priority within the international agenda.

The objective of Rugova and the LDK was to change this perception and raise the profile of Kosovo through internationalization. 'Internationalization' here is understood as a process characterized by a series of purposeful actions to draw international political and public attention to the status of Kosovo. This meant overcoming a series of challenges, such as widespread stereotypes about Kosovo and Albanians like those notably portrayed by Yugoslav and Serbian propaganda. Other such challenges included widespread global sympathy for Yugoslavia, which necessarily marginalized the role of Albanians, and also the obstacles posed by Marxist-Leninist groups that advocated radical approaches but had no strategies in place for advancing their cause, or that were indeed liable to take action when the conditions were conducive neither to upgrading Kosovo's status to that of a republic within Yugoslavia, nor to seeing it join Albania.

This chapter will analyse these challenges in more detail and show how Rugova's strategy of non-violence successfully neutralized them while presenting Kosovo to the outside world via a different political and cultural lens. This was achieved through an information campaign targeting a series of international actors, such as the media, politicians, intellectuals, activists and the Catholic Church.

Stereotypes

In the second chapter of this book, I elaborated in detail on the phenomenon whereby Yugoslav and Serbian authorities and institutions, both political and academic, portrayed the presence of the Albanian population in Kosovo and in the former Yugoslavia by ascribing to them a plethora of stereotypes that had persisted for much of the last century, at different intensity at different times. In the 1980s and 1990s the stereotypes most widely entertained in Serbian public discourse were the presentation of the predominantly Muslim Albanian population as jihadist and intolerant of non-Muslims (Serbs). According to this discourse, 'Their [Albanians'] alleged aim is to Islamize the area and to expand the Muslim faith further north into the heart of the Balkans'.[1] It should be reiterated here, though, that these stereotypes led to a general perception among regional and international political actors that the Albanian population was backward and unimportant, a perception also fuelled by the fact that Kosovo was the most underdeveloped entity within Yugoslavia, which was ultimately the principal reason that led to political and social unrest in Kosovo. However, political repression took priority over economic development, and therefore the Yugoslav authorities used the unrest as a justification for further suppression of Albanian rights. A prime example of how this was manifested is the Albanian civil unrest of 1981, which surfaced for economic reasons. However, the Yugoslav authorities used the unrest as a pretext for supressing the Albanians with draconian measures, while adding to them a long list of negative stereotypes.[2] The reality of the province of Kosovo, according to Albanian politicians and political commentators, had been distorted by the Serbian nationalist propaganda often employed by Yugoslav federal institutions; that is, the information that circulated about Kosovo was largely selective and based on stereotypes, so that it would negatively affect the image of Albanians globally. Chapter 2 addressed these issues in more detail; however, it should be emphasized here that the crux of these stereotypes revolved around a narrative already in circulation since at least 1913 when, at the London Conference of Ambassadors, Serb diplomats presented a memorandum claiming a 'Serb historical and religious right to Kosova; the moral right of the more civilized Serb nation; and the ethnographic right against *the recent invasion by the Arnauts*'.[3] This narrative has been present in more recent decades with the questioning of the origins of Albanians in Kosovo,[4] while in the 1980s this discourse frequently included the ascription to Albanians of such terms as 'rape' and 'genocide' among many other negative terms employed by Serb political propaganda.[5]

International sympathy for Yugoslavia

With a strong legacy built during the Cold War, and having been among those key states that led the non-aligned organization that helped to preserve the peace during that period, Yugoslavia still enjoyed widespread international support, and so any attempt to break the status quo was not viewed sympathetically by the main international actors. The political turmoil surrounding the disintegration of Yugoslavia and the lack of any vigorous attempt to stop the bloodshed in the conflict in Bosnia and Herzegovina during the 1990s are testimony to how rigid the international community was in its perception of the Yugoslav crisis, let alone its views about Kosovo Albanians. When the Kosovo government in exile applied to the Badinter Commission, sponsored by the European Peace Conference for Yugoslavia, for recognition in December 1991, along with four other republics of the former Yugoslavia (Croatia, Slovenia, Bosnia and Herzegovina and Macedonia), its request was not considered, despite Kosovo having met the principal criteria – being a constituent member of the SFRY.[6] Thus, there existed in the world an image of the political, legal and historical realities surrounding Kosovo that 'justified' the 'right' of the Serbian authorities to treat the province as they saw fit, including the use of violent means in the managing of Serbian interests in Kosovo. It is the heavy reliance on this perception by the Serbian authorities that, despite the overwhelming refusal of the majority of Kosovo's population, the autonomy that it once enjoyed was removed in March 1989. Despite this controversial act, Serbian legitimacy over Kosovo was not questioned at the time, and Serbia suffered no significant detriment at either the national or international level.

Competition from Marxist-Leninist and Enverist groups abroad

The presence of Marxist-Leninist and Enverist groups formed one of the most important challenges to Rugova's policy of non-violence. I have already spoken (in Chapter 3) about their role and how their political agitation was contained by Rugova in Kosovo, but for the context of this chapter, I will briefly summarize their activity abroad. Different groups that campaigned for the improvement of Albanian rights in Yugoslavia were present during the post-1945 period. However, the 1981 demonstrations throughout Kosovo, with their demands for better economic conditions and the elevation of Kosovo autonomy into a republic, were attributed to the Marxist-Leninist groups[7] and brought them prominently into the public domain. The massive clampdown by the Yugoslav authorities led to many of the participants being persecuted; those who either escaped persecution or who had served their prison terms then emigrated to various European countries and to the United States to launch political activities there. These were carried out by a number of Marxist-Leninist groups and by those loyal to the Albanian communist leader, Enver Hoxha – the so-called Enverist groups[8] – and in February 1992 they formed a joint organization known as the LPK. However, a common denominator persisted among all of these groups, including the LPK: the conviction that Albanian rights could only be achieved through an armed uprising. They principally targeted Albanian workers abroad, most frequently by attending their cultural clubs as part of their effort to spread publicity and to recruit members to their organizations. Although the Yugoslav secret services and other state agencies constantly pursued these militants and punished them for their activities, those involved remained obstinate in denouncing Yugoslavia while promoting their cause. However, owing to their Marxist ideology they failed to attract significant support in the West. When a few prominent activists sought to move outside of these far-left ideologies or to form a more united national front, they were physically eliminated.[9] The assassinations of four prominent activists in Germany and Brussels in the 1980s and early 1990s, and the failure of the respective governments to bring the perpetrators to justice, arguably demonstrated a lack of interest on the part of Western governments in supporting the cause of these Albanian activists. The LDK and Rugova, therefore, had to 'de-throne' the Marxist-Leninists and Enverists from the leading role in promoting the Albanian cause abroad and at the same time demonstrate that they themselves were different, a progressive force that was based on Western democratic principles and political culture.

It is the challenges outlined above that Rugova and the LDK were faced with from the outset of their political campaign.

The strategy to overcome the challenges

In order to overcome the obstacles outlined above, Rugova facilitated his policy of non-violence by developing an information and diplomacy infrastructure. Its primary objective was to change international understanding and garner support for the Albanian cause in the Kosovo conflict. To achieve this objective, Rugova's LDK and other Albanian political activists targeted a series of international actors, such as international media, politicians, intellectuals and activists, including such religious organizations as the Holy See and the Community of St Egidio. I now address each of these separately.

Rugova's weekly media conferences

The seeds of Rugova's non-violence movement may arguably have been sown by his media presentations, in which he drew the attention of the international media to the situation in Kosovo. Even before Rugova became formally involved in politics, this aim was noted in a number of interviews he gave to international media in which he drew attention to a bleak future for Kosovo.[10] In an interview for the German magazine *Der Spiegel*, published on 26 June 1989, Rugova warned of a possible conflict between Serbs and Albanians, stating:

> If Serbia insists on violating our national cultural identity, then there will be an uprising. I can only warn the Serbs: they too are a small nation. In the past, whenever a small nation has tried to play the role of a big power in the Balkans, it has ended in tragedy for them.[11]

The interview referred to the 600th anniversary of the Battle of Kosovo, which Milošević instrumentalized for public consumption by inviting a massive number of Serbs from the whole country to commemorate this event in Kosovo, but also to consolidate public support for his constitutional changes that would be implemented several months later.

Rugova's media conferences followed his weekly meetings with the heads of LDK branches and sub-branches throughout Kosovo, which were held regularly at the same time every week. 'It was obligatory for every chair of LDK branches to participate in the weekly meetings on Friday at 11:00 in the LDK headquarters presided over by President Rugova', says Skender Zogaj.[12] At these meetings, the heads of the LDK's branches would present their reports on the situation in their respective areas, but they also took onboard recommendations from the LDK's headquarters and from Rugova.[13] The first-hand information provided by the local activists at these meetings provided Rugova with the assurance that he was releasing accurate information in his media conferences, as well as providing him with the opportunity to use the platform to appeal to the international community for attention. His most important slogan, in which he insisted on 'the independence of Kosovo, neutral and open towards Albania and Serbia, with a provisional international protectorate, and with all guarantees for the Kosovo Serbs',[14] was repeated in these media sessions and helped consolidate local perceptions of his policy of non-violence. The success of his visits abroad and in hosting international visitors would also be addressed during these media occasions with carefully crafted language. For instance, commenting on the visit of the Kosovo delegation to the International Peace Conference for Yugoslavia on September 1992, Rugova stated:

> We are happy with the discussions we have had with the members of the Group for Kosova and with co-chairs Vance and Owen. We informed them about the situation in Kosova and demanded action to prevent the conflict but also proposed our views for the resolution of the Kosova issue.[15]

Statements like the above were characteristic of Rugova's media style, where he used this platform to maintain the tone of his discourse of non-violence. However, the bulk of the information on events in Kosovo was delivered by the LDK's Commission for Information, to which I now turn.

Kosovo Information Centre – Qendra e Informimit të Kosovës

The Commission for Information of the Democratic League of Kosovo (Komisioni për Informim i Lidhjes Demokratike të Kosovës – KILDK) started with a public statement on 23 December 1989 announcing the formation of the LDK.[16] The Commission, which was later to become the Kosovo Information Centre (Qendra e Informim të Kosovës – QIK), consisted of prominent LDK founders such as Ibrahim Berisha as head commissioner, Xhemajl Mustafa, Rugova's information advisor, and Mehmet Kraja, a writer, and became a significant part of the LDK's philosophy in the presentation of Kosovo to the world.

Its prominence grew after 5 July 1990, when the Serbian authorities introduced administrative measures against the Kosovo media that resulted in the closure of the only daily newspaper, *Rilindja*, radio and TV stations, and publishing companies.[17] *Bujku*, a periodic newsletter devoted to agrarian affairs, was the only one allowed to circulate after the Albanian media in Kosovo were shut down, but in time it eventually started to cover politics. However, the QIK became the most reliable source of information, with a daily bulletin known as *Informatori* (Informer). Typically, news released by the QIK was published with a brief description and arresting headlines covering every incident or piece of information relevant to the public, or information deemed important for both local and international audiences. It also diligently picked up on any piece of information published anywhere in the world about Kosovo and reprinted it for the Albanian readership.[18]

The effectiveness of the QIK was largely due to many former journalists who joined the LDK and became part of the LDK's Commission for Information. Safet Zejnullahu, a QIK activist, describes how this information network operated: 'It was impossible for anything to happen in any village or district of Kosova without the news reaching Prishtina, while the accuracy of the reports was 99 per cent unquestionable.'[19] As its role grew in significance, the number of the QIK's informants and journalists increased to a dozen or more, including translators into English, German and French, characterized by high levels of professionalism, speed and efficiency, which ensured that *Informatori* reached important global destinations. It was published in printed version and distributed free to political activists, international diplomats and journalists, and to the public, as well as online to thousands of internet websites (by the late 1990s) through a twenty-four-hour uninterrupted process.[20]

Kosovo's parallel-state information agency, the QIK, became even more prominent when Enver Maloku became editor in 1993. Under Maloku's editorship, the QIK intensified its activity in terms of both quality and quantity, increasing the publication of *Informatori* from initially one issue a day to several, and as the Kosovo crisis developed, in the latter stages it came out up to seventeen times a day, according to Zejnullahu.[21] In an interview with Maloku himself in December 1998, he reported that the QIK's publication of *Informatori*, and other news articles, in Albanian and other languages, including books, had reached well over 100,000 by December 1998. Sadly, on 11 January 1999 he was assassinated, and, ironically, this interview of his was published in *Informatori* just four days after his death.[22] It is safe to argue, therefore, that the QIK was the principal source of the distribution of information and a facilitator of the LDK and of Rugova's policy of non-violence throughout its existence.

This consistent information strategy, which covered practically every incident committed by the Yugoslav authorities, drew the attention of many Western media outlets, such as the *New York Times*, *Washington Post* and *Christian Science Monitor* in the United States, *Le Monde* in France, and of course British, German and Italian media, and many others throughout Europe. In addition, local Kosovar journalists worked as reporters for such international outlets as *Deutsche Welle*, *Radio Free Europe*, *Radio France International*, *Voice of America*, *Reuters* and so on.[23] In line with information sources inside Kosovo, the international media and human rights organizations reported the increased number of incidents in Kosovo, which earned it the status of the most dangerous aspect of the dissolution of the former Yugoslavia.[24] In a lengthy article by Robin Lodge with the tantalizing headline 'Kosovo Smells War', which appeared in the *Sunday Telegraph* in October 1992,[25] Lodge recollected graphic images of Albanian victims he had seen during his long visit to Kosovo and that the Human Rights Council in Prishtina had collected for international visitors. The central message of the article was that Kosovo was on the brink of violent conflict.

This information discourse also reached such international political experts as Henry Kissinger, who in September 1992 published an article in the *Los Angeles Times* to which he devoted an analysis of the crisis of Yugoslavia. In the article he suggested that although NATO members did not perceive the conflict in Bosnia as so threatening that they would intervene, they should intervene when it came to Kosovo in order to prevent an international conflict there and to stop the ethnic cleansing.[26] A statement of that nature from former Secretary of State Kissinger demonstrated the effectiveness of the Kosovo media information and human rights agencies' reports, which had reached the world and its most competent experts.

Within this framework, political analysts familiar with Balkan politics, such as Elez Biberaj, a *Voice of America* editor, called the Kosovo crisis the *Balkan Powder Keg* in an academic paper published in 1993, a phrase that came to be used frequently by journalists and political commentators. In his paper, Biberaj proposed that both the United States and its Western allies take appropriate measures to prevent Kosovo from drifting towards war.[27] He suggested that 'the international community should either halt Serbia's aggression in Kosova or face the consequences of a general Balkan war, with reverberations as far as Central Asia'.[28] This account by Biberaj, a well-informed individual both within the Albanian information campaign in Kosovo and in the Albanian-American community's campaign in the United States, credibly echoed the QIK and Rugova's information objectives.

Diaspora activity as a source of information

The LDK's information strategy was enhanced by news of diaspora activities, which became an extended agent of the LDK both in Kosovo and abroad. Hafiz Gagica, a post-1981 émigré, instrumental in the formation of the LDK's branch in Germany and later a co-ordinator for all LDK branches in the Albanian diaspora, describes the significance of the QIK's information role as follows:

> Whenever there were meetings, discussions, or any gatherings in Europe, we delivered correct and accurate information about Kosova based on the QIK, whose credibility, once tested, was never questioned again. Thus, it became our principal hub from which we used to distribute our information to the rest of the world.[29]

The founder of the LDK's branch in Switzerland, Shaip Latifi, testified as to how the QIK's information capacity was realized by using the Albanian diaspora and by efforts to establish its own information sources. With their vigorous organization and activity, the LDK's branch in Switzerland established a newsletter, *Informationblatt*, which circulated among such high-profile officials as the chair and members of the Swiss Parliament, NGOs and so on.[30] Furthermore, with remarkable speed and efficiency the personnel of this LDK diaspora branch distributed information coming from Kosovo to the capitals of the world. An incident that involved the LDK's number two, Professor Fehmi Agani, is testimony to their efficacy: upon Agani's return to Kosovo from a trip in Europe, he was arrested by the Yugoslav authorities. 'Within 30 minutes of his arrest, the news reached the offices of Helmut Kohl (the then German chancellor), John Major (the British prime minister), Boutros Boutros-Ghali (the secretary-general of the United Nations), and so on',[31] reports Latifi.

As far as the parallel government was concerned, it too sponsored several information providers. Xhafer Shatri, minister for information in Bukoshi's government, reports:

> After the Belgrade authorities closed the Kosovo media – radio and television – the government improved the information gap: it financially supported a 15-minute programme in Albanian that some Kosovo journalists had succeeded in negotiating with Radio Zagreb, as well as a half-hour satellite television transmission of Albanian Radio television, where the Kosovo government had established its own editorial board.[32]

Shatri was an émigré, who, prior to joining the parallel government as a minister, was a Marxist-Leninist activist and an editor of *Zëri i Kosovës*, the newsletter of the Movement for the Republic of Kosovo in Yugoslavia (Lëvizja për Republikën e Shqiptarëve në Jugosllavi – LPRSHJ), before splitting from the LPRSHJ and co-funding a campaigning entity named Komiteti.[33] He passionately stated that 'although the outbreak of the war in Croatia and Bosnia got the attention of the international community, due to our collective co-ordination and relentless action we succeeded in undoing Serbian propaganda'.[34]

How Albanian diaspora activities aided the internationalization of the Kosovo conflict will be elaborated further in the next section, where I examine the role of political actors.

Political actors

Identifying and influencing various international political actors formed perhaps the most important part of Rugova's information campaign. Efforts to target political actors, especially at the parliamentary level (since the parallel state of Kosovo was not recognized, a ministerial level was not available during these early days), were made soon after the declaration of independence on 2 July 1990 and the approval of the constitution on 7 September. This activity was characterized by various obstacles, described earlier in this chapter, which the LDK sought to overcome by inventing a new cultural identity. At the heart of this philosophy was the idea of conveying a perception to Europe and the United States that Albanians were a European nation that belonged to Western civilization: Albanians were arguably among the (if not the) most outspoken in post-communist southeastern Europe in adopting democratic principles, a commitment to dialogue and the peaceful resolution of conflict. They were praised for their non-violent approach by international authorities, including the US ambassador in Belgrade, Warren Zimmerman, on a visit to Kosovo on 9 September 1991. In a lengthy meeting with representatives from Kosovo Alternative (Alternativa Kosovare), in which he was presented with their detailed views on the conflict with Serbia, Zimmerman praised the Kosovo Albanian leaders for their peaceful resistance against Milošević, and pledged the US support.[35]

The LDK leadership were particularly interested in conveying a pro-Western image. In the LDK's programmatic concept, they intentionally formulated a strategic triangle based on 'equality, democracy, and association (belonging) to the West', argued Jusuf Buxhovi.[36] With these formulations, the LDK began its diplomatic mission aimed at enlightening a largely uninformed international community about Kosovo, which Edita Tahiri in her interview with me described as follows:

> When we started our diplomacy, in the late 1980s and 1990–1, Kosova was *terra incognita* for the world. This is from my own experience with my meetings with diplomats, some of whom did not even know where Kosovo was. They did not know the history, the root causes of the conflict, and did not even know Albanians existed in Yugoslavia, although Albanians constituted the third-largest population in Yugoslavia.[37]

The absence of information about Kosovo at the international level also hampered the parallel government, which by the autumn of 1990 found itself in exile. In the beginning they were not even able to gain access to foreign governments, which necessarily meant they would target lower-ranking political actors. Prime Minister Bujar Bukoshi stated: 'Initially we tried to contact members of Parliament in various countries, because at the beginning we could not access international governments.'[38]

While the parallel state was still in its very early stages, Albanian diaspora campaigners, mostly consisting of Marxist-Leninists and Enverists, had been active since 1981, and more so after 1989, when many Albanians emigrated abroad to avoid Yugoslav repression. They had created a network of media contacts, which gave them a sense of a self-perceived 'monopoly' on speaking about Albanians' interests abroad. When the LDK began to establish its branches abroad, Marxist-Leninist and Enverist groups perceived it as a challenge to their 'monopoly', which saw them engaged in an unwelcoming campaign. While most remained loyal to their ideology and political structures, some joined the LDK and the government of Kosovo in exile. Xhafer Shatri, a pragmatic activist, was one of them, who was sponsored by the PPK.[39] He joined the government of Kosovo in the capacity of minister for information.

Hafiz Gagica, another activist, and among the first of this contingent to join the LDK and help establish its first branch in Germany, said:

> Our first task was to create contacts with the institutions of the countries where we lived. For example, Ibrahim Rugova visited Germany (the Bundestag) for the first time in June 1990. Or the first interview that Rugova gave to *Der Spiegel* in 1989, which was arranged by us, and we organized his first visit to the Bundestag in June 1990.[40]

Even though Germany was considered to be one of the best informed on the Yugoslav crisis, it was not easy to break through the wall built around certain circles in Germany that Yugoslav propaganda about Kosovo had created, in order to pass on the information that the LDK representatives wanted to impart. Gagica provided a prominent example of this challenge when, in March 1991, he met the head of the Commission for Foreign Policy in the Bundestag, Dr Hans Sterke, a conservative from the Christian Democratic Union:

> I spoke with Dr Sterke about the violence of the Serbian authorities in Kosova, and I suggested that it would be really good if a delegation from the German authorities could visit Kosova. He was looking at me and, after a moment, burst out: 'You want to destroy Yugoslavia, you are connected to the Islamist fundamentalists and your people assaulted that nun', etc. It was such a difficult

meeting [...] He was such an important person to hold that kind of view about the Albanians [...] He was so influenced by Serbian circles against the Albanians that you cannot imagine. Those days, German TV programmes were running a documentary about a nun of Serb nationality who claimed to have been sexually assaulted by Albanians at the Graçanica Monastery in Kosovo. Although the incident was completely fabricated, Sterke had absorbed the incident as a true event committed by 'Albanian fundamentalists'.[41]

Unable to contain his rage, and lacking any diplomatic experience, Gagica reportedly asked Dr Sterke:

'Are you an ambassador for Yugoslavia or head of the Commission for German Foreign Affairs?' Of course, this was not a tactful move, but I felt like I had nothing to lose.[42]

However, to his astonishment, two days afterwards Gagica received a phone call from Dr Sterke's secretary inviting him to another meeting, which resulted in a dramatic turnaround of events:

At this meeting Dr Sterke inquired if I was able to arrange for him a visit to Kosova and to meet Rugova himself, which I duly did, by calling Rugova then and there.[43]

Soon afterwards, Dr Sterke led a delegation to Kosovo, which resulted in a radical change of his views about the reality there. 'From the day he returned from Prishtina we became friends', reported Gagica.[44]

There were other factions within German politics, of course, that were more familiar with the reality of Kosovo. However, the role of the activities of the Albanian diaspora was significant in sensitizing German political actors as to the plight of the Albanians. Gagica reported that he personally delivered to the then German foreign secretary, Hans Dietrich Genscher, a letter in which the Kosovo leadership pleaded for (among other things) concrete assistance from the German authorities. One of these demands was permission to establish a residence for the Kosovo government in Germany, which duly happened.

Targeting political actors in the United States

Despite the political weight of European powers such as Germany, France and the UK, it was on the United States, as the principal international superpower, that the Albanian leadership and diaspora activists focused their attention. Traditionally, the United States had been more sensitive to the plight of Albanians in southeastern Europe and had played an influential role on behalf of their interests on more than one occasion during the twentieth century. This role was first demonstrated by a positive response to demands from the Albanian community in the United States, shaped by the Pan-Albanian Federation Vatra, led by the prominent Albanian intellectual and priest Fan Noli,[45] who had emigrated to America in 1906. Owing to Noli and Vatra, among other factors, US president Wilson's role was instrumental in ensuring the existence of the Albanian state during the Paris Peace Conference in 1919 and in ensuring it a place at the League of Nations.[46] During the years under communism, the United States maintained a permanent interest in Albania and at times attempted to influence changes there. After the fall of communism, the United States provided immediate support for the democratic forces led by Sali Berisha and pledged a long-term relationship with the democratic regime in Albania, confirmed by the highly publicized visit of former Secretary of State James Baker in June 1991.[47]

From a few dozen Albanians recorded to have emigrated in 1894,[48] by 2011 the number had grown to about half a million according to some sources[49] from all Balkan areas. Many of these were political emigrants, who, longing for change in their homeland, actively campaigned and provided information to the American government, Congress and the Senate, about Albanian affairs. In the post-1980s period, Albanian Americans frequently spread information and sent letters to American institutions about the plight of Kosovo Albanians under Yugoslavia, and also through public gatherings and protests.[50] As a result of this campaign, in October 1983 congressman Broomfield of Michigan reported in the House of Representatives on the abuse of Kosovo Albanians in Yugoslavia.[51]

However, the Albanian intellectual, author and human rights activist Dr Sami Repishti was perhaps the most involved during the Cold War years in feeding American institutions with information about Kosovo. A young scholar, and son of a deputy from Shkodra (north of Albania) in the 1920s, with pro-Kosovo political convictions, Repishti was arrested by the communist regime because of his calls for the unification of Kosovo with Albania in 1945. He explains:

> I was arrested in 1946. One of the reasons was that I had proclaimed the unification of [Albania] with Kosova in 1945: 'You want to destroy our fraternity with comrade Tito, etc., was among the accusations.'[52]

After he was released from prison, Repishti escaped to Yugoslavia (1959–60), where he witnessed the persecution of Albanians. 'When I came to the United States I pledged to myself that I would fight to free Kosova, and so I did', Repishti stated.[53] With that aim in mind, he embarked on his mission, and as early as April 1964 he delivered testimony to the House of Representatives, which was the first time that the issue of Kosovo had reached Congress. Many years later he sent a formal request to the US vice-president:

> In September 1986, I addressed a formal request to Vice-President George H. W. Bush asking for the opening of an American Information Office in Prishtina, which was later accepted, and the office was opened in 1997.[54]

The invigoration of Albanian-American activities in the United States

The escalation of the Kosovo crisis saw an intensification in Albanian-American efforts to campaign effectively to US institutions about Kosovo. Towards that end, a major success was achieved when Joseph DioGuardi, an energetic Republican congressman from New York (1985–8) and the son of an Albanian/Arbëresh immigrant from Italy, started to campaign on behalf of the Albanian-American community. Within an year of his election as a Republican congressman, in June 1986 DioGuardi tabled a resolution in the House of Representatives in which the abuse of Albanian rights in Kosovo and elsewhere in Yugoslavia was documented.[55] Having lost his race for re-election in 1988, he then decided to devote his time to the issue of Kosovo, and in May 1989, along with several activists, including Sami Repishti, established the Albanian-American Civic League (AACL).[56] DioGuardi and Dr Repishti were elected to the leading roles of president and executive director, respectively, and generated an impetus to Albanian-American-community lobbying.

The experience gained during his years as a congressman enabled DioGuardi to network and campaign effectively, and he established the AACL office on Capitol Hill. The AACL achieved remarkable results within a short time related to the internationalization of the Kosovo issue in the United States. DioGuardi established critical contacts with Democrat congressman Tom Lantos, an American Jew – a Holocaust survivor who, together with Republican John Porter, had established the Congressional Human Rights Caucus.[57] Already engaged in several human rights issues around the world, Lantos incorporated the Albanian human rights issue into his caucus agenda. This was a prelude to two successive events that marked the turning point in the internationalization of Kosovo's human rights in US institutions. On 24 April 1990, the AACL sponsored a Congressional Human Rights Caucus Hearing for Kosovo in Washington, DC. The hearing involved both sides: the Albanians and the Serbs. Kosovo Albanians were represented by newly established party representatives – often known as the Kosovo Alternative – and the chair of the Council for Human Rights in Prishtina, whereas the Serbs were represented by the Serbian head of the Academy of Sciences and Arts Dobrica Ćosić and Serbian Orthodox Bishop Artemije.[58]

The visit of the Kosovar Albanian intellectuals to the United States was celebrated by Albanians both in Kosovo and in America as an event with historical significance, and it had multiple effects. First, it provided an opportunity for the Albanian representatives to lay out their views on the situation in Kosovo before one of the most significant institutions in the United States, along with their counterparts, the Serbs. The Albanian speakers gave testimony on human rights violations, illegal imprisonment, the isolating of Kosovo intellectuals and politicians, assassinations and attacks on Albanian culture and history, all using documented evidence. This also gave the Albanians the opportunity to reaffirm their pledge to democracy and non-violence, and to their commitment to resolve the Kosovo crisis by democratic means, which, according to Rugova, found support among their American hosts.[59] By contrast, Rugova argued that the Serb side presented their views:

> in their typical propagandistic fashion, justifying their policies in Kosova based on historical myths and absurd statistical data about the presence of Serbs in Kosovo in the Middle Ages; those statistical data did not even exist then.[60]

Repishti, himself one of the Albanian-American speakers at the hearing, judged the organization of the hearing of Rugova and other Kosovar Albanian intellectuals' testimonies to the US Congress as a great public relations success:

> The hearing was held at the House of Representatives, Washington, DC, April 1990. The US authorities gave Dr Rugova a standing ovation in treating him as a 'statesman', elevating his international status and reputation to new levels.[61]

Repishti went on:

> Of eight members of Congress present at the meeting, only one, Mrs Helen Delić Bentley, of Serbian origin and a close friend of S. Milošević, was against us. The next day, we held a seminar at the Roosevelt Hotel, New York City, where all fourteen Kosovar intellectuals spoke and expressed their opinions, and again this was a huge success. The LDK became overnight the dominating force for the Albanian-American community in the United States.[62]

An additional positive aspect to the visit relates to Albanian unity in the United States. Although Albanians were heavily invested in their campaign, the community was struggling to harmonize their views. Repishti reported: 'I gave Rugova a summary of the situation of our community, which we followed with the arrangement of a meeting with a large group of activists, to whom he wanted to explain how things were proceeding in Kosova and demanded joint action to advance the cause of Kosova.'[63] The meeting reportedly proved fundamental in harmonizing Albanian elements within the United States and also encouraged the formation of LDK branches there.[64] In this speech, Rugova reportedly drew the attention of the participants to the fact that Kosovo Albanians wanted democracy, freedom and equality, which would bring Albanians closer to Western values, principles that were enshrined within the LDK programme. He said that these principles should be a common goal for all Albanians, irrespective of political affiliation, including calls for the Albanian-American community to act within that framework when lobbying US institutions and political figures.[65] He went on to say: 'our delegation from Kosova represents a pluralist spectrum (left, right and centre) with parties such as the LDK, Agrarian Party and the Social-democratic Party',[66] which was an example for them to follow.

A negative element in all this activity, according to Repishti, who was the most familiar with the dynamics within Albanian circles in the United States, 'was the Communist Albanian Delegation to the UN and their servile agents. Everything was done to break the sense of unity and the activities organized following the instructions given by Dr Rugova. However, the overwhelming number of Kosovars remained faithful to the instructions from Prishtina'. Repishti himself went on to testify fourteen times before both Houses of Congress.[67] Eventually disagreements between Repishti and DioGuardi emerged. A proposal by DioGuardi to represent Albania and Kosovo in the United States was refused by Repishti for as long as Prishtina or Tirana did not authorize DioGuardi. Thus, their relationship suffered, which led to Repishti's resignation; from 1996 he carried on his lobbying activity as head of another Albanian Community organization – the National Albanian-American Council (NAAC). In 2003, Rugova awarded both Repishti and DioGuardi the Golden Medal of the League of Prizren for their contribution to Kosovo's independence.[68]

In May 1990, shortly after the April hearing, Lantos and DioGuardi travelled to Kosovo for a human rights fact-finding mission, where Lantos wanted to witness for himself the reality in Kosovo. The extensive visit and meetings with various political leaders, human rights activists, journalists and ordinary people provided Lantos with evidence showing the reality of human rights in Kosovo. On his return, on 1 June 1990, a hearing was organized at which Lantos gave powerful testimony to Congress, enumerating the brutal violations he had witnessed by the Yugoslav regime of Albanians' fundamental rights.[69] Lantos was (as stated above) a Democrat congressman and human rights activist, but in the case of Kosovo, US politicians of both parties were engaged in a uniquely bipartisan fashion.

Robert Dole as a political factor

The internationalization of the Kosovo conflict in the United States may have achieved its greatest success, however, with the 'recruitment' of the prominent US Republican leader of the Senate (1985–96) and former presidential candidate Robert (Bob) Dole (1923–2021). He was introduced to the problems of Albanians in Yugoslavia, reportedly, by an Albanian-American businessman from South Serbia, Xhimi Xhema.[70] He then independently followed developments pertaining to the Yugoslav crisis in the late 1980s and early 1990s, becoming a fierce critic of Milošević's policies towards Albanians. Dole's initial stance was aligned with the official position of US foreign policy, which was oriented towards the preservation of Yugoslavia. However, reports from Kosovo of the violent crackdown by Yugoslav authorities on peaceful protests promoted by the LDK and Rugova, on the one hand, and the effective campaign by the Albanian-American lobby in the United States, on the other, influenced the American leadership towards having a more critical view of the Serbian authorities in relation to Albanians.[71]

Dole's perceptions about the political reality in Kosovo may have changed fundamentally with the Congress hearing on 24 April 1990, which was followed up by Dole hosting a meeting in his office with Rugova and Buxhovi, from the Albanian side, and Ćosić and Bishop Artemije, from the Serbian. A fierce discussion reportedly took place between Senator Dole and Ćosić, who insisted that the Serbs would refuse any concessions to Kosovo Albanians, with the justification that '[the Albanians] violated Serbian graves in Kosovo, threatened the existence of Serbia with their separatist ambitions and so on'.[72] Dole reportedly replied to Ćosić:

> 'I have not seen anything threatening in the Albanian pronunciations of any kind, while in the program of the LDK they appear to be defending Yugoslavia, and they want democracy and equality, so where do you see their threat?'[73] 'From their behaviour against us [the Serbs], from their violations of our graves, against our saints … from everything', Ćosić responded.[74]

But there is more to this dynamic conversation, in which two of the most trusted proponents of Serbian official policy vehemently defended their position on

Kosovo Albanians. Senator Dole asked whether Serbia would solve the Albanian problem by democratic means, as the Albanians demanded, or by different means. Ćosić responded:

> 'The Serbian people couldn't accept any changes that resulted in the change of their position, including democratic changes.' Dole subsequently followed up with the next question: 'So you don't accept democracy?', to which Ćosić responded: 'We don't accept anything that would mean self-destruction … this right is in harmony with natural law.'[75]

Ćosić's reference to natural law seemingly aggravated Dole, who then reacted by saying:

> This is enough, sir, for you don't apply the laws of civilization but those of nature. If you continue in this way you will destroy Yugoslavia and Serbia. The United States won't accept violence as an alternative to democracy.[76]

Turning to Rugova and Buxhovi, Dole reaffirmed:

> You, on the other hand, will continue your path to democracy even after what you witnessed today.[77]

To confirm that they were on exactly the same page as Senator Dole, Rugova swiftly took the opportunity to repeat his slogan:

> 'Sir, we want democracy, freedom and Western values', after which Dole concluded the meeting by saying: 'The US is on the side of those who seek freedom and equality', and indicated the meeting was over.[78]

The April 1990 testimony to the US Congress and the ruthless, violent response against the Albanians by the Yugoslav authorities following the declaration of independence by the Kosovo Parliament on 2 July 1990 was followed by a visit to Yugoslavia from a group of US Republican senators in August 1990. The delegation, led by Senator Dole, included Alphonse D'Amato, Connie Mack, Larry Pressler, Don Nickels and John Werner, first visited Zagreb and Belgrade, and then, despite objections from the Serbian authorities, headed to Prishtina on a military plane on a fact-finding mission.[79] At the Grand Hotel of Prishtina Senator Dole organized a hearing at which Rugova and other Albanian leaders testified. The significance of the visit for Albanians is recollected by Alush Gashi, a senior LDK leader, who judged it 'the most significant meeting ever held in Kosovo until that point'.[80] In their testimony, the Albanian leaders elaborated extensively on the violent conduct of the Serbian authorities against the Albanian population, but Gashi stated 'we also re-affirmed our commitment to live in peace and freedom in a sovereign Kosova and free from any form of Serbian jurisdiction over Kosova.'[81] The evidence, now also published in a recorded video, confirmed Senator Dole's views about the condition of Kosovo Albanians, while also endorsing their political discourse of non-violence: 'If you follow this discourse you will not be disappointed.'[82] Having completed the visit to Prishtina, on the way to the airport Dole is quoted as having issued a statement for the Serb media: 'Do not touch the Albanians while they continue their work peacefully, because otherwise there will be consequences.'[83]

Thus, Rugova's diplomatic strategy of non-violence for the internationalization of the Kosovo issue had scored another major success – warranting endorsement by so outspoken a US politician as Dole. From then on the latter remained a consistent supporter of Kosovo and particularly of Rugova's discourse of non-violence, which led also to a cordial relationship, as already noted. Dole was instrumental in many US resolutions on Kosovo and was a driving force in pushing the Kosovo issue onto the US foreign policy agenda.[84] He was among the first heavy-weight politicians to publicly endorse the independence of Kosovo in the early 1990s.[85] Later on, Rugova nominated Dole an 'honorary ambassador' to represent Kosovo interests to the United States, and in 2004 he awarded him the Golden Medal of Freedom. In August 2020, a statue devoted to Senator Dole was unveiled in Prishtina.

But, as with Lantos, Albanian-Americans had targeted many Democrat congressmen, the most prominent being Eliot Engel from New York. Harry Bajraktari, a Kosovo Albanian businessman and founder of an Albanian newspaper, *Illyria*, is considered responsible for 'identifying' Engel as a supporter of Kosovo. In a recent article devoted to Engel, who had been in Congress for thirty years, Bajraktari described the moment when he first knocked on the door of the newly elected New York congressman. Bajraktari recollects how Engel patiently listened to his report about the conditions of Kosovo Albanians, and then said:

> It was a beginning of a great friendship between us … he became a friend of the Albanian community in the United States and a great advocate for freedom and democracy in the Albanian-inhabited lands in the Balkans.[86]

Engel became a very active supporter of Kosovo through an Albanian-issues caucus in Congress that he founded. In a long list of Engel's contributions to the issue of Kosovo, a 1994 hearing at the House Foreign Affairs Committee that Engel himself chaired is noteworthy. Partnered by Republican congressman

Benjamin Gilman, Engel pressed the Clinton administration for more support for Kosovo against Milošević's repression of the Albanians.[87] Like the Republican Dole, Engel was among the first to consistently support Kosovo's independence and visited Kosovo several times, most prominently in 1996 when he officially inaugurated the opening of a US Information Office in Prishtina.[88] He too was awarded the Golden Medal of Freedom by Rugova.

Sensitization of political actors in Albania

Before I conclude this section, it is also worth noting the relationship between Kosovo Albanians and Albania. Traditionally, the expectation of Kosovo Albanians and Albanians living outside the borders of Albania had been higher than Albania was able to commit to in her foreign policy. During the four decades under communism, Albania played a controversial role regarding Kosovo Albanians. However, after the fall of communism the situation seemingly changed: Albania began its co-operation with democratic political forces in Kosovo. The Berisha government declared its unreserved support for Rugova's LDK by harbouring many Kosovars, while also creating space for LDK activities. Tirana became a frequent destination for Rugova, who would use it as a destination to fly from to Western capitals in his diplomatic activity, and a representative office covering embassy-like duties was also established there. Skender Zogaj, office representative from 1993–4, described its activities, which 'included a diplomatic relationship with Albania and liaison with all the international embassies and diplomatic representations in Tirana. Official representatives were invited regularly to events with the diplomatic corps, and I had the honour to represent the views of Ibrahim Rugova'.[89] Furthermore, Berisha's government in Albania placed Kosovo on its foreign policy agenda and made it a central reference point in many international diplomatic forums, including in the UN. Once the democratization of Albania had begun, while the former Albanian communist leader Ramiz Alia was still in power, Albania even allowed the training of Kosovo Albanian military forces to take place. This will be addressed in the next chapter, but suffice it to say here that, during the first half of the 1990s, the relationship between Prishtina and Tirana had strengthened; however, with the arrival of the Albanian left to power in 1997, the controversial relationship between Tirana and Prishtina returned once again. This will be elaborated on in more detail in Chapter 5.

Activists and intellectuals

So far, I have examined how Rugova's strategy targeted the media and international political actors with a view to internationalizing the Kosovo conflict. I now address how this activity was manifested with respect to intellectuals and human rights activists.

Human rights campaigners were active from the early days of the Kosovo crisis in 1989 and even more so in 1990, when the violent crackdown by the Serbian authorities against Albanian protests was taking place. The Council for the Defence of Human Rights and Freedoms in Prishtina (Këshilli për Mbrojtjen e të Drejtave dhe të Lirive të Njeriut – KMDLNJ) was among the first entities that formed Kosovar civil society, and it became very active in collecting and reporting human rights abuses. Many international agencies were part of the contingent that comprised this body of information, and some activists stayed in Kosovo for a prolonged period to gather information about it. One such activist was Howard Clark, co-founder of the Balkans Peace Team in 1994, who spent years of research in Kosovo that eventually resulted in a wide-ranging publication.[90]

The KMDLNJ liaised closely with LDK activists, and the two actively shared information relating to the violent conduct of the Serbian authorities against the Kosovo population: in fact, it was standard practice for the KMDLNJ representative to participate in all relevant LDK leadership meetings with international diplomats, human rights activists or journalists. As a result of this activity, human rights organizations were engaged in Kosovo from the beginning of 1990. In an interview for an Albanian newspaper in August 1990, Rugova summarized a series of reports by international organizations, such as the Helsinki Federation for Human Rights, Amnesty International, the International Federation for Human Rights of Paris, the American Federation for Human Rights, the American Congress and others, that reported extensively on the abuse of human rights in Kosovo and also reported on the role of Kosovo activists in their meetings with international visitors.[91] Helsinki Watch (of Human Rights Watch) published two early reports, one in March 1990 and the other in September 1992, detailing abuses of Albanian rights in Kosovo.[92] Rugova considered these reports complementary to the activities of the political leadership and the other forms of media reports that they harnessed, and expressed his satisfaction: 'The West is now informed, it has examined the situation in Kosova, and we expect that the historical "injustice" against Kosova will be reviewed, and we expect concrete steps in due course.'[93]

The Albanian diaspora was also active in targeting various activists. In Switzerland, for example, which had a large Albanian diasporic population, the formation of the LDK revolutionized the effectiveness of information regarding Kosovo. Shaip Latifi, who emigrated to Switzerland in 1990, was instrumental in establishing the LDK branch there in April of the same year. He was a driving force in changing how Albanians operated in Switzerland. In his words:

> When Marxist-Leninists protested in Swiss streets they carried pictures of Marx, Engels and Lenin, which got negative reactions from the Swiss public. I have myself witnessed situations when members of the public would react against this kind of iconography and tell them to 'go and protest in your own country'.[94]

Albanian protests were then accepted more positively, eventually to be joined either in person or in solidarity by many Swiss intellectuals, members of Parliament and religious organizations:

> Albanians started to join us [in LDK activities] and the Swiss people not only began to accept our protests positively but even joined us physically. In 1991 we organized a hunger strike near the premises of the UN in Geneva, where we found the support of Geneva's Protestant Church. Ulie Laurberger, a Green Party member of Parliament, became our supporter and advisor out of sympathy for our demands.[95]

This event was the first Albanian activity in Switzerland to have gained the attention of Swiss TV. On the seventh day of the strike, Latifi reported that the Albanian strike organizers had been invited by the UN office in Geneva to meet Michael Stopford, who served in the office of Secretary-General Boutros Boutros-Ghali.[96]

Several authors in their publications about Kosovo had prominent roles in enlightening an international readership about the historical and political realities in Kosovo. Rugova himself was particularly considerate to those authors who wrote sympathetically about Albanians. They included Noel Malcolm, whose *Kosovo: A Short History* (1998) represented a major challenge to established views about Kosovo historiography, and also Robert Elsie and Michel Roux, who were given awards by Rugova for their contributions.[97]

However, specific attention should be paid here to the efforts to win over the sympathies of the French, who traditionally had pro-Serb sympathies.[98] The evolution of French understanding and perceptions of Kosovo began in very rudimentary style in the 1980s and early 1990s, becoming reasonably positive in favour of Kosovo Albanians after the mid-1990s; this was due to several factors. As in Germany and Switzerland, modest diaspora activity in France was notable. One activist was Musa Jupolli, a post-1981 immigrant who was initially a member of the network of Marxist activists. Conscious of his fruitless previous activity under Marxist-Leninist ideology, Jupolli seemed to have reinvigorated his efforts after an influential meeting in 1985 with Rugova, who at the time was attending a research course in Paris.[99] With his friends among French intellectuals, Jupolli established *Albakos*, an association engaged in the defence of Albanian human rights, which he registered in the International Federation for Human Rights.[100] Inspired by reports in *Albakos* on human rights abuses in Kosovo, the French secretary of the International Federation of Human Rights, Antoine Garapon, led a delegation of activists to Kosovo as early as autumn 1989. Upon their return, he organized a media conference in Paris and published an influential article in *Le Monde*, in which he documented the abuse of Albanian rights, such as torture, isolation and 'differentiations'.[101]

The most prominent factor was, however, Rugova's discourse of a peaceful political strategy. According to Muhamedin Kullashi, a Kosovo intellectual in Paris, this strategy surprised many and provoked questions that required a review of long-standing stereotypes held about Albanians.[102] Having studied in France under the celebrated intellectual Roland Barthes, Rugova had created a formidable relationship with the country. His tactful approach, combined with his specifically cultivated aesthetic outlook, helped shape recognition and sympathy among the French, and earned him the status of a 'francophone and Francophile', according to a French journalist at *Le Monde*.[103] His political discourse was further reiterated through a series of interviews conducted by two French journalists, resulting in a book published in 1994 (and since reprinted).[104]

The role of the famous Albanian writer Ismail Kadare[105] and Kullashi himself, both associated with French intellectual circles as well as with their own contributions in the French media, may also be considered significant factors. The establishment of the Kosovo Committee in May 1992 by several famous French intellectuals who worked for the magazine *Ésprit*, such as Olivier Mongin, Antoine Garapon and Pierre Hassner, and Albanian intellectuals who lived and worked in France, was another critical factor in educating French public opinion on Kosovo. The committee's role was enhanced by the adherence of such famous philosophers as Paul Ricoeur, Edgar Morin, Claude Lefort, André Glucksmann, Alain Finkielkraut and others, who, in their frequent and publicized articles, articulated, according to Kullashi, 'the thesis that the Yugoslav crisis did not start in Bosnia but in Kosovo, and that it might return to Kosovo with even greater magnitude'.[106]

Another factor that contributed to the shift in viewpoint among the French media and intellectuals becoming more favourable towards Kosovo was linked to the Serbs' ongoing war and atrocities being committed at the time against civilians in Bosnia and Herzegovina, which inadvertently helped the Kosovo Albanian narrative.[107] Thus, from a very obscure political reality in the French media and total insignificance in regard to French foreign policy in the late 1980s and early 1990s, by 1993 and 1994 Kosovo had become a well-known part of the Former Yugoslavia, one that was being subjected to inhuman treatment by the Serbian authorities, a situation that required attention. France, which itself was in the process of redefining its role within the new dynamics of EU integration during the 1990s, would eventually become one of the key actors in shifting international support in favour of Kosovo Albanians in the late 1990s.

Religious activists – the Catholic Church

The last grouping to be discussed in this chapter that Rugova's movement of non-violence targeted in their strategy for the internationalization of the Kosovo conflict is the Catholic Church (the Holy See), and its political wing, the Community of St Egidio. Rugova's 'special relationship' with the Holy See and the Community of St Egidio certainly forms part of his gallery of specific relationships cultivated and used in order to enhance his non-violence discourse and to promote the independence of Kosovo. This relationship was examined in more detail in Chapter 2; however, a short summary is of benefit here. The Catholic Church and the Community of St Egidio in particular became heavily involved in the Kosovo conflict, mostly owing to Rugova's discourse of peace and a tactful approach that led to a unique relationship with Pope John Paul II, as evidenced by a series of meetings between them. Don Lush Gjergji, who acted as a mediator and interpreter between the two men, reported a telling episode during the first meeting between Rugova and the pope at which the latter told Rugova:

> You have no state, no diplomacy, no ambassadors, or representatives, so from now on all the Vatican's nunciatures in the world will be in your service.[108]

Turning to the archbishop of Kosovo, Nik Prela, who had also joined the meeting, the pope added: 'Please send us the materials and information that we can use in order to present your case.'[109] However, Gjergji argued that in order to remain within the Holy See's tradition of political impartiality, the case should be delegated to the secretariat of the Vatican State, as well as to the Community of St Edgidio, which was just being established at the time.[110] The Community of St Egidio thus became actively involved in the Kosovo crisis, with two prominent leaders and activists – Andrea Riccardi and Don Vincenzo Paglia – at the heart of that involvement. Their perseverance eventually resulted in an agreement between President Milošević and Rugova on the issue of the normalization of education in Kosovo.[111] However, the agreement failed, owing to unwillingness on the part of Serbian president to implement it.

As with his 'affair' with Senator Dole, Rugova exploited his relationship with the pope, hanging a picture of the two of them together in his office. Many Kosovo Albanians also had the same portrait in their homes or business offices, to demonstrate their unanimity. Eventually, when Rugova was held hostage by Milošević during the military confrontation in 1999, St Egidio, in the person of Monsignor Paglia, in collaboration with the Italian government and the Italian embassy in Belgrade, intervened with Belgrade to ensure free passage for Rugova to Italy.[112]

Conclusion

One of the principal goals of Rugova's strategy of non-violence was the internationalization of the Kosovo conflict. The strategy was determined by the necessity to avoid a violent conflict, bearing in mind the radically disproportionate power structures with its opponent, but also by the calculation that a diplomatic and information campaign would be more effective in pushing Kosovo onto the agenda of the major international powers. The strategy proved remarkably successful over a long period first by neutralizing internal obstacles, partly by incorporating radical political elements within Kosovo and the diaspora within the LDK, and hence marginalizing local critics and factions, and second, by managing successfully to refute the stereotypes that Serbian propaganda had ascribed to Albanians over a long period, while at the same time putting out a positive, non-violent image of Albanians to the world. Alongside this, through a well-organized campaign, Rugova's parallel state was able to inform world institutions, organizations and political actors about the violation of Albanian rights in Kosovo committed by the Yugoslav/Serbian authorities, and also to suggest a resolution to the conflict by non-violent means.

The success of the strategy of the internationalization of the Kosovo conflict is owed to a large degree to the personal relationships developed by Rugova and

LDK personnel and diaspora activists with various political actors and activists around the world. A personal letter that the former US ambassador to Albania, Bill Ryerson, sent to Sami Repishti after the successful NATO campaign against Serbian forces in 1999 is testimony to the role these diaspora activists played:

> [The liberation of Kosova] could not have prevailed had not you and the others spent years patiently educating the American public, and more importantly our political leaders, of the serious problem posed by Serb repression of the Albanians there. You may be justly proud of what you have accomplished. No, you did not do it single-handedly, but I doubt that without your long efforts American leaders could have acted as they did.[113]

As a result, Kosovo's parallel state, with its political organization, created an exceptionally effective information and diplomatic campaign, which eventually succeeded in elevating Kosovo from an issue that required improvements in the human rights domain to an international one requiring specific international attention. Failing to force the Kosovo issue into the Dayton Accords, which concluded the violent conflict in Bosnia and Herzegovina in 1995, may in fact have meant that major international actors (the Contact Group, consisting of the United States, the UK, France, Russia, Germany and Italy) probably realized that a different form of international attention to the Kosovo conflict (other than that of Dayton) was necessary, and possibly a shift in Albanian political strategy. Edita Tahiri, a former minister for foreign affairs in Kosovo's parallel state, said: 'What I can say is that by 1996 Washington started to signal to us that time had come to shift the strategy.'[114] The next chapter will examine the transformation of the Kosovo conflict from non-violent to violent.

5

Transformation from a non-violent to violent conflict

After every war we all are less.
Ibrahim Rugova, in Presidenca e Kosovës, *Presidenti Rugova*, 23.

Introduction

So far, this book has established that Rugova's strategy of non-violence led to remarkable success in a number of key areas – for example, channelling the sentiments that drove the massive protests on the streets into an institutionalized form of politics and organizing a parallel state, which provided basic social and healthcare assistance and access to education for the majority of the population. Furthermore, it established the core components of a state, which in return delegitimized the presence of the Serbian state in Kosovo and internationalized the Kosovo conflict through organized information and diplomatic campaigns. However, this influence fell short of rousing the international community into intervening more vigorously, as Rugova had explicitly advocated, with a political process for preventing escalation of the conflict into violence, and placing Kosovo under an international protectorate for a transitional period. This chapter deals with the change in dynamic: the transformation of the conflict from non-violent to violent confrontation.

The first section of this chapter outlines the challenges that Rugova's strategy of non-violence was faced with. It then examines the origins of the armed resistance and an analysis of the politicization of the armed groups by the Marxist-Leninist/Enverist organization, the LPK, and its efforts to acquire control over them. The discussion then moves to the Forcat e Armatosura të Republikës së Kosovës (FARK – the Defence Forces of the Republic of Kosovo) and Albania as a contributing factor in the power struggle between Rugova's LDK and the LPK, and its military wing, the KLA. Next, Rugova's parallel state between the armed conflict and international diplomacy is covered before examining the KLA, and the international diplomacy that followed with the Rambouillet Conference on Kosovo.

Challenges to the strategy of non-violence

Despite years of a successful strategy of non-violence (see Chapters 2, 3 and 4), Rugova's approach began to be questioned post-1995. Several reasons can account for this. First, both the Yugoslav authorities' violence and unemployment had resulted in hundreds of thousands of Albanians leaving the country, which arguably counted as a success for Belgrade's strategy in emptying Kosovo, and a factor that went against Rugova's strategy of preserving the population of Kosovo. Second, diplomatic efforts to internationalize the Kosovo conflict had reached a point from which it was difficult to see any international mobilization that would rescue Rugova's strategy – international intervention.[1] Although the Kosovo crisis was linked to the beginning of the disintegration of Yugoslavia, it never received adequate treatment from the international community. Successive international initiatives and conferences, such as the European Peace Conference for Yugoslavia (EPCY), which lasted for years, did not confer on Kosovo the same status as other Yugoslav constituent republics. More notably, though, when the Dayton Conference (1995), organized under the leadership of the United States to end the years of fighting in Bosnia and Herzegovina, where Serbia and Croatia were also involved, ignored Kosovo almost completely, alarm bells started ringing for Kosovo Albanians.

But, according to Peter Russell, the expectation that the Dayton Conference would have dealt with the Kosovo crisis was unrealistic, for several reasons. It was not ignored, however, for the lack of knowledge or concern about the situation in Kosovo:

> Western policymakers knew perfectly well, and had known for years, what was happening in Kosovo. This was, if anything, especially true in the United States, the prime mover of the Dayton talks, because Kosovo had been the main focus of American human rights concerns in Yugoslavia until well into 1991.[2]

Among the principal reasons Kosovo was not placed on the Dayton agenda was because Dayton was designed principally to stop the tragedy in Bosnia; therefore, 'the emphasis on Bosnia worked against the inclusion of Kosovo through the perception in the West that Slobodan Milošević was the indispensable figure at the talks'.[3] A quotation from the former US ambassador to Belgrade, Warren Zimmermann, reaffirms this argument: 'Milosevic "defined his political identity by his nationalism on Kosovo," and his interest was very much in keeping Kosovo off the agenda at Dayton'.[4] The only aspect in which the Dayton conference related to Kosovo was through the so-called 'outer wall' of sanctions, which the United States managed to incorporate into the final text of the accords. The outer wall of sanctions stipulated conditions related to a series of terms that the FRY was required to fulfil in Kosovo before sanctions could be lifted.[5]

Another factor was the growth of internal opposition against the status quo. Despite the success of the parallel state, the situation in Kosovo was not improving, for which Rugova and the LDK were held responsible on account of their allegedly 'passive' resistance.[6] Up until the mid-1990s, Rugova's strategy had been effective by incorporating the Marxist-Leninist radicals by means of power-sharing within the LDK. However, their relentless efforts gained impetus when they found an ally in Prime Minister Bujar Bukoshi. After years in exile, and having accumulated considerable sums from the government's '3 per cent fund', Bukoshi's perception grew to the extent that he now thought that he should be leader. Edita Tahiri, in an interview with the author in March 2018, said: 'As you know, we [the LDK] had created the "3 per cent fund", but Bukoshi was running it from abroad, and so somehow he thought that he was the leader of the movement, but you cannot be a leader from the outside'.[7] Around the same time Rexhep Gjergji told me: 'Bukoshi stimulated the LPK structures, financed them, and followed up with a series of his interviews against Rugova, stating among other things that "the LDK had become a swamp, etc.",[8] an approach that eventually led Bukoshi to restrict funds for Rugova's diplomatic visits, hence making the latter's position even more vulnerable.

Officials in Tirana, led by the Democratic Party and the Albanian president, Sali Berisha, who took over power from the communists in Albania's 1992 general elections, had unreservedly supported Rugova (and part of Albania's diplomatic objective had been to campaign in favour of Rugova's strategy), but now they suddenly developed a cold stance towards him. Under US pressure due to the alleged role of his party in the 1996 elections, and also due to an internal social and political crisis, Berisha shifted his attention to Kosovo and switched his support from Rugova in favour of the radicalization of political activities in Kosovo, which Demaçi and his Marxist-Leninist followers, such as Hydajet Hyseni, were advocating.[9] Demaçi, a relentless critic of Rugova, was against the

LDK's stance that Kosovo should not meddle in the internal politics of Serbia, and in 1996 he voiced his support for the coalition of opposition parties called Zajedno (Together), with hopes that it would contribute to the democratization of Serbia. He stated:

> By supporting these protests we assist the democratization of Serbia, and in the process we could win our freedom. The resolution of the Kosovo problem depends also on what kind of Serbia we will have to deal with – democratic or dictatorial. It is wrong to think that by having Milošević in power the situation will get worse, but we will be nearer to freedom.[10]

As stated briefly in Chapter 3, in 1996 Demaçi unveiled his political proposal for a confederation of Serbia, Montenegro and Kosovo, namely Balkania, but found no support in Kosovo. He then brought these ideas back to the table in March 1997[11] and embraced Berisha's support for a change in the dynamics of Kosovo. Considering all the above factors, the escalation of the crisis in Kosovo seemed inevitable, with violent action from what would come to be called KLA guerrilla groups as the dominant factor. Demaçi eventually joined the KLA in the capacity of a political representative in Kosovo, although his relationship with and influence over the KLA was somewhat controversial, as this chapter will reveal.

A political process was triggered in 1996 under the auspices of the Community of St Egidio, leading to an agreement between Milošević and Rugova on 1 September that same year on the issue of higher education in Kosovo. The refusal of Milošević later to implement it led to more disillusionment among the public, particularly among young students and some within the academic community in Kosovo. This led to student protests organized by the 'Independent Students Union' of the University of Prishtina (Universiteti i Pavarur i Studentëve të Universitetit të Prishtinës – UPSUP). Led by such leading figures among the students as Albin Kurti, and also accompanied by a respected law professor and the rector of the university, Ejup Statovci, the students marched peacefully in Prishtina to demand the return of university premises taken over by the Serbian authorities. However, they were met with harsh police violence. Despite this, the students and the academic community continued with intermittent demonstrations in order to show their growing frustration with the status quo.

So, during the period 1996 to 1997, several factors challenged existing circumstances. However, it was violent radicalization, in the form of armed groups, that threatened the status quo the most, a fact to which I now turn.

The origins of armed resistance:
The parallel state's defence structures

There is a common misperception in public opinion and among political analysts both inside and outside Kosovo that associates the origins of the armed resistance that came to be known as the KLA with the Marxist-Leninist–Enverist organization, namely the LPK.[12] The reality is much more complex, however. In fact, the origins of the armed resistance should be traced back to the early years of the parallel-state organization, which provided the initial, formal military training for some of the main military figures who later formed the core of the KLA. In this section, I will try to disentangle these ambiguities to facilitate a better understanding of the political processes that followed.

As with the development of most other aspects of the parallel state, conditions on the ground also necessitated the organization of a self-defence capacity within Kosovo. There was little doubt among senior LDK activists I interviewed that Kosovo could not have achieved freedom from Serbia through peaceful means alone. Therefore, some political activists with a more pragmatic mindset engaged in creating some form of defence structures in case the Serbian authorities pushed Kosovo Albanians beyond a point where a policy of non-violence could be sustained. From this way of thinking two forms of self-defence mechanisms resulted. The first was somewhat spontaneous and was linked to July 1990, soon after the Serbian authorities launched their onslaught on Kosovo institutions, using violence in various forms, which bred fear and uncertainty among the Albanian population. A number of incidents occurred during this period involving Yugoslav police raids against Kosovo villages, including one incident at the end of July 1990 that forced thousands of residents in a region to the north of Kosovo on the border with Serbia to leave their homes, and another police raid in Pollatë (northern Kosovo) in September 1990 that resulted in two young people being killed. A senior LDK figure, Rexhep Gjergji, visited the area, and in discussions with local political activists, it was decided to organize a form of self-defence patrol in order to make sure the inhabitants were not subjected to unexpected Serb police violence or paramilitary attacks.[13]

As similar incidents kept occurring, LDK activists decided that this self-defence model had to be extended throughout Kosovo. A responsible body of activists was formed, overseen by Gjergji himself, and within two months or so this form of self-defence was indeed extended throughout Kosovo. This usually involved unarmed (but in some instances armed) citizens guarding villages, towns and large residential buildings.[14] 'It was an extraordinarily efficient organization, not that we knew what to do, but circumstances dictated that we should do something', Gjergji told me in an interview in 2020.[15] It is this self-defence model that was applied in December 1991 when Yugoslav forces attacked Adem Jashari's family for the first time, but were met by Prekazi villagers in support of the Jasharis, along with intervention from the LDK, which resulted in the withdrawal of those Yugoslav forces.[16]

The second defence mechanism was of greater significance and requires a more detailed examination. The armed struggle, as a 'plan B', was often discussed among senior LDK figures during the early 1990s. The idea of organizing military defence structures was conceived by LDK political activists in Switzerland and Germany and by senior leaders in Prishtina. However, because of the tight control over Kosovo by the Serbian authorities, it was not possible to undertake such an operation in Kosovo: the risks associated with it could have jeopardized the entire project of non-violence. For these reasons, Albania was chosen as the location for this enterprise.

The arrangement with the Albanian authorities has been attributed to a meeting between Rugova and the Albanian communist president, Ramiz Alia.[17] However, no evidence has been produced to support such a claim. It is likely that, owing to pressure from different groups within the LDK, and the imminent threat from the Serbian/Yugoslav military, Rugova remained 'silent' or tacitly approved the efforts to develop defensive military capabilities as part of the parallel state. While doing this, he trod carefully, so that these actions would not compromise his policy of non-violence. 'He [Rugova] cared so much about keeping non-violence intact', Ali Aliu told me. Aliu, who eventually oversaw this enterprise in Albania, explains how the arrangement took place:

> Here is how this happened with some form of [Rugova's] semi-approval: at the beginning of 1991, through the Albanian Embassy in Bonn, and one of Bukoshi's contacts, Ramiz Alia requested meeting Rugova somewhere in Europe. Then, Bukoshi and I spoke with Rugova, who, concerned about what would happen to his non-violence movement, refused to meet Alia, but was happy for me and Bukoshi to meet whomever Alia delegated.[18]

Subsequently, Bukoshi and Professor Aliu met Alia's chief advisor, Sofokli Llazri, in a tourist resort outside Vienna. But to Aliu's disappointment, the meeting with Llazri did not meet the LDK's expectations, and no agreement was reached. President Alia had reportedly laid down a condition that Rugova visit him in Tirana and allow him to bask in his reputation: following the formation of the LDK, Rugova had become the most popular Albanian political leader in the region, enjoying international sympathy, which Alia sought to benefit from. Professor Aliu continues:

> Ramiz Alia insisted on meeting Rugova and complained, 'You are meeting the whole world but not us, etc.' [...] At some point [during the meeting in Vienna] we moved to Llazri's rented villa in the vicinity, and looking him straight in the eye I asked him: 'Look, sooner or later, Kosova will be involved in a military conflict. When, we don't know, but one day it will happen. What can we expect from you?' His answer was most depressing: 'To be honest with you, you would put us in a difficult situation.' They had nothing. So, the meeting was concluded.[19]

A few months later, in February 1991, Aliu, Bukoshi and Rugova visited Tirana, and met President Alia and Llazri, and a tacit agreement was reached for the LDK's parallel institutions to organize military training on Albanian soil.

> The result of the visit was that we reached an agreement so that Albania would help us make some military preparations. It was Perikli Teta, the minister of defence, who got this process going by appointing a high-ranking military officer to facilitate it.[20]

On 15 August, Professor Aliu and the diaspora activist Gagica met in Tirana with Ramiz Alia, and then Sali Berisha, which resulted in a finalized agreement. This also resulted in Kosovo establishing an information office in Tirana with Aliu in charge, which by default made him responsible for liaising with the Albanian authorities for military training.[21]

The concluding of the agreement was then followed by the arrival of two contingents of selected young volunteers from Kosovo and the diaspora, no matter their political differences,[22] at Albanian military bases to undergo military training. The first contingent was recruited from the region of Llapi (northeastern Kosovo), and included such leading soldiers as Zahir Pajaziti (Podujevë-Llapi), and also from a part of the Dukagjini region (southwestern Kosovo), including the prominent soldier and leading LDK political activist Sali Çeku.[23] The second contingent was represented by volunteers from the Drenica region, Ana-Morava, Ferizaj and Kaçanik (eastern, central and southwestern Kosovo). In other words, the entirety of Kosovo provided trainees, including Adem Jashari, now a celebrated and legendary hero, and recruits from his close family members and other relatives. By the end of 1991 and into early 1992, a small group of the best soldiers who had just successfully completed training, under the supervision of Çeku, who had shown a high level of military skill to become their leading commander, and who was also the central link between the senior LDK leadership and these military groups, smuggled a contingent of armaments into Kosovo: conflict in Yugoslavia was now looming, and there was a high probability it would extend to Kosovo as well.[24]

In this view, another initiative for the organization of the defence structures of Kosovo emerged from Albanian military officers serving in the Yugoslav People's Army (YPA). It started initially as an effort on the part of a number of Albanian military officers to assist and protect Albanian soldiers, many of whom, after the YPA's attack on Slovenia and then Croatia in 1991, had been put in danger of their lives. While many Albanians fought for the Croatian and, later, Bosnian armies, others prepared for Kosovo. One of these officers, Ismet Ibishi, told me:

> I myself, Rrustem Berisha, Afrim Beka and Skender Hasanxheka undertook an initiative to remove the Albanian soldiers and military officers from the war zones and shelter and feed them, and assist them with documentation. We contacted institutional figures such as the chair of Parliament, Ilijaz Ramaijli, and then the prime minister in exile, Bukoshi, who, after a visit in 1992 of our contingents in compounds hired from the Croatian authorities, nominated his deputy prime minister for defence and security, Ramush Tahiri, and then his successor, Nikë Gjeloshi, to liaise with us.[25]

After contacts with the institutions of Kosovo had been established, this group of educated military officers went on to elaborate plans for an army, pledging their loyalty to the Kosovo government and the president of Kosovo. Ibishi went on:

> We pledged our allegiance to the government and president of Kosovo, who by default was the head of Defence Forces of the Kosovo Army (Forcat e Armatosura të Republikës së Kosovës - FARK). Within a short period of time we had prepared our plans and handed them over to the deputy prime minister, Tahiri, and continued to work with Gjeloshi when he later took over the role of deputy prime minister.[26]

Their contingents numbered several hundreds of soldiers and ex-Yugoslav military officers, and they remained on standby to fight for Kosovo if the circumstances required. However, since the Albanian leadership was not prepared to enter the military conflict at the time, the aforementioned initiative remained mostly inactive until 1997 and the beginning of 1998.

Explaining in full the efforts for the formation of defence capacities remains somewhat unclear amidst the silence of the former prime minister Bukoshi. However, we know that practical efforts for the creation of defence capacities were developed in Kosovo by the LDK leadership, involving also Prime Minister Bukoshi. All the self-defence capacities developed until then within LDK branches throughout Kosovo were handed over in 1992 to the newly appointed defence minister, Anton Kolaj. In Gjergji's words:

> All the structural organization, including the personnel that managed the self-defence structures of which I was in control (a top-down organization), were handed over to the newly appointed minister of defence, Anton Kolaj, who then integrated these within a new structure that consisted of Yugoslavia's territorial defence recruits who had deserted the Yugoslav Army, and then the same were integrated into the Ministry of Defence.[27]

Having transferred the self-defence structures to the Ministry of Defence, Gjergji was then assigned to establish the Ministry of Interior Affairs.

> After discussions I had with Rugova, we decided to target contingents of the Albanian police, who, after being removed from the police force by the Serbian authorities, self-organized in the form of a 'police union', but in fact the 'union' served these figures also as a shelter for their covert police activities.[28]

Gjergji nominated an educated officer, Jonuz Tërrstena, as a key contact to report to Gjergji himself.

Subsequently, Minister of Defence Anton Kolaj, in co-operation with Chief of the Defence Staff Hajzer Hajzeraj, a former lecturer on defence affairs, went on to design a military programme aimed at having an army to be counted in the tens of thousands. Kolaj remembered:

> After consultations with Professor Agani, and his consultation with President Rugova, I was appointed minister of defence in March 1992, and soon afterwards I started to work with Major Hajzeraj, who was appointed chief of the general staff. We would meet regularly, in complete secrecy, to work on our project, which was a serious effort, and we believed in it. We would discuss the dynamics and the process of how to form and develop defence mechanisms at regional and municipal levels. We worked under extraordinarily difficult conditions, including financial barriers and a lack of infrastructure. The risks of being discovered were extremely high, given the total control and surveillance that the Milošević regime had imposed on us.[29]

Hundreds of Albanian military officers who had served in the Yugoslav Army had left owing to the break-up of Yugoslavia, some opting to fight for the Croatian and Bosnian Armies against the Serbs.[30] The Ministry of Defence intended to engage these military professionals in leading roles within its defence organization. 'Our goal was to form a professional defence organization by placing Albanian officers in leading positions. There were hundreds of them, who were trained in the Yugoslav Army and who were ready to answer our call.'[31]

The organization moved fast and effectively: by early 1993 the Ministry of Defence had reached a level where they were prepared to bring in armaments and distribute them to those municipal personnel who were more prepared.

> In a meeting with Hajzeraj in April 1993, he told me that the general staffs in the majority of municipalities were now prepared to receive armaments. A month or two later, [Hajzeraj] went to Tirana to meet with Prime Minister Bukoshi in order to discuss how to proceed with this matter.[32]

However, this enterprise was short-lived. Before Rugova's parallel institutions were able to implement anything, on 23 September 1993 the Yugoslav authorities arrested Hajzeraj and some other leading personnel. However, a number did manage to escape arrest and detection, including Kolaj, who was ordered by Rugova to leave urgently.[33] As later developments proved, the LDK neither recuperated from this defeat nor replicated these defence initiatives.

On the other hand, the small group of Salih Çeku, Adem Jashari and Zahir Pajaziti stayed in Kosovo and continued with sporadic action over the years, with Gjergji and, in some instances, Professor Agani maintaining limited contacts with some of those figures. 'I maintained contact with Sali Çeku continuously, throughout the 1990s until a few days before he was killed in April 1999', Gjergji said.[34] The three main figures, Çeku, Pajaziti and Jashari, who eventually went on to form the core of the KLA, did not act within a chain of command but alongside a very small number of individuals or indeed alone, liaising among themselves horizontally and infrequently. Their actions focused on executing individual, small-scale ambushes of Serbian police officers known for their violent conduct towards the local population, but in some cases they also targeted so-called Albanian 'traitors', those who were believed to have worked for the Yugoslav authorities.[35] These small groups came to be perceived as the origins of the KLA. After the war, Rrustem Mustafa, known as Remi, a KLA commander who operated in the Llapi operational zone, was also involved in political activity in Thaqi's Democratic Party; he concurs that 'the groups who conducted the early actions in Kosova are the genesis of the KLA.'[36]

Politicization and control over the armed groups

The politicization of armed groups, in this context, refers to efforts to establish control over armed groups and to ensure their allegiance to a specific political entity.

While the LDK's efforts to create defence organizations were institutional and aimed at including personnel from all interested groups, including the LPK, the latter had different intentions.[37] Although they were heavily represented within the LDK, the LPK and Enverist groups within Kosovo were modest in number and operated underground. At its general conference of 27 July 1993, the Lëvizja Popullore për Republikën e Kosovës (LPRK) dealt with two main issues: changing its name to Lëvizja Popullore e Kosovës (LPK) and deciding to establish a military wing. Sabri Kiçmari, one of the LPK's political ideologues during the 1990s, said:

> In 1993 the LPRK changed its name, hence becoming Lëvizja Popullore e Kosovës (LPK) as the political wing, and within the LPK we also established a military wing, which would organize armed resistance. [...] At the same conference it was decided that I would remain on the political side, and with my political analyses and through publicity justify the demand for armed resistance, whereas Xhavit Haliti, Azem Syla, Hashim Thaqi and Ali Ahmeti, among others, lined up for the military wing.[38]

Kiçmari went on to say: 'Then, between 1993 and 1996, we structured the military system, built our connections with Adem Jashari, and Zahir Pajaziti thus created the first formations.' However, this account is disputed by senior LDK leaders. Gergji, Kolaj and Zogaj, among many others, contend that the LPK has no credible evidence that either of the mentioned guerrilla leaders had pledged allegiance to the LPK, or subscribed to the LPK-led KLA ideology. Even though the LPK had close ties with the Jasharis, some sources close to both sides indicate a breakdown of relations between the LPK leadership and Jashari,[39] while LDK sources documented Jashari's allegiance to the LDK, including his presence on Rugova's visits to Tirana and Switzerland, and photographs of Adem Jashari with LDK political activists alongside Rugova. Çeku, on the other hand, consistently maintained relations with the LDK throughout this same period.[40] LDK sources claim that the main LPK-led KLA leaders responsible for the narrative that associates the three aforementioned group leaders with the LPK is 'post festum'. A factor that has not been discussed when analysing these disagreements makes the debate even more interesting. Çeku, Jashari and Pajaziti's groups operated in complete secrecy, and therefore claiming responsibility for their actions against the Yugoslav police would have exposed their lives to risk. Aware of this reality, the LPK capitalized on their actions and claimed responsibility by issuing a series of communiqués from abroad. In the next chapter I will discuss this in a little more detail; however, it should be stated here that as violent incidents became more frequent, this modus operandi of the LPK successfully continued until they succeeded in establishing their control over the guerrilla groups. A number of incidents preceded this. On 26 November 1997, Adem Jashari's group had ambushed Serbian police forces that had surrounded the villages of Vojnik and Lludeviq, inflicting serious losses. Gjergji says:

> Following the incident, Fatmir Sejdiu and I visited the village and witnessed destroyed cars and loads of shells, etc., which indicated heavy fighting between Adem Jashari's men, who had attacked from two sides, and the Serbian police force.[41]

In retaliation, the Serb police, shooting randomly, killed an Albanian teacher, Halit Geci, on his school premises, an event that provoked outrage among the population, but also inspired the KLA to go public for the first time. On 28 November, at the teacher's funeral, one of the speakers was the senior LDK figure Fatmir Sejdiu, who, on behalf of President Rugova, read a statement. This statement ended: 'While we say farewell to [Halit] Geci, and others [recently killed Albanians], I invite you to continue the path we have started.'[42] However, what makes this event more significant was the appearance in public of three KLA soldiers (two of whom were masked) in uniform for the first time. A short, open declaration was read by Rexhep Selimi, who stated, among other things, 'From the bosom of the nation the KLA has been born as the only force for the realization of national ideals', a speech that was received with emphatic approval from those attending the funeral.[43] The soldiers' appearance eliminated any doubt about the KLA's existence. Until that point there had been speculation, including by Rugova himself, that the violent acts attributed to Albanians had in fact been committed by Serb forces, who then blamed the Albanians.

The KLA's appearance in public influenced, almost instantly, the rate of volunteer recruitment to armed groups and hence led to an intensification in the KLA's actions against the Serb police. The Yugoslav forces retaliated with disproportionate force, which subsequently precipitated the armed conflict quicker than KLA leaders were prepared for. In January 1998, Serbian/Yugoslav special police forces commenced exercises in the Drenica region, and at the same time Serb civilians were armed by the Serbian authorities, and paramilitary groups entered Kosovo from Serbia.[44] On February 27, Yugoslav forces attacked two Drenica villages, Likoshan and Qirez, in which four policemen were killed and many more Albanians, including twenty-four Albanian civilians, were massacred.[45]

The biggest blow to the guerrilla groups was, however, the fall of the Jasharis. Adem Jashari, who had become the central reference point for the whole military resistance in Kosovo, was among the most prominent of the participants in the military training programme of 1991 (organized by the parallel institutions) and formed the 'Jashari Group', along with his father, Shaban, and brother, Hamëz, and some other relatives. As mentioned earlier, their first confrontation with the Yugoslav police force dates to 29 and 30 December 1991, when a large contingent of Yugoslav forces surrounded the village of Prekaz but were met with resistance from the whole village;[46] the Jasharis were unscathed on this occasion. They were attacked again on 22 January 1998, when Serbian police tried to arrest Adem Jashari, but fierce KLA resistance forced the police to retreat.[47] But the next attack was the most ruthless. On 5 March 1998, Serbian forces using tanks and heavy artillery launched an attack that lasted three days and ended with fifty-six members of the extended Jashari family dead, including women, children and the elderly, together with Adem Jashari, his brother, Hamëz, and father, Shaban.[48] It is this event, along with previous violent Serb police raids, that inspired many youngsters to join the KLA, especially since the events in Albania in 1997 resulted in an increased availability of weapons on the market, in which Kosovo Albanians were buyers. As Perritt argues, 'A flood of arms after the collapse of the Albanian state in 1997 was followed by a flood of volunteers after the Jashari massacre of 1998.'[49]

Paradoxically, the loss of the Jasharis created the conditions for the LPK to fill the gap left and extend their influence over other groups that they had not previously controlled. The LPK's efforts to assume control over the guerrilla groups was perceived by some guerrilla factions close to the parallel-state institutions as being facilitated by the Albanian government of Fatos Nano. In his book *Lufta pa Maska* (War without Masks), Gani Geci, a Drenica regional commander who had been close to the Jasharis from the early days, said, referring to LPK efforts to establish control over authentic guerrilla groups:

> With the physical elimination of Hamëz and Adem Jashari and their uncle Osman, [Fatos] Nano's wrestlers[50] finally assumed control over the KLA and inherited the efforts and the eight years of guerrilla fighting led by Adem Jashari, Zahir Pajaziti and Salih Çeku.[51]

The efforts of the LPK to stamp their authority on the existing guerrilla groups in Kosovo was also demonstrated through the introduction of their Marxist ideological methodology, and thus further politicized the guerrillas. In a TV interview in March 2019, Geci described how this transformation came about:

The change occurred when on 24 March 1998 twenty-eight volunteers arrived from Switzerland. They brought the 'ideology', 'greeting with the communist fist', etc.[52]

The politicization often took on a violent character along political lines. Geci's brother, Halil, a local LDK activist, had nearly become one of the victims. Here is how Gani further explained how these splits in Drenica (the guerrillas' heartland) involving his own brother took place:

> The critical moment [of the split along political lines] was when Halil [Geci] left for Albania for armament supplies. In Deçan, an LPK group stopped him and wanted to kill him, on the justification that he was a Serb who spoke Albanian. Luckily, he was saved by friends who knew our family, and soon after members of the Sali Çeku group accompanied him to Albania.[53]

As a powerful family, the Gecis appear to have been an obstacle to the establishment of LPK influence in Drenica – the main region of resistance against Serb forces. Geci, who was also the subject of assassination attempts, in his already cited publication explains how LPK intelligence managed to influence and jeopardize the unity of guerrilla groups in Drenica and instigate inflammatory language against such guerrilla activists as the Gecis.[54] Geci reports that one of his colleagues, Sabit Geci, a KLA commander (their shared surname is coincidental), approached one of the village gatherings and specifically demanded that

> LDK members should not participate in the war, although for us the main thing was the willingness to fight, and not who belonged in which political party.[55]

To neutralize the credibility and the power of the Gecis further, the KLA's HQ released the infamous 'communiqué number 59' from abroad that proclaimed Gani Geci was a 'traitor, who in a masked uniform led the Serb forces against the Albanian villages', a statement that Geci and his local zone commander disputed categorically.[56] However, by mid-1998 the LPK-led KLA had already established considerable domination over the guerrilla groups, especially after the LPK had announced the formation of the general staff. Ibrahim Kelmendi, a senior LPK leader, told me that 'between April and 11 June 1998, LPK activists worked with local commanders in the war zones to establish the general staff, which was announced by Jakup Krasniqi, a KLA spokesperson, on 11 June 1998'.[57]

Excited by the change of atmosphere and modest success, KLA military figures, who were often self-appointed commanders, defined the rules on how violent conflict was to be conducted, including the selection of personnel with close LPK connections to be in charge, and managed finances from the so-called 'Vendlindja Thëret' (Homeland Calling), which was created to facilitate the guerrilla fight. However, the distribution of financial resources was dogged by controversy. Gani Geci explained in detail how their group, including Adem Jashari himself, struggled for funds to purchase armaments and was let down by both Prime Minister Bukoshi and the LPK:

> One day, along with Sejdi, Xhevahir and Safet Geci, I went to the Jasharis. Hamza [Adem Jashari's brother] told us: 'Things are not good, because our fight is being controlled by Fatos Nano and the LPK, while the Kosovo government [Bukoshi] doesn't want to take responsibility. We have communicated with the prime minister, but he has remained silent. Rexhep Selimi [a KLA commander who until recently had been a frequent visitor to the Jasharis] has not visited us for over six months. Dad [Shaban Jashari] and Adem are very irritated. He [Selimi] seems to have made money and is paying others to take action.'[58]

The above statement illustrates that by this time LPK activists had successfully achieved control over the guerrillas and designated strategies of war, and that, seemingly, the Jasharis, even before their elimination, were not part of those strategies.

Through the military campaign against the Serbian/Yugoslav forces, the LPK-led KLA saw their propaganda strategy as a legitimate tool in their efforts to establish the upper hand over the LDK. They had been doing this since 1996, when the LPK started to spread negative information about the LDK leadership, including KLA communiqués that contained threatening language. Henry Perritt argues:

> KLA communiqués issued during 1996 and 1997 consistently cajoled and threatened the Albanian political class to stop propaganda against the KLA, and to avoid bargaining away Albanian territories.[59]

Clearly, with statements like this, the KLA-led LPK leadership aimed at mispresenting the LDK. It was well-known that Rugova's institutions were steadfast in maintaining the territory of Kosovo intact and were far from bargaining with Serbia. Incidents involving LDK victims at the hands of LPK-led KLA members were countless, but the assassination of core LDK political figures, including two individuals among Rugova's most loyal colleagues, Xhemajl Mustafa and Enver Maloku, and the serious injury of Dr Sabri Hamiti, as well as a number of assassinations of LDK figures after the war, led the LDK and some media groups to point the finger at the LPK-led KLA.[60]

This same attitude was also asserted regarding the FARK, a military structure established by Colonel Ahmet Krasniqi under a mandate from Prime Minister Bukoshi in early 1998. The next section will explain the emergence of the FARK and its co-existence with the LPK-led KLA.

Forcat e Armatosura të Republikës së Kosovës (FARK)

When the parallel-state defence structures of Kosovo were dismantled after the arrests of 1993, most military officers migrated to Europe. One of them, Rifat Haxhiaj, had settled in Geneva, where he joined the Ministry of Information led by Xhafer Shatri. Eventually, a society that gathered together Kosovo Albanian military officers who had deserted the Yugoslav Army was formed, numbering around seventy members in Switzerland alone; it met three times a year to discuss pertinent military issues in case they were summoned to fight for Kosovo.[61] When violent incidents in Kosovo became frequent towards the end of 1997, and even more so at the beginning of 1998, they met more frequently. Then, a day after the incident with the Jasharis happened, the group was summoned by a military officer who, according to Haxhiaj, introduced himself as Ahmet Krasniqi and stated:

> I have been appointed by Prime Minister Bukoshi as minister of defence, and from now on you will receive orders from me. [...] As minister of defence, my task is to assist you to work closely with the tactical units of the KLA that are in the field in order to strengthen and professionalize them.[62]

Clearly, military organizations that were operating in several geographical zones in Kosovo were communicating poorly among themselves at the time, and, as a first step, Krasniqi sought to remedy this. A high-profile military officer with the rank of colonel in the Yugoslav Army, and a high reputation among most Albanian military personnel, Krasniqi was considered a formidable nominee to lead the Ministry of Defence during a war situation. His first action was to train a group of ten senior officers with the most up-to-date military knowledge, who would lead units consisting of more than 1,000 troops each.[63] This meant that in a short period the Kosovo Army would count well over 10,000 men, equipped with the most modern professional and technical abilities. At the beginning of May 1998, Krasniqi, along with his close team, moved to Tirana, from where he had begun contacting all Kosovo Albanian military professionals scattered throughout Western Europe, and while in Tirana he instructed Haxhiaj to establish a directorate for information, and a team of military and civilian experts, who within a short time started to circulate a military magazine.[64]

In a matter of a few months, the FARK gathered highly professional officers and soldiers for a project that was intended to sustain a long-term military confrontation with Serbian forces on many levels. The FARK was a long-term project, which contrasted with LPK-led KLA short-term plans that had no professional planning. Kiçmari best described this approach:

> The war had started like, let's start a guerrilla warfare first and in the process we will progress to all-out war as well. But the all-out war was imposed on us because of the attack on the Haradinajs.[65]

While seemingly a positive development towards a more coherent armed resistance, the establishment of the FARK was equally perceived with scepticism by the KLA–LPK leadership, who saw Krasniqi and the FARK as Bukoshi's effort to undermine their long-term project, despite Bukoshi and LPK leadership flirtations in the past. Aware of the existing animosities, Krasniqi undertook his actions for unifying the LPK-led KLA and those groups that were closer to the institutions of the parallel state. The relationship had deteriorated to the degree that the Albanian media were hooked more on competing Albanian factions than on the conflict with Serbia. Krasniqi himself, in an interview for the FARK magazine *Revistë Ushtarake*, warned:

> Regrettably, I have to say that, very often, when reading the Albanian media, one gets the impression that the biggest conflict is among us [the Albanians], and not with our occupier. This is tragic. Our journalists should be engaged with the historic moment of where we are, when half of the nation and its territories are being threatened with annihilation. In these conditions, journalists should be focused on the Albanian conflict against the Serbs, and in this context win the propaganda war against Serbia instead.[66]

He undertook a creative role in bringing the two groups together to build a united Kosovo Army. To realize the idea, a meeting between the KLA leadership, including Xhavit Haliti and Adem Demaçi, who later became the KLA's political representative, and the FARK/Ministry of Defence led by Krasniqi and his deputy, Agim Mehmeti, was held in Oslo on 21–3 May 1998. This resulted in an agreement, known as the Oslo Agreement, that stipulated a military structure with the KLA as part of the FARK and the Ministry of Defence. The Ministry of Defence would incorporate the general headquarters, and Demaçi, as a KLA representative, was given the opportunity either to replace Krasniqi and become minster of defence or to be nominated chief of the general staff. The agreement also stipulated that once the general headquarters was fully functional, a professional military officer would be allocated to every command structure with existing personnel that did not currently possess a military professional of the rank of commander or a deputy commander.[67]

Clearly, Krasniqi thought a milestone had been achieved towards unification; however, the terms of the agreement were subject to LPK-leadership approval. Within two weeks Demaçi had reportedly responded to Krasniqi, saying, 'What we have agreed won't work for now.'[68] Nevertheless, Krasniqi did not stop pursuing the idea of unification, and a series of meetings between himself and Haliti are reported to have been held in Tirana, often in the presence of Albanian officials, including Fatos Klosi, the head of the Albanian information service. Although Klosi admits having been present at these meetings, he does not provide any information as to the exact nature of these discussions, but stated that 'he [Krasniqi] was a serious person, but our differences rested on our being interested to know when they would enter Kosovo to fight, but they were hesitating.'[69]

The fact that Albanian territory had become a theatre of military preparations by Kosovo Albanians made Tirana the determining factor in who would come out on top in this battle between factions within Kosovo. This is examined below in the next section.

Albania as a factor

Since her creation in 1913, Albania has almost always, in one way or another, influenced political outcomes in Kosovo. Sharing a common culture, language and historical legacy, it gave Albania some form of moral 'obligation' to fulfil the 'big brother' role regarding Kosovo, albeit not successfully. However, the emergence of Rugova and the LDK in 1989 resulted in Prishtina being the epicentre of Albanian politics in the region. Rugova's popularity extended also to Albania, which at the beginning of the 1990s was making its first steps towards democratization. Those on both the left and the right of the political spectrum strove to attract Rugova to their political parades for purposes of internal consumption, including the Albanian communist leader Ramiz Alia.[70] This is how Rexhep Gjergji commented on the Albanian leadership's feelings towards Rugova:

Albania was in a transitional stage, and the old regime saw Rugova as an opportunity somewhat to clear their conscience about their past. Everyone wanted to at least shake Rugova's hand, and they even begged for Rugova's presence at a political parade of the Democratic Party, because Rugova at that time was an absolute authority for Albanians throughout the whole world.[71]

Undeniably, the Kosovo leadership did play a constructive role in the democratic transformations in Albania in the early 1990s, but the Democratic Party of Berisha gained more from flirting with Rugova and the LDK. However, instability crept into Albania when Berisha pressed for more control over Albanian politics in the 1996 elections, coupled with the economic crisis caused by the 'pyramid-scheme' economy in 1997.[72] A provisional government led by left-wing parties was formed, and later that year the Socialist Party won the elections, Fatos Nano becoming prime minister. Once Nano came to power, Rugova was no longer Tirana's most favoured politician: the left-wing government in Tirana saw the rising importance of the LPK-led KLA in Kosovo as an opportunity to switch its allegiance from Rugova and the LDK to the LPK, which owed its existence in large degree to Albania's Socialist Party's predecessor, Partia e Punes së Shqipërisë (Albanian Labour Party), the ruling party in the communist years.

The change of Albanian discourse on Rugova and his parallel state became transparent at a summit of Balkan leaders on 4 November 1997 in Crete. On this occasion a separate, behind-closed-doors meeting of Nano with the Yugoslav president, Milošević, was held, followed by a media conference at which Nano, among others, declared that the 'Kosovo issue should be resolved within the context of Yugoslav/Serb institutions', a statement that was met with vigorous reactions in Kosovo.[73]

In the meantime, Nano's government had intensified its relationship with the LPK leadership through his newly appointed head of the Albanian information service (Shërbimi Informativ Kombëtar – SHIK), Fatos Klosi. He became instrumental in assisting the LPK-led KLA, particularly its leadership stationed in Albania, gaining the upper hand over Rugova's institutionalists. Xhavit Haliti, a figure with long-term influence on the LPK, who was now operating from Tirana, and who had reportedly been working for the Albanian secret service, the Sigurimi, for many years,[74] became the most trusted individual. In an interview for a Kosovo TV programme, Klosi stated:

> I met many [Kosovar Albanians] because I was in a new role and was curious to get to know them, but the most serious of them was Xhavit Haliti, whom I met at the very beginning of my appointment. I then spoke to members of our agency, and we created the file for Kosova.[75]

On the political front, Nano's foreign minister, Paskal Milo, was also active in promoting an anti-Rugova discourse by assisting the LPK-led KLA leadership. Subsequent developments proved that Nano's government would play a decisive role in enabling both the political and the military structures of the LPK to conduct the war and win the battle to establish supremacy in Kosovo politics, an approach that led to Rugova's deep distrust of Nano and his government.[76] With regard to post-war Kosovo, the Albanian Socialist Party saw the LPK and KLA as safe allies, and once the dust in Kosovo had settled, their grip on power in Albania would become easier with an ally in Prishtina. Rifat Haxhiaj, familiar with the Albanian politics of that period, commented:

> The battle for power in Albania was very uncompromising, and the Socialist Party saw the LPK as a tool to stay in power, so they assisted the LPK, who had financial resources and military power, with all their influential human resources and contacts. The Albanian Socialist Party saw the FARK's affiliation to the institutionalists [LDK], which traditionally supported the Democratic Party of Albania, as much more dangerous, and a threat to their grip on power in Albania. In that respect they were successful.[77]

The period around 1998 in Albania was characterized by instability, with Berisha striving to return to power, whereas the Socialist Party was determined to consolidate its grip. There were high stakes riding on the outcome of negotiations between the LPK and FARK; the head of the Albanian SHIK, Klosi, or personnel close to the Socialist Party acted as interlocutors, and possibly defined the outcome of the discussions for the unification of the KLA and FARK. Thus, it is believed that the official government of Tirana or elements within the state actively destabilized Krasniqi's safety. He became subject to police searches, survived an assassination attempt and was removed arbitrarily from his residence by the Albanian police, and the premises of the directorate for information (which Krasniqi had established) were searched and personnel taken to local police stations for interrogation.[78] More tragically, however, Krasniqi was executed in the vicinity of his new residence five days after the police raid on the directorate for information.

Poor handling by the Albanian authorities of Krasniqi's killing and the lack of a proper investigation into the case left a bad feeling within Kosovo, leading to a strong belief in a joint plot to remove Krasniqi by elements within the Albanian state and the LPK.[79] In a 2018 TV debate entitled *Kush e Vrau Ahmet Krasniqin?* (Who Murdered Ahmet Krasniqi?), speakers such as Anton Quni, a FARK military officer, and a former Kosovo minister of defence, concluded, 'If indeed the Albanian authorities did investigate Krasniqi's death at all, they did so only superficially.'[80] In the same debate, Skender Zogaj, Krasniqi's information advisor during his tenure, provided written evidence showing that the Albanian authorities had opened an investigation into the death of Krasniqi on 10 January 1999 and closed it the same month – on 29 January. Zogaj argues:

> Even an ordinary crime would have been investigated for a lengthier period, let alone the murder of a personality such as Ahmet Krasniqi. This irresponsible approach makes me suspect that the Albanian state had a role in Krasniqi's death.[81]

He went on:

> My anger against the Albanian state grows particularly due to the fact that it [Krasniqi's murder] happened in the most sensitive circumstances for the destiny of Kosova [...] given the fact that he was judged even by Albanian military personnel themselves as one of the best military experts in the entire Albanian geography.[82]

The elimination of Krasniqi clearly left the FARK in disarray, and from then on their status as an institutional military structure lost its aura, with some sections integrating into the LPK-led KLA. However, the expertise and professionalism of FARK personnel came to be pivotal in arguably the most important all-out battle with Yugoslav forces, the so-called Beteja e Koshares (Battle of Kashare). During this battle, which was reportedly masterminded by FARK military experts, the border between Kosovo and Albania was removed. FARK military experts were also instrumental, among others, in the success of the Battle of Loxha (July 1998), in which Yugoslav forces were defeated.

In the end, whether the Albanian state deliberately participated in the elimination of Krasniqi or did not made little difference: Tirana came to be instrumental in defining the balance of power in Kosovo politics and continued to exert its influence even after the war by directly assisting the dominant KLA faction, now transformed into the Democratic Party, while the LPK lost its significance and was eventually dissolved. They even assisted ex-KLA leaders to establish, unofficially, an information agency, namely the abovementioned SHIK, with a name similar to that of the equivalent agency in Albania. Tirana's friendly relations with the most significant countries or entities involved in the Kosovo conflict, such as the United States, the EU and NATO, which also included joint military exercises in Albania in August 1998,[83] may have allowed Tirana some degree of discretion in the dealings with Kosovo actors as long as it stayed uninvolved in the conflict with the FRY.

Rugova's parallel state between armed conflict and international diplomacy

The appearance of the KLA in the public eye, the increase in the number of armed incidents and above all the massacre of the Jasharis forced reactions from international organisms, such as the reactivation of the Contact Group (the United States, the UK, France, Russia, Germany and Italy) for the Former Yugoslavia. President Clinton's envoy to the Balkans, Robert Gelbard, visited Kosovo in February 1998, an occasion on which he branded the KLA a 'terrorist organization,'[84] a qualification that was interpreted by many as a green light for Milošević to go ahead with violent actions in Kosovo.[85] At the same time, Gelbard reportedly urged Rugova to hold a general election in order to ensure the legitimacy of Kosovo's institutions and the continuation of political and diplomatic processes under new circumstances.[86] The last general election in Kosovo had been held in May 1992, which meant a full electoral circle had been completed.

However, navigating the election process at a time when military radicalization had triumphed in many areas was not a simple task. The LDK elections held in February 1998, which preceded the general election, were a challenge that Rugova had to get through first. Having learned his lesson from previous party elections in which the Marxist-Leninist groups had nearly 'won the castle from within', but also under pressure from the Agani Group,[87] Rugova appeared more cautious in selecting delegates for the LDK General Council, which, according to the party's rules, selected the leadership. Then, unhappy with Rugova's selection, the Marxist-Leninists, led by Hydajet Hyseni, left the convention of the General Council; they perceived his selection as an effort to remove Marxist-Leninist elements from the LDK. In March 1998 their groups tried to block the organization of parliamentary elections in Kosovo by boycotting the meeting at which LDK deputies were selected.[88] Their boycott failed, and a month later the Marxist-Leninists withdrew completely from the LDK. The most outspoken from within the Marxist-Leninists, and Rugova's vice-chairman, Hydajet Hyseni, along with several other Marxist-Leninists joined with Rexhep Qosja and formed their own party, the LBD.[89]

The atmosphere was tense in 1998 when a number of villages were de facto at war, and the elections were boycotted by some of the smaller political parties, such as the newly formed LBD. However, on 22 March 1998 the second parliamentary elections in the parallel state were held, which confirmed Rugova's legitimacy, and

Parliament was constituted for the first time on 16 July 1998.[90] With reconfirmed legitimacy, Rugova hoped the conflict would remain manageable and that the international community would force Milošević to resort to diplomatic means. The reinvigorated Contact Group had held two meetings, in February and March, in which it condemned the violence on both sides, and, referring to the Contact Group meeting held in New York the previous year (24 September), they urged the Belgrade authorities and the Kosovo Albanian leadership to join together in peaceful dialogue. They also expressed concern about recent events in Kosovo:

> We note with particular concern the recent violence in Kosovo that has resulted in at least eighty fatalities, and we condemn the use of excessive force by the Serbian police against civilians and against peaceful demonstrators in Pristina on 2 March.[91]

Furthermore, on 31 March 1998 the UN Security Council approved Resolution 1160, which reiterated demands for a political process and laid the ground for a series of meetings between the Serb and Albanian political leaders.

Under the sponsorship of the Contact Group, a political process ensued. This was spearheaded by the US ambassador to the Former Yugoslav Republic of Macedonia (FYROM),[92] Christopher Hill, the EU envoy, Wolfgang Petritch, and the Russian diplomat Boris Mayorski. Now that the KLA had appeared on Kosovo's political landscape, Rugova and the LDK were not the only authority to negotiate on behalf of Kosovo; therefore, it became necessary to create a unified Albanian negotiating team to deal with the Yugoslav authorities, a task that proved extremely challenging. During the process, the American diplomats Hill and Gelbard, and later Holbrook, spent considerable time facilitating the formation of a broad, representative body of Albanians. Initially, a small LDK-led team was formed; however, a larger group was also formed in the background. This larger group satisfied the smaller political parties and such independent figures as Demaçi, Shala and Surroi, but also demonstrated some form of Albanian unity, which came to be known as the Group of 15 Albanians (G-15), that could engage in a political process with Belgrade.[93]

The dynamics of the conflict had now changed substantially, and under these new circumstances the American diplomats Christopher Hill and Richard Holbrooke, who was a senior diplomat and former envoy involved in the Bosnian conflict and who had replaced Gelbard, urged a reluctant Rugova to meet Milošević on 15 May 1998.[94] The meeting paved the way for the Serbian and Albanian delegations to continue the political process, but, as subsequent events confirmed, meeting Milošević was fruitless and detrimental to Rugova's reputation. However, as Holbrooke had promised, President Clinton received Rugova, Agani, Bukoshi and Surroi on 29 May 1998 in an historic visit during which Clinton (among others) promised Rugova, 'I reassure you that Bosnia will not be repeated in Kosovo.'[95] Clinton's statement seemingly strengthened Rugova's position and the continuation of the political process. However, the much-anticipated Serb–Albanian talks failed when Serbian forces continued their offensive in Kosovo, forcing Kosovo's leadership to withdraw from negotiations.[96]

While the international community appeared more intent on diplomatic means, the continuation of the conflict was making Rugova's policy less sustainable. At the same time, Milošević was refusing to yield to the Albanians, even insisting that Kosovo was an internal Serbian issue.[97] The lack of results on the diplomatic front gave rise to demands for the inclusion of the KLA in the political process. Referring to the prospect of success in the Serb–Albanian negotiations in May 1998, Blerim Shala, a former editor of the weekly magazine *Zëri* and a member of G-15, stated:

> As the war was expanding, the political process without KLA representatives included on the Albanian team made less and less sense. Whereas on the Serbian side there was one single address for both, war and negotiations, in our case the warriors and negotiators were 'residing' in two different places. It was impossible for this situation to continue for much longer.[98]

Indeed, as intensification of the fighting between Yugoslav forces and the KLA continued, the latter's inclusion in the political process became inevitable.

The KLA and international diplomacy

Although the international community still addressed the LDK and Rugova as the principal actors, it was the guerrillas' actions that triggered international diplomacy. Despite many shortfalls, by the summer of 1998 the KLA had improved its infrastructure: it announced the creation of a political directorate, with Hashim Thaqi as director (abroad) and Adem Demaçi as a political representative in Prishtina. It also announced the formation of a general staff and later, its supreme headquarters, and an official spokesman. On the ground, the KLA gained control over substantial parts of Kosovo mostly rural areas; at various times they controlled as much as 40 per cent of the territory.[99] The KLA's elevated profile seemed to have swayed US diplomatic calculations. Therefore, the American diplomats Holbrooke and Hill realized that some form of KLA representation on the Albanian negotiating team had to be devised.

A semi-governmental coalition deriving from the elections of March 1998 almost succeeded, only to be rejected by Demaçi, who as a KLA political representative now sought to play a more prominent role in Kosovo politics. In this bolstered role, Demaçi insisted on the removal of Rugova from the equation, among other conditions. He reportedly told Shala, 'He [Rugova] should go away completely, if you want my help.'[100] Efforts to unite the Albanian political and military wings continued. A compromise seemed to have been reached by the second half of July 1998, with Rugova having approved a candidate for prime minister, Mehmet Hajrizi, a moderate Marxist-Leninist, who was among the few to have stayed in the LDK after the exodus of Hyseni's group in March 1998. However, Thaqi refused the proposal, saying, 'Kosova now needs a government that will take responsibility for leading the war.'[101] Hence, the formation of a coalition government failed again.

Faced with these difficulties, Hill and Holbrooke decided to work with both sides in a parallel process. This meant going into war zones and meeting the KLA, which by default raised the KLA's profile. One particular visit that Hill and Holbrooke paid to the village of Junik (western Kosovo) on 24 June 1998 is considered as having represented a major effect in raising the KLA's profile. They were met by a group of KLA soldiers in a local village house, and a picture of Holbrooke with a KLA soldier quickly made the headlines in the press. Shala told the author in an interview:

> This showed that the Americans wanted to work with the KLA. As a matter of fact, during May and June 1998 Gelbard, having retreated from his earlier qualification of the KLA as a 'terrorist organization', had been engaged in secret talks with the KLA's political wing, the LPK, in Switzerland.[102]

Describing Holbrooke's meeting with KLA soldiers, Shala asserted that 'they [the Americans] realized that without the inclusion of the KLA in the political dialogue, it was not possible to have an agreement between Kosova and Serbia.'[103]

The diplomatic path pursued by the Americans built upon a series of international diplomatic efforts expressed on several fronts: following the first UN Security Council Resolution on 31 March 1998, four more resolutions were passed that same year – on 21 July, 24 August, 23 September and 24 October – in which concerns over the worsening situation in Kosovo were expressed. UN Security Council Resolution 1199 of 23 September 1998 stated that the council was

> Gravely concerned at the recent intense fighting in Kosovo and in particular the excessive and indiscriminate use of force by Serbian security forces and the Yugoslav Army which have resulted in numerous civilian casualties and, according to the estimate of the Secretary-General, the displacement of over 230,000 persons from their homes.[104]

As stated earlier, the Contact Group endorsed Ambassador Hill to formulate a document that sought to reach a political settlement, which came to be known as the 'Hill process'.[105] In the meantime, the activity of the Organization for Security and Co-operation in Europe (OSCE) was reinvigorated through its monitoring process. Since 1993, the OSCE mission of long duration had been excluded from Kosovo, and now that international pressure on Milošević had increased, the latter agreed to accept its reinstatement, in exchange for the FRY's readmission to the OSCE. This resulted in a diplomatic mission on 6 July 1998 to establish a so-called Kosovo Diplomatic Observer Mission (KDOM) to monitor developments in Kosovo, which was agreed on by the United States, Russia and the EU.[106] Shortly afterwards, the OSCE established its mission, namely the Kosovo Verification Mission (KVM), with the deployment of 2,000 OSCE 'verifiers', most of whom were based in Prishtina and in every municipal district in Kosovo, with a liaison office in Belgrade.[107]

NATO, which was already involved in the security of the region, represented another front. In April 1998, NATO 'confirmed its willingness to support UN or OSCE monitoring activities and indicated that it was considering NATO preventive deployments in Albania and in the Former Yugoslav Republic of Macedonia, and further "deterrent measures"'.[108] In a gradual but systematic fashion, NATO was scaling up its language with threats to use force, President Clinton announcing that he had instructed his delegation to NATO to vote for the authorization of 'military strikes against Serbia in case President Milošević continues to defy the international community'.[109]

After the Serbian Parliament had declared the end of a successful military campaign against the KLA, on 28 September Holbrooke and Hill sensed the opportunity for a ceasefire. However, since Rugova had no influence over the KLA, and because of Demaçi's obstinacy, they were faced with a dilemma. Holbrooke reportedly told Albanian representatives, including Shala:

> I know Rugova can't do anything in this respect, because he does not control the situation on the ground. Also, we know that Demaçi is a KLA representative here in Prishtina, but neither I nor ambassador Hill can agree anything with him.[110]

The American diplomats therefore decided to sideline Demaçi and successfully obtained a statement from the KLA, whose supreme headquarters issued a political declaration on 8 October in which the KLA pledged a commitment to accept the terms of UN Security Council Resolution 1199, as well as to suspend its military activity as of 9 October.[111] This paved the way for a ceasefire agreement that Holbrooke achieved with Milošević and that was also backed up with a threat to use force by NATO.[112]

The Holbrooke agreement was an important development for Kosovo. By this time, the number of Kosovo Albanian civilians who had been displaced had reached over 300,000, with the KLA well defeated and desperate for some form of respite. Indeed, as we know from new evidence that has emerged, the KLA's political leaders had never intended to wage full-on war with the Serbian forces. Their intention was to provoke the international community to act on the Kosovo issue, unlike the leaders of the FARK, who were preparing for a serious confrontation with the Yugoslav military. Expressing their sense of desperation, this is what one of the KLA's key political leaders, Haliti, told Shala and Veton Surroi in Tirana in the summer of 1998:

> It is difficult to win the war. Despite the exceptional will of the KLA's soldiers, our armaments are far behind what the Serbian forces possess. Our position is becoming even harder, since Serb forces are killing civilians and destroying entire villages, with the intention of wiping the KLA out, and without the population the KLA can't survive.[113]

He went on to say:

> We created the KLA because we realized the West did not care about Kosova [...] Our goal, therefore, is through armed resistance to create circumstances such that NATO can come into Kosova [...] That is the maximum we could achieve.[114]

Thus the deployment of the OSCE's KVM mission to monitor and report on compliance with UN Security Council Resolution 1199 and the Holbrooke ceasefire agreement were both great achievements for Kosovo and the KLA. However, while Hill was working on a proposal on behalf of the Contact Group for a provisional political settlement, combat resumed. A recuperated KLA swiftly resumed action against Yugoslav forces, the latter accelerating their punitive measures against civilians. By late autumn, Yugoslav forces had carried out several massacres of Albanian civilians. Milošević's successful outmanoeuvring of the international community, which had relied on the norm of non-interference with respect to Serbia's internal affairs, appeared to have come to an end. Western leaders appeared more and more prone not to adhere rigidly to this international principle. Referring to the conditions in Kosovo, in October 1998 the French president, Jacques Chirac, observed: 'the humanitarian situation constitutes a reason that can justify an exception to a rule, however strong and firm it might be.'[115] The British prime minister, Tony Blair, also echoed this view in a speech given in Chicago in April 1999: 'the principle of non-interference should not be jettisoned too readily [...] it must be qualified in important respects by opposition to genocide and oppression.'[116]

One incident in particular was to come to represent a strong motive for the international community's changing course. In the early morning of 15 January 1999, at least forty-five ethnic Albanians, including women and children, from the village of Reçak were found dead, shot at close range; what investigators found, including severed body parts, was particularly gruesome. The Serbian government claimed that 'the police had returned fire on armed terrorists'; however, OSCE observers stated that the massacre was in retaliation for the death of a Serbian police officer.[117] The KVM's chief, William Walker, promptly visited the village and, at a press conference, called the event a 'massacre' and a 'crime against humanity'; he then invited the International Criminal Tribunal for the Former Yugoslavia (ICTY) at The Hague to undertake a criminal investigation.[118] Condemnations followed from other international bodies, including in a Security Council presidential statement that reflected the view that the FRY was responsible for the atrocity,[119] and on 29 January the Contact Group announced the organization of a conference on Kosovo that would come to be known as the Rambouillet Conference, the prelude to a more intrusive international approach.

The Rambouillet Conference, 6 February–22 March 1999

The dedication of a peace conference represented the highest level of the internationalization of the Kosovo conflict to date. Rugova's peaceful political movement had for many years, through campaigns of information and diplomacy, engaged the international community in the Kosovo crisis, while exposing Milošević's repressive policies regarding Kosovar Albanians. However, since there was no open violent conflict, the international community had failed to devise a political solution for the situation in Kosovo. This changed when violence threatened a human catastrophe and a spill-over of the conflict into neighbouring countries. Representing the views of Western leaders, President Clinton had stated that 'we will not allow a second Bosnia in Kosovo.'[120] This change of dynamics in the conflict saw international mechanisms such as the Contact Group involved in months of negotiations through shuttle diplomacy, but they failed to achieve even an interim political settlement. Only when NATO threatened the use of force was a ceasefire achieved, in October 1998. This indicated that only a credible use of force could facilitate the end of the conflict.

The Rambouillet Peace Conference, therefore, was designed to adopt a more effective political process associated with a threat of the use of force justified on humanitarian grounds: many Albanian civilians had been killed, and hundreds of thousands of displaced people were being threatened with a humanitarian catastrophe, a fact that was reiterated by the French president, Jacques Chirac, in his opening remarks at the Rambouillet Conference: 'You must know that France and her European, American and Russian allies will not tolerate this conflict to continue to violate the fundamental principles of human dignity.'[121]

While the opportunity for Albanians to make historic progress towards a successful parting from Serbian control over Kosovo was unique, creating a united Albanian delegation that would be accountable to a binding political agreement was nonetheless equally challenging. American diplomats had been engaged for months in trying to achieve this, but the KLA's representatives would not accept a leading role for Rugova. Therefore the conference was also a unique opportunity for the anti-Rugovists to gain the upper hand over the institutionalists, represented by Rugova and the LDK. At the Rambouillet Conference, Rugova's elegant efforts to maintain power were manifested through his selection of key institutional figures, such as his right-hand man, and vice-chairman of the LDK, Professor Agani, Edita Tahiri in the capacity of foreign minister, academic Idriz Ajeti, who was chairman of the Kosovo Parliament, Prime Minister Bukoshi and of course Rugova himself.

However, the international negotiators were instrumental in the composition of the remaining Albanian representatives,[122] which appeared to have formalized a shift of support away from Rugova. Most anti-Rugovists, however modest their political groupings in terms of the numbers of supporters they represented, were now allowed to participate in the Albanian delegation. Qosja, who along with several Marxist-Leninists had recently formed the LBD, and Bajram Kosumi, a former LPK activist and now leader of the parliamentary party and a close ally of Demaçi, had only a handful of supporters each. They all gravitated towards the KLA, represented here by Thaqi in his capacity as the KLA's political director.

The plot to oust Rugova from his leading role was evident on the first night after their arrival at Rambouillet. Rugova's interpreter, Skender Hyseni, in whom Rugova had vested various political and diplomatic tasks and who attended the conference as an advisor to Rugova, said in an interview with me in July 2021:

> The first evening at Rambouillet was unpleasant, with many dirty calculations. The next morning, I heard rumours that most of the delegation was in favour of a KLA representative as the head of the delegation. When I met Chris Hill [the following day] he tested my reaction, saying: 'I hear that some members of the delegation are not happy with Rugova as head of the delegation. What do you think?' Of course, I was not happy, and I went to Rugova and told him that Qosja and others were plotting this! He said, 'I know, I don't care, let anybody head the delegation, who cares, just tell them let's finish it and go home.'[123]

Hyseni believed that if it had been up to Rugova, the Albanian delegation would have signed the accords on the first day:

> He [Rugova] was convinced, as I was, that Serbia would never sign the accords with that military annex [see below] [...] We were handed over the Rambouillet draft accords three days before we left for Paris.[124]

And so the anti-Rugovists, led by Qosja, succeeded in installing Hashim Thaqi as head of the delegation to lead negotiations on behalf of the Albanians; Rugova and Qosja, along with Thaqi, formed a steering committee, while a group of experts, including Agani and international lawyers such as Marc Weller and Morton Abramovitz, were hired by the Albanians as legal advisors. The role of the international diplomats in installing a KLA representative as the central negotiating partner may have been, in the end, a pragmatic choice. Hill, Holbrooke and Petritch had struggled for months to get Albanians to work together on a homogenous team that represented all party and military entities.[125] Rambouillet was an opportunity not to be missed.

Now that a unanimous Albanian delegation had finally been built, the central issue for the Contact Group remained the achievement of a provisional political settlement for Kosovo. This had to be devised in such a way that the settlement preserved the sovereignty of Yugoslavia,[126] satisfied Serbian ambitions of retaining control over Kosovo, and also offered a provisional status for Kosovo that gave the Albanians a path to independence after a period of three years.[127] The implementation of the political settlement included a military annex, which stipulated a NATO-led implementation of the agreement and the withdrawal of FRY forces from Kosovo, including the establishing and deployment of an international (military) force (KFOR – the Kosovo Force) operating under the authority and political control of NATO.[128]

This was to be achieved either by the two sides agreeing to the Rambouillet Accords, whereby NATO troops would be deployed by agreement, or through military intervention in the case of the FRY not agreeing. If the Kosovo Albanians did not agree to sign the accords, neither NATO troop deployment nor intervention would be forthcoming. 'In order to move towards military action, it has to be clear that the Serbs were responsible', James Rubin had stated at a press briefing during the conference.[129] But that proved to be a very challenging task: in the last few days of the Rambouillet Conference, international mediators, including US Secretary of State Madeleine Albright, appeared acutely desperate 'to get across the finishing line with the Kosovo Albanians', in Rubin's words.[130] As part of the pressure on the Albanians, Secretary Albright is quoted as having told them: 'If you accept [the proposal], you will move toward a future of prosperity, democracy, and integration with Europe. Reject it, and the outcome will be a war you will lose, along with international support.'[131]

After a long battle with the international mediators, the Kosovar delegation succeeded in obtaining a concession in the final draft of the accords. This concession at least partially satisfied Albanian demands with an important addition being made to the final section of the agreement referring to 'the will of the people', which ambiguously indicated the right of the Kosovo people to a referendum.[132] With this last-minute concession, the majority of the Albanian delegation agreed to sign the accords, except for the KLA's representative, Thaqi. In a chilly atmosphere in which the Albanians were contemplating their own failure, Rugova, who until then had reportedly been completely quiet, volunteered to sign the accords himself in his capacity as the elected president of Kosovo.[133] However, since the Kosovo delegation acted through an arrangement based on consensus, the Albanians finally submitted a document that stated:

> The Delegation of Kosova by consensus understands that it can sign the agreement in two weeks after consultation with the people of Kosova, and political and military institutions.[134]

Thus, the deadline was extended for two more weeks, during which consultation at home was to be sought before the delegations returned to Paris to sign the accords. But, as Christopher Hill commented, 'the Kosovo Albanians returned to Kosovo to prepare for peace, and to get others in Kosovo to do the same. The Serbs went home to prepare for war.'[135] These two weeks, in which consultation between various bodies was to be sought to determine whether or not the peace accords should be signed, Milošević instead used to deploy more forces in Kosovo. So, when the conference resumed in Paris for the purpose of signing the accords, on 19 March 1999, only the Albanians turned up. They signed the draft accords, named 'the Interim Agreement for Peace and Self-Government in Kosovo (Rambouillet Accords)'. A summary of the accords states:

> This agreement aims to end the violence in Kosovo and facilitate the return of refugees and displaced persons. It also calls for the adoption of a new constitution for Kosovo that respects the territorial integrity of the Former Republic of Yugoslavia while simultaneously establishing the principles of democratic self-government for three years until the final status of Kosovo is determined. This agreement has not been signed; however, it has been given effect by Security Council Resolution 1244.[136]

The American diplomats Holbrook and Hill flew to Belgrade on 22 March and spent hours trying to find a last-minute solution to the implementation of the Rambouillet Accords, but it was not possible. Hill concluded that 'Milošević – and many other Serbs – were not prepared to host foreign troops'.[137] On 23 March 1999 NATO forces began their campaign against Yugoslav forces.

Following the realization of his miscalculation that the NATO campaign would not last long,[138] Milošević attempted one more trick – Rugova himself. On the eighth day of the bombing campaign, 31 March 1999, a contingent of security and military personnel broke into Rugova's residence and placed him, along with his extended family and bodyguard, under house arrest.[139] The following morning, Rugova was taken to Belgrade to meet Milošević and was forced to sign a joint statement on an agreed political process, which sought to resolve any political problems by peaceful means alone;[140] he was also made to appear with Milošević on TV, including a short media appearance where Rugova was pressed on whether 'the NATO bombardments should stop'. He answered: 'All [sides] should stop'.[141]

With his image already damaged following the Rambouillet Conference, at which he was relegated from the position of uncontested elected leader, Rugova suffered a devastating effect on his reputation on account of the staged meeting with Milošević. Condemnations from his opponents poured in on all sides, from Albanian political and intellectual circles, including the famous Albanian writer Ismail Kadare. On 2 April 1999, the KLA leadership in Tirana released a statement declaring Rugova a 'traitor' for having been seen with Milošević and allegedly requesting NATO to stop the bombing.[142] However, years later, when Milošević was indicted at the War Crimes Tribunal at The Hague, Rugova was invited to testify against Milošević, which also gave him the opportunity to clarify his opinion about the statement he had been forced to sign. In his witness statement, among other things, Rugova said:

In my opinion, my meetings in Belgrade and Prishtina and the push for me to sign a declaration about a peaceful resolution of the conflict were all intended to discredit me politically. They were hoping to incite internal conflict among Albanians.[143]

During the forty-three-day-long hostage situation, Milošević forced Rugova to meet the Serb president, Milutinović, Milošević's close associates Nikola Šainović and Ratko Marković, the Russian patriarch, Alexei, and the Russian ambassador to Belgrade, Jurij Kotov, who visited Rugova at his residence.[144] Eventually, after continued international demands, in particular from the Italian government and the Community of St Egidio, on 5 May 1999 Rugova and his family were released to travel to Rome, from where a shattered Rugova started his political recuperation. Unprecedented political activity commenced, Rugova meeting the Italian prime minister, Giuliano D'Amato, and the foreign minister, Lamberto Dini, and many other high-ranking Italian officials. This was followed by a meeting with the American ambassador, Christopher Hill, who had arrived in Rome to meet him, and also a visit to see Pope John Paul II in the Vatican. In short order, Rugova had been invited to visit Paris, Madrid and London.

While these visits indicated a reinvigorated Rugova and a possible reinstatement of his leadership role in Kosovo, a meeting that Albright arranged between Rugova, Qosja and Thaqi, on 8 June 1999, in Germany, did not give that impression. A proposal that the Albanian government had been working on with the KLA and Rexhep Qosja for a Kosovo National Security Council (NSC) surfaced at this meeting.[145] If successful, the NSC would have overridden Rugova's parallel-state institutions, and it would have meant anti-Rugovists having a primary role in events in Kosovo. Apparently, Albright was on board with this. However, Rugova refused to buckle.[146] He also confirmed his earlier indication at a meeting with Paskal Milo in Rome, immediately after he was released from Milošević's arrest, that he would not consent to a coalition government that was negotiated hastily in Rambouillet with Thaqi's self-appointment as prime minister.[147] Soon afterwards, on 13 June, at the premises of the College of St Egidio in Rome, Rugova met the leaders of parties represented in the Kosovo Parliament and released a communiqué[148] that confirmed his determination to stay put in his institutional approach, following the procedure of the parallel state, of which he was the formally elected president.

When the Yugoslav authorities finally agreed to NATO's terms to pull their forces out of Kosovo, the KLA quickly moved in to occupy the political space. In doing so, they also claimed the victory, implying that it was their joint campaign with NATO that had brought freedom to Kosovo, and that therefore they should rule Kosovo. All of a sudden, almost ten years of Rugova's policy of non-violence were condemned as a failure, thus consolidating the widely held perception that violence remained the only model for resolving ethnic conflict in the Balkans. The same international players that had supported Rugova's policy for almost ten years now shifted their support in favour of the KLA over the LDK, thus contributing to a further strengthening of the KLA's grip on power. This new constellation of powers enabled the KLA to exploit the political and institutional vacuum created by the withdrawal of FRY forces, on the one hand, and the neutralization of Rugova's parallel-state structures, on the other. Thus began a new chapter in the history of Kosovo, which was seen by many that everything had started with the LPK-led KLA's rise to power shortly before; Rugova and the role of his LDK were forgotten. The necessary co-operation of key international players, including NATO, with the KLA powerholders seemingly placed the two parties on the same page, bestowing on the latter the much-desired legitimacy of their claim that it was the KLA that had won the war and set Kosovo on the path to independence. In line with this view, a set of changes, including the renaming of Kosovo's cities and streets, began,[149] while the mere mention of Rugova's name and that of his party, the LDK, was associated with failure, and was at times even risky.[150]

It was against this background that the international community went on to establish a provisional UN administration over Kosovo, suspending Yugoslav and Serbian control over the province, before sponsoring its independence in February 2008. The independence of Kosovo, as a political outcome, was thus attributed to the international community and the LPK's military wing KLA.

Conclusion

In this chapter, I have examined the political processes that turned the Kosovo conflict from non-violent to violent. While creating a parallel state that delegitimized the Yugoslav presence in Kosovo, and a diplomatic and information campaign through which he was able to build relations with the most powerful Western powers and international human rights agencies, Rugova, with his policy of non-violence, fell short of achieving his political objectives – the peaceful settlement of Kosovo's political status.

Following a series of challenging factors during the Kosovo crisis, of which the guerrilla movement was the most significant, Rugova's policy of non-violence alone could no longer be sustained, and the conflict became violent. When the escalation of the conflict threatened a humanitarian catastrophe and risked spilling over into the rest of the Balkans, the international community reacted more vigorously than ever before. First, a political process ensued that fostered the hope that Rugova would once more get the chance to reassert his political authority and achieve his political goals without further violence, only for the Yugoslav forces and guerrilla groups, in the form of the KLA, to get involved in the fighting and eclipse Rugova. Under these circumstances, the international community stepped in again, but this time NATO was invited to facilitate, using the threat of force to implement a political settlement. Thus, a peace conference for Kosovo was organized.

During the conflict, the international powers thought that the involvement of KLA representatives was necessary for the purpose of furthering the political process. Therefore, they intervened and facilitated the creation of a unified Albanian political delegation, which resulted in the replacement of Rugova as the chief representative of the Albanians with the KLA leader, Hashim Thaqi. Thus, suddenly, the character of the international involvement changed. Just when it finally looked as though Rugova had succeeded, following his long-term lobbying activity, the same lobbyists shifted their support to the KLA. However, when the KLA and the political actors close to them thought that they had consolidated their grip, Rugova returned and, through elections administered by UNMIK in 2001, regained power, which thus revived the debate as to who was actually the real founder of the state of Kosovo. This will be examined in the next chapter.

6

The epilogue

Introduction

As I announced at the outset of this book, the arguments put forward here take an alternative perspective: although the LPK-led KLA escalated the conflict, which eventually led the international community to intervene in Kosovo diplomatically and militarily, and forced Yugoslav forces to leave Kosovo, it was Ibrahim Rugova, with his strategy of non-violence, who created the state structures and a frame of domestic and international political support that laid the groundwork for the independent state of Kosovo.

In this chapter I intend to consolidate my proposition with five main arguments. First, I show how Rugova's strategy of non-violence transformed the political environment in Kosovo by institutionalizing Albanians' demands and averting violent conflict at a time when the international community knew hardly anything about Kosovo, let alone what was really going on there. In the process, a culture of non-violent resistance was shaped that drew on Albanians' cultural and historical foundations. The second argument is built around the capacities that Rugova's policy developed through the formation of the parallel state in Kosovo, which consolidated the Kosovo Albanians' state culture and their political and cultural identity. The third factor reaffirms the claim that Rugova's policy of non-violence internationalized the Kosovo conflict to the extent that the international community had to address it, notwithstanding the fact that they fell short of preventing the conflict from escalating from non-violence to violence. The fourth argument focuses on violence as an 'internationalization variable', and on the intervening factors in the (temporary) shift in the balance of power from Rugova and his parallel institutions towards the LPK and their military wing, the KLA, which led to their claiming the credit for the positive results of international intervention and, later, independence for Kosovo. The chapter concludes with a brief summary of Rugova's political legacy, which forms the fifth argument.

Political transformations in Kosovo as a variable

In March 1989, the republic of Serbia, at the end of a process that had included bullying the political establishment in Kosovo amid silence from the federal institutions of Yugoslavia, forced constitutional changes that brought the province of Kosovo firmly under Serbia's control. Albanians, who made up over 90 per cent of the province's population, considered this political outcome intolerable, with potential long-term consequences for their political and cultural existence. Having lost hope in the communist leadership, which had failed to defend Kosovo's autonomy of 1974, the Albanian population resorted to fierce protests on the streets of the Kosovo capital, Prishtina, and other towns, resulting in the murder of around 100 Albanians by the Yugoslav/Serbian police.

It is this political background that determined the rise of Rugova and his political party, the Democratic League of Kosovo, founded in December 1989. The LDK was formed from a particular section of the intellectual community, largely from the fields of culture, and a smaller number of 1981-era Marxist-Leninist veterans and communists. While accommodating different political views, the core of the LDK's ideology was shaped by the cultural intellectuals, who had earlier clashed with Serbian intellectuals in defence of the cultural and political rights of Kosovo Albanians – the famous clashes between the two respective writers' associations in 1985 and 1988 (see Chapter 1). Within several months of its formation, the LDK had grown into a massive political party with over 600,000 members. In a tense political atmosphere, the LDK, under the leadership of Ibrahim Rugova, took on the responsibility of the concerns of Kosovo Albanians and channelled their political demands through an innovative political approach that came to be known as Ibrahim Rugova's policy of non-violence.

I reaffirm the argument that through the policy of non-violence, Rugova represented Albanians as non-violent and the Albanian nation as a secular force that was well equipped to enshrine the new democratic principles in their political life and to build a state, despite the constraints that Serbia had placed on Kosovo through its monopoly on violence. Rugova, as a literary writer, was well placed to draw on the Albanian culture of resistance at certain periods of political history, and cultural tolerance at others, and turn these into a new paradigm – that of a new culture of resistance. In a series of interviews that were published in book form by two French authors, and that became one of the most cited publications about Kosovo in the 1990s, Rugova stated:

Being against violence corresponds somehow with our character, a tradition of endurance regarding all foreign domination [...] We have found our way by means of our active resistance based on non-violence and solidarity. We have now succeeded in tapping into this feature of the Albanian spirit.[1]

While tapping into these cultural traditions and embedding them in his policy of non-violence, Rugova and the Albanian political elite were now able to present Kosovo Albanians as a moderate force, who were prepared to resolve conflict by non-violent means. At the same time, through this approach the Albanians gave themselves an opportunity to formulate their long-term political goals and play along with other intervening factors, such as the Yugoslav crisis and the international stakeholders. This transformation of their political approach led the Albanians towards the idea of independence that came to be structured in the form of the parallel state of Kosovo.

The (parallel) state and legitimacy

Despite efforts throughout history, an independent political identity separate from Yugoslavia or Albania had not, prior to Rugova's policy of non-violence, developed in Kosovo. Rugova's arrival in Kosovo politics marked a new era in this regard. There had consistently existed Albanian cultural and historical foundations deeply rooted in the territory of Kosovo. Rugova's political approach was based on and consolidated further these foundations in the form of the parallel state. While it lacked the classic means of the monopoly on violence, the parallel state built under Rugova's leadership nevertheless enjoyed an unprecedented popular legitimacy. The concept of legitimacy as developed by David Beetham is used here (see Chapter 3 for a more detailed analysis) to show how Kosovo Albanians waged a battle to delegitimize Serbian control over Kosovo by sidelining their institutions, and, through elections and a plebiscite, create legitimacy for their own (parallel-)state institutions.[2] The evidence from the interviews I conducted with political figures who participated in these events shows that, as a result of a changed cultural environment, the Albanian political elite had successfully built a synergy with the existing provincial institutions (the executive and the Parliament) in order to create a legal and political infrastructure and to push forward the idea of independence for Kosovo. This synergy led to a radical change in circumstances. The new deputies who had been 'hand-picked' by the Serbian authorities, and were now under Rugova's influence, and the LDK' s agitation, declared Kosovo's independence on 2 July 1990, which was followed by the approval of its constitution within two months.

Nevertheless, the conditions for functional political activity remained extremely difficult. Therefore, to compensate for the activity of the government, which was forced to operate in exile, the Albanian political parties devised a *sui generis* political body, namely the CCAPP, in order to support the creation of parallel institutions. This became a platform where power was shared among the Albanian political parties for the purpose of consensual decision-making, but it also served as an instrument for maintaining unity among those factions. Although their role is perhaps underappreciated, the evidence shows that between 1990 and 1992 the CCAPP and the Parliament in exile accomplished three vital political tasks. First, they organized a referendum for the independence of Kosovo in September 1991, in which 87 per cent of some 1,051,357 eligible voters endorsed Kosovo as an independent and sovereign state.[3] Then, general elections were held the following year to elect members of the Kosovo Parliament, as well as elections for the president of Kosovo in May 1992, which formally produced a pluralist Parliament and confirmed Rugova as president.[4]

The massive participation of the Kosovo population in electing their political representatives demonstrated that Kosovo's parallel institutions had gained popular legitimacy. At the same time, the LDK and the parallel-state institutions were able to persuade the population to refuse to recognize the institutions of the FRY and boycott their elections in Kosovo, which further eroded Serbian legitimacy over the territory. The interviews I conducted with senior LDK political figures illustrate their conviction, within the political project, that they were engaged in achieving Kosovo's independence. A senior LDK member described the erosion of Serbian legitimacy in Kosovo as follows:

> The parallel state reduced Serbia's presence in Kosovo into only as far as a policeman could reach with his truncheon. Thus, Serbia was present in Kosovo only as far as a police truncheon could strike. It was not present in the public sphere, in education, in culture, health care, or the administration. Its authority was zero.[5]

The parallel state, therefore, gave further cohesion to the idea of the state of Kosovo, and it empowered the Albanian leadership with legitimacy in representing Kosovo on the international stage. From there Kosovo Albanians gradually forced themselves into the workings of the European Conference for Yugoslavia, which was dealing with the Yugoslav crisis, and their leadership now found themselves being received as dignitaries of state around the world.

Internationalization as a variable

The third most significant factor associated with Rugova's policy in creating Kosovo's political identity and preparing the ground for its independence is its role in the internationalization of the Kosovo conflict. Internationalization was in fact one of the key strategic aims of Rugova and his policy of non-violence. It is through internationalization that Rugova sought to bring the international community to the rescue of his project. This objective derived from two main factors. First, as has already been argued, the Albanians in Kosovo and in the region of the Former Yugoslavia were marginalized and suffered from a negative image[6] as a result of the propaganda that Serbian political and cultural institutions were able to transmit to local and international audiences about the Albanians. The latter were presented as backward and incapable of creating their own state, and, capitalizing on a global political discourse that gained currency in the 1990s, Albanians were also presented as an 'Islamic extension into Europe, which the Serbs actively prevented'.[7] But the Albanians were also powerless to compete in any sense with Serbia as the most powerful republic that had the most effective access to the federal institutions of the SFRY, including the army, as well as being able to capitalize on the widespread international reputation that Yugoslavia enjoyed. Therefore, all these factors added to the challenges the Albanians faced in their mission to change world opinion on the political and cultural realities of Kosovo.

Having placed the information and the diplomatic campaign at the heart of its activity, the LDK and Rugova were able to shape a different image and perception of Albanians in the world by exposing Serb violations of Albanian cultural and political rights and raising the international profile of Kosovo. Through the strategy of internationalization, Rugova was able to draw the attention of international powers, institutions, human rights agencies, and international media and intellectuals, including the Catholic Church (the Holy See), to Albanian rights and their political status (see Chapter 4). From having a very low international profile when the Kosovo crisis emerged with the removal of its autonomy in 1989, by the mid-1990s this had changed radically. As a result of a very successful campaign in representing Kosovo through a different political and cultural lens, but also by creating formidable diplomatic contacts with Western political centres, Kosovo had now been recognized as a major international political issue that had to be dealt with. Alongside this, the deadlock reached between repression by the Yugoslav authorities and a non-violent political movement equally stubborn in the pursuit of its political goal – independence – compelled the major powers to perceive the Kosovo crisis as a threat to the peace and stability of the region. Prominent among such powers stood the United States, where, as a result of the internationalization of the Kosovo issue, between 1986 and 1992 the House and the Senate approved fourteen resolutions in which Yugoslav conduct towards Kosovo Albanians was condemned.[8] As a result of this trajectory of the internationalization of the Kosovo crisis, the US president, George H. W. Bush, issued the so-called 'Christmas warning' on 24 December 1992 that stated: 'In the event of conflict in Kosovo caused by Serbian action, the United States will be prepared to employ military force against Serbians in Kosovo and Serbia proper'.[9]

The impact of President Bush's statement, which was also repeated by the incoming president, Bill Clinton, in January 1993, is taken for granted in this book, in which I assume that the president's Christmas warning may indeed have prevented the Serb leadership from waging an open, violent conflict against the Albanians, and I am in fact led to conclude that it did allow Rugova to continue with his policy of non-violence and continue building his parallel state. His frequent visits to the United States demonstrate an increased interest in and concern from American institutions over the situation in Kosovo, and those institutions' commitment to preserve Kosovo's ethnic and political survival.[10] All four or five official visits to Washington, including a meeting between Rugova and Secretary of State Warren Christopher in May 1996, demonstrate the United States' increased concern about Kosovo and were a sign that the Americans were committed to not allowing Serbia to ethnically cleanse Kosovo.

That US foreign policy had already implemented such an approach became most acutely transparent with President Clinton's invitation of Rugova and a team of Albanian political representatives to the White House on 29 May 1998. On this occasion, President Clinton reaffirmed the US position that 'Bosnia [i.e. the crimes in Bosnia] should not be repeated, and will not be repeated [in Kosovo]'.[11] President Clinton's awareness of the danger that Kosovo Albanians were exposed to from Serbian aggression is also echoed by General Wesley Clark, the commander of NATO forces against Yugoslavia in the 1999 campaign. Recalling a meeting with President Clinton for the National Defence University on 15 September 1998, which traditionally discusses military defence priorities, Clark states: 'As he [the President] came by to shake hands, he touched my shoulder and said: "You will be ready to take care of the Kosovars, won't you?" "Yes sir," I said. It was his way of showing he knew what was on my mind. And I hoped it was on his mind, too'.[12] At this stage, violent conflict in Kosovo was still latent, and, as Daalder and O'Hanlon argue, even by 24 March 1999 the levels of violence were modest by the standards of most civil conflicts, but there was good reason to believe that without intervention things would get much worse.[13] This shows that the international approach spearheaded by the United States was driven by an educated political elite that accurately anticipated the aims of the Serb leadership, which came to be exposed overtly over the coming months, and especially during the NATO campaign.

Rugova had been constantly warning Western leaders of a scenario in which Serbia would try to ethnically cleanse Kosovo of Albanians. And his warnings almost proved prophetic when a blueprint, namely 'Operation Horseshoe', which Serbia's secret service and military close to Milošević had formulated for wiping out Albanians from Kosovo, was discovered by Western governmentS.[14] Operation Horseshoe was designed to start from the north, where Kosovo's borders with Serbia are hundreds of kilometres long, and so to the southeast and to the southwest – the term signifying the shape of the operation in the form of a horseshoe.[15] Despite the loss of thousands of Albanian civilians, the relatively swift international intervention under the leadership of the United States in early 1999 justifies Rugova's political battle in urging the international powers, particularly the United States, in preventing a well-prepared Serb genocide on a massive scale.

In Europe, the reaction was slower than it was in the United States. This was partly due to the plurality of the decision-making centres: the EU had not yet developed its common institutions, let alone a common foreign and security policy. However, the case of France is pertinent for showing how Rugova's policy of non-violence transformed French perceptions from being traditionally pro-Yugoslavian, and perhaps more specifically pro-Serbian, to being in favour of Kosovo Albanians. I have already explained in Chapter 3 how French perceptions changed over several years as a result of the campaign of non-violence and the efforts of Albanian diaspora activists and their lobbying of French intellectuals to sensitize French media and the public sphere about the reality of Kosovo. But it is worth re-emphasizing here that French intellectuals, particularly those involved in the magazine *Esprit* and in a lobbying group, namely the Kosovo Committee, founded in 1992 with a number of prominent French intellectuals and philosophers, were foremost in promoting the Kosovo Albanians' cause.[16] Their contribution, along with Rugova's policy of non-violence, influenced French institutions and the public to review long-standing stereotypes held about Albanians, as a Kosovar Albanian intellectual in France has observed.[17] In line with this trajectory of increased understanding of the urgency of the Kosovo conflict, the French president, Jacques Chirac, received Rugova on 13

June 1998 and, standing next to him at a press conference, stated among other things that 'Yugoslavia's "brutal intervention" in the province and its "desire for ethnic cleansing" are totally "unacceptable" to the West, which is prepared to use "all means" to end these offences'.[18] Although Rugova's visit to the Champs-Élysées took place at a time when the KLA was fighting Yugoslav forces, the reaction of the French president can hardly be dissociated from the influence of Rugova's information and diplomatic approach over the years. It was significant confirmation that France had now reached a full consensus with the United States and the UK, which were accelerating their Contact Group–approach for a tougher stance on Serbia.[19] France would eventually become one of the key actors in shifting international support in favour of Kosovo Albanians in the late 1990s by hosting a peace conference – the Rambouillet Conference of February to March 1999 – and participating in the military campaign.

A similarly perceived urgency in the Kosovo crisis as a result of Rugova's political battle can be noted in British politics. Debates about Kosovo had been held at various times during the 1990s in the British Parliament. However, the best example that encapsulates the understanding of and sympathy for Rugova's policy and his pleas to Western politicians to save Kosovo and its population is illustrated by testimony from the former prime minister, Tony Blair. Addressing the Kosovo Parliament on his visit in July 2010, Blair recalled a touching exchange with Rugova at his office in Westminster:

> My friends, I recall a visit from Rugova to Downing Street in 1998. He was a quiet, modest man. He came in with a white and purple crystal, which I kept in my desk at Downing Street throughout the years I served as prime minister; now I keep it in my collection of souvenirs at home. He told me the truth about Kosovo, of the duty of the world to listen to this people. He did not shout or make his case with slogans or extravagant gestures. He just spoke softly, but with the most impressive sincerity. And as he left, he said to me, 'Please, I ask only this: do not let my people suffer any more. Feel for them as you would feel for your own people and help us'. I said Britain would help. I gave him my *besa* – the honour word [an Albanian traditional institution, which consists of a ceremonial promise to do or not do something], and I kept it.[20]

Indeed, Prime Minister Blair and his foreign secretary, Robin Cook, played an extraordinarily active role in the mobilization of the Western alliance in support of Kosovo, along with the United States.

The progressive internationalization of the Kosovo crisis should also be noted in relation to international institutions. For instance, following a fact-finding visit to Kosovo, the European Parliament addressed the Kosovo crisis on 11 October 1990, when it approved a resolution expressing deep concerns over the human rights situation there.[21] When the EPCY was created in August 1991, the European Parliament supported the desire to allow participation by Kosovo and Vojvodina, which had been excluded from the EPC statement's list of participants. It 'explicitly endorsed the claim that the republics and the autonomous provinces enjoyed the right of "democratic self-determination" [...] "which it considered could only be negotiated within ... new processes of voluntary co-operation"'.[22] Although Parliament's resolutions had no powers of enforcement, they recognized the significance of the Kosovo crisis. After the formation of Kosovo's parallel institutions, the EPCY eventually incorporated Kosovo into the work of the conference by allocating the so-called Kosovo Working Group, led by the German ambassador, Geert Ahern.[23]

The internationalization of Kosovo was gaining more impetus, while its leader, Rugova, was being treated as the uncontested leader of Kosovo and was frequently received officially in Western chancelleries, including Washington, Paris, Bonn, Rome and Brussels. This, among other things, led to the EPCY's co-chairmen, Lord David Owen (UK) and Cyrus Vance (US), travelling to Prishtina on 29 October 1992 to meet Rugova in an effort to reinvigorate the dialogue between Prishtina and Belgrade when a new Yugoslav prime minister, Milan Panić, came to power temporarily.[24] Now that Kosovo was represented in some form at the EPCY, the Conference for Security and Co-operation in Europe (CSCE – renamed the OSCE in January 1995) became involved as well. From July 1990 the CSCE/OSCE began to issue statements in which it denounced Serbia for its treatment of Kosovo Albanians. This eventually ended up with the establishment of a CSCE long-duration mission in Kosovo, Vojvodina and Sandjak in September 1992.[25] Although the mission was in fact short-lived, the OSCE continued its regular reporting on Kosovo over the years and dispatched a more prominent mission in 1998, namely the KVM.

A series of resolutions from the UN's Security Council represented perhaps the highest form of the internationalization of the political crisis before the conflict escalated. However, owing to the permanent UN seats reserved to Russia and China (who had their own internal issues), as well as Yugoslav diplomacy, Kosovo struggled to achieve any desirable success.[26] Nevertheless, a successful lobbying campaign and diplomacy targeting the UN Human Rights Commission located in Geneva earned the Albanian leadership a breakthrough onto the UN's agenda. They first secured support for a text on Kosovo, with a broad statement on the 'Situation of Human Rights in Yugoslavia', including Kosovo, which was adopted in August 1992.[27] Meanwhile, owing to the grave human rights situation in Yugoslavia at the time, the UN Human Rights Council established a special rapporteur for human rights in the territory of the Former Yugoslavia, and the former Polish prime minister, Tadeusz Mazowiecki, was appointed as the first rapporteur. Mazowiecki went on to produce ten reports on the territory of Yugoslavia, one of which, from February 1993, detailed the violation of human rights in Kosovo.[28] Over time, developments in Kosovo became regular affairs in the UN General Assembly. In the period between December 1992 and December 1998 it approved twelve resolutions, and there were many more from the UN Commission on Human Rights and the Security Council.[29]

Considering all the above, the evidence gathered from interviews and other literature sustains the argument that Rugova's policy of non-violence and the parallel-state institutions successfully elevated the subject of Kosovo to an international issue that required specific international attention. However, the ongoing war in Bosnia and Herzegovina, in which the Serbs, Bosnian Muslims and Croats were involved for years, prevailed in the international pecking order, and Kosovo was not considered at the Dayton Conference of 1995 that concluded the conflict there. But some political analysts, political actors and military figures in Kosovo perceived this absence from Dayton as evidence of a failure of Rugova's policy of non-violence. Therefore, since 1995 the impression has been created that only a military conflict could have propelled the issue of Kosovo to the top of the relevant international actors' agenda.

Authors who pursue this line of reasoning when writing about these events fail to acknowledge the factors elaborated above, that by 1995 Kosovo's leadership had successfully argued its case at the international, primarily Western, decision-making centres, that the issue of Kosovo required specific, international attention. Therefore, a conference such as Dayton, at which the interests of several parties were at stake, could not have resolved Kosovo successfully. Peter Russell, as discussed previously, has addressed this matter quite succinctly. The fact that Kosovo was not discussed at Dayton did not mean that it was not recognized as a crisis that required specific attention. The vigour with which the Contact Group for Yugoslavia was reactivated, and the ramping-up of the threat by NATO to use force against Serbian forces during 1998 and early 1999, together show the determination of the main Western decision-makers to prevent Serbia from ethnically cleansing Kosovo of its Albanian population and to address the issue of Kosovo once and for all.

Armed resistance as an internationalization variable

Judging by events prior to NATO's intervention in Kosovo in 1999, the impression is that the international actors were indeed well prepared for the impending consequences of violent conflict in Kosovo. However, armed resistance seemed a necessary step in order to inject some pace into the international mobilization. As I will argue later, it is impossible to say whether Rugova's non-violence alone would have succeeded in gaining full independence without the military component. That said, we already know (see Chapter 5) that Rugova's party, the LDK, had not ruled out violent confrontation with Serbia: they had put in place rudimentary contingency plans for waging armed resistance against Serbia if circumstances dictated. We must bear in mind that Rugova's strategy was to free Kosovo with as few losses as possible, but freedom from FRY/Serb domination was an imperative. Viewed from this perspective, therefore, the existence and the role of these embryonic military structures that Rugova's parallel institutions had created in the early 1990s require further detailed elaboration here, for it is from these rudimentary cells that the KLA later grew.

From the interviews I have conducted with senior LDK leaders, it appears that despite their orientation towards non-violence, some form of controlled violent resistance was preferred by the LDK and Rugova's parallel state – so long as it did not get out of control. It helped the LDK to act as a 'peace-broker' between its own military figures and the Serbian authorities and to suggest that it was best if both sides restricted themselves to political means.[30] This is best explained by Mentor Agani, the son of Rugova's vice-chairman, Professor Fehmi Agani, hailed by most people in Kosovo as the LDK's most effective politician, who was killed by Serbian police in 1999:

> Look, my father worked for the military resistance, but the whole idea was to have a controlled violent resistance in order to achieve the result without major loss of life [...] The principal idea was to move through the political process, but given that Milošević was a demagogue, he did everything possible to block the political process. So, in case the process was to be blocked, the idea was to activate these groups [the military groups] in sporadic actions here and there and unblock the political process.[31]

Indeed, senior LDK figures, including Professor Agani, had brokered an agreement with the Yugoslav forces in December 1991 after they had surrounded the Jashari family on 29 and 30 December that year. In response, the villagers had formed a cordon around the Yugoslav forces when a possible larger conflict was imminent. Agani went on to say:

> My father had negotiated with the Jasharis and the Yugoslav forces, on which occasion the main protagonist of the Jashari family, Adem, was allowed to leave the village and go to Albania. Then, soon afterwards, my father went to meet Jashari in Tirana.[32]

In very covert fashion, the senior LDK leadership, including Gjergji and Professor Agani, had liaised mostly with Sali Çeku, who had been the leading figure in the early military structures that the LDK had prepared.[33] However, the specific circumstances under which Adem Jashari, Sali Çeku and Zahir Pajaziti operated forced them to remain silent, which gave the LPK the opportunity to claim the credit for their actions by issuing a series of so-called communiqués.[34] It is through these communiqués that the LPK started to monopolize actions committed by others, and, as events proved later, their strategy worked in their favour extremely well.

As the frequency of armed incidents by small guerrilla groups grew, so did the LPK's self-identification with them, and eventually the LPK gave a name to these guerrillas – the KLA. However, there is no evidence to say what percentage of conscripts were actually loyal to the LPK. The KLA did not grow as a result of the LPK's propaganda or the political alternative they offered. In fact, the LPK had no alternative except to provoke violence; their political demands echoed Rugova's and the LDK's – independence. The bulk of the conscripts came from sections within the LDK, from which in most cases members joined the guerrillas en masse, despite the misperception that the LDK and Rugova had lost support among Albanians. Amid confusion as to where support for Rugova stood during the months when the guerrilla struggle against the FRY was intensifying, the US ambassador to the Former Republic of Macedonia (now the Republic of North Macedonia) recounts a telling story. In his published memoirs, Christopher Hill describes a touching experience he witnessed in the autumn of 1998, when Rugova and he visited a village in the area of Drenica, the region where the conflict was most active.

> The reaction [of the villagers] to the sight of Rugova was extraordinary. People, hesitant at first at the sight of their leader of more than a decade, approached him and draped their arms around his neck, kissing him on his cheeks. Some hugged him and dropped to their knees, kissing him on his hand as if he were the pope. I stood back to absorb the totality of the scene. For those who had written him off, I wished they could see him now.[35]

Whereas Rugova and the LDK remained extremely cautious about embracing the war, the LPK exercised ruthless methods to monopolize it, which often included threats against and possibly the murder of figures within the LDK and conscripts affiliated to it. So, during 1998 the battle for power moved from the political arena, where the LPK had constantly lost, to the armed-struggle arena, where LDK elements loyal to Rugova refused to engage in an internal battle among Albanians. Preserving unity and internal peace had all along been one of Rugova's demands, and so the LDK was never going to endorse a violent internal confrontation, no matter what. It is this determination that reportedly held Rugova back from sacking his prime minister, Bujar Bukoshi, who had over a long period created a rift with Rugova on the grounds that he wanted a 'more radical resistance'.[36] Kolaj, one of Rugova's vice-chairmen, who left his post as minister of defence after the arrests of 1993, told me that:

> The principal reason Rugova did not sack Bukoshi was out of fear that the Albanian movement might have degenerated into tribalization or, even worst, Palestinization. So, he thought it was better to keep Bukushi in, rather than give him any motive to align himself with other groups such as the LPK, with whom Bukoshi had dealings, or form his own faction.[37]

Bukoshi might have proposed a more radical approach than Rugova; however, since the effort to activate the Ministry of Defence and military structures in the early 1990s failed to materialize, it was mostly down to him to re-energize those efforts. Only in the spring of 1998 did he appoint a new minister of defence, Colonel Ahmet Krasniqi, who formed the FARK, but the fate of this belated enterprise was also defined by the dynamics of the internal power struggle. Shortly before Krasniqi's well-trained, professional military forces were to enter Kosovo, he was assassinated in Tirana in September 1998, leading many to believe that Albania's left-wing government, or agents close to it, had had something to do with his elimination. A common, dominant perception among the public in Kosovo was that this was done to consolidate the shift of power from the institutionalists to the LPK-led KLA, which was favoured by the Albanian government. With the elimination of Krasniqi, the FARK and the institutionalists seemed to have silently accepted the LPK's upper hand, and that in the interests of the nation they would conduct the fight jointly.

The above analysis demands a response to the question: how and why did factions close to the LDK, Rugova and the institutions of the parallel state, despite their overwhelming supremacy in numbers, practically hand power over to the Marxist-Leninists? The simple answer is, to avoid a bloody intra-Albanian conflict, which Rugova had successfully managed up until this point. Resorting to violence within Albanian groups would have had fatal consequences for the Albanians' struggle for freedom. The culture of unity that Rugova and the LDK had been nurturing for nearly a decade in the face of a ruthless Serbian regime eventually prevailed in wartime as well. Despite the hits that Rugova and the LDK took, large sections of the LDK who had joined in with the guerrilla warfare refused to fall into the trap of confrontation with their political rivals – the LPK-led KLA. This toleration was also shown at the political level. Rugova had silently accepted that the KLA's representative Hashim Thaqi would lead the Albanian delegation at the Rombouillet Conference, despite the fact that he (Rugova) had been elected the legitimate president of Kosovo with an overwhelming majority.

In the end, playing down the political differences among Albanians paid off all the while they faced an adversary prepared to use the most unconventional methods and tools to achieve its objectives. These include the incident that left six young Serbs murdered at the 'Panda' cafeteria in Pejë/Peć (western Kosovo) on 14 December 1998, which was masterminded by Serbia's secret service with the aim of pinning the incident on the Albanians,[38] and blaming the KLA for breaking the ceasefire agreement brokered by Holbrook on 13 October 1998.

The gruesome massacre of forty-five Albanian civilians in the village of Reçak on 15 January 1999 added to the sequence of the same sort of events that the Serbian authorities committed as part of their strategy. However, the swift qualification by the head of the KVM, William Walker, of this incident as a 'crime against humanity' is the most pertinent evidence of an international community already enlightened as to Serbia's intentions, and also validated Rugova's constant pleas to the international community to prevent an imminent genocide at the hands of the Serbs.[39] The Reçak massacre, therefore, forced the international community to intervene more decisively, first through the organization of a peace conference for Kosovo at Rambouillet in February 1999, and eventually with NATO's intervention in order to end the ethnic cleansing and humanitarian catastrophe in Kosovo.

After months of a military air campaign, FRY forces were forced to withdraw from Kosovo, implying thus that Kosovo was freed as a result of a joint campaign between NATO and the KLA, a perception that placed the latter in a favourable position regarding the LDK and Rugova. With his reputation tarnished by having been kept under house arrest by Milošević and forced to appear on Serbian TV, Rugova was compelled to spend months in Italy and on a diplomatic mission in Europe to recuperate, while the KLA and the political structures close to it captured the political space left by the withdrawal of Serbian forces and the loss of influence of Rugova's parallel state. Within a short period, municipality names, street names and those of cultural institutions were reviewed and renamed, while KLA and LPK personnel occupied official roles immediately after the conflict. This implied that they had freed Kosovo and that therefore it was they who should rule it.

However, despite the KLA's role in accelerating international intervention and the dramatic conclusion of the conflict in favour of Kosovo Albanians, I maintain that the KLA's military battle would have stood no chance without the political battle waged by Rugova, and eventual independence might not have been achieved. The evidence presented in this book shows that, through his innovative policy of non-violence, Rugova transformed the political environment of Kosovo following its occupation by Serbia/Yugoslavia in 1989. He had stood up to Serbia, which had access to arguably the fourth-largest military power in Europe (the SFRY), formed a parallel state under almost impossible circumstances, built an alliance with the most powerful states in the international community, pulled Kosovo out of marginalization and internationalized the Kosovo conflict. The groundwork for the state of Kosovo, therefore, was built on Rugova's policy. However, the LPK-led KLA, which became responsible for escalating the conflict, gained all the benefit from Rugova's hard work, stealing the glory of victory from him.

But Rugova was not going away until his 'mission' was seen out, unless death prevented him. In her memoirs, former US Secretary of State Madeleine Albright offered an account of her experience of Rugova in Washington, which perhaps best describes his uniqueness and tenacity.

> I have been around a lot of dissidents in my life, in Central Europe and elsewhere. Usually you can sense the fervor with which they approach their cause. Rugova was an anomaly. Although he often proved bewildering, I came to believe that one of his strengths was that he was constantly underestimated. People disregarded him, but he didn't go away, and when Kosovars voted, they did so more often for him than for anyone else.[40]

Albright's accurate account was confirmed soon afterwards. The first general election organized by the UNMIK administration in 2001 demonstrated clearly where popular allegiance rested and what the final political status of Kosovo would be. The presence of Rugova at the political helm symbolized that objective – the independence of Kosovo. Therefore, such events as the March 2004 riots,[41] which some argue set in motion the political processes ahead of the declaration of independence,[42] may have accelerated the necessity for the definition of the political status of Kosovo, but were not a decisive factor. There was no doubt in the minds of the vast majority of Kosovo Albanians that the idea of independence that Rugova had instilled in their psyche had no alternative. This political reality warrants a discussion of Rugova's lasting political legacy.

What is Rugova's political legacy?

In discussing this subject, we ought first to distinguish between the objective of Rugova's policy, namely to achieve political independence for Kosovo while preserving its substance – the Albanian population and its modest (in size) territory, and the achieving of this objective purely by non-violent means. This book provides an affirmative answer to the first part, while allowing discussion of the second. However, it is difficult to say whether Rugova's strategy would have triumphed by non-violent means, or with fewer human lives lost, if the LPK-led KLA had not entered the conflict.

Throughout this book, it has been documented that Rugova, by his policy of non-violence and the parallel state, internationalized the Kosovo conflict to the extent that resolving it, with or without armed conflict, would eventually have become necessary for the international community. A hypothetical question remains, however: Could an approach with a comprehensive sanctions package[43] after the Dayton Accords of 1995 have yielded the same results as the military intervention of 1999? The answer remains hypothetical as well. However, as some political analysts predicted, as the Yugoslav crisis started in Kosovo, so it would end in Kosovo, and therefore so long as the Kosovo crisis remained unresolved, the Yugoslav crisis would continue to cause instability in the region and among the international community. Except for speeding up the dynamics of the conflict, the ultimate political outcome that was brought about as a result of international intervention, and then facilitation through UNMIK,[44] has a strikingly common feature with Rugova's expressed option throughout his political strategy: 'an independent Kosovo with an international protectorate for a transitional period'.[45] In February 1993 Rugova launched a *Working Peace Plan of Ten Objectives* requesting, among other things, the deployment of UN or NATO troops in Kosovo, placing Kosovo under an international protectorate and the prevention of ethnic cleansing.[46] International figures approached the Kosovo crisis with this same attitude; in all the political scenarios that the Contact Group proposed for the Kosovo crisis in the period 1998–9, a provisional settlement featured as a necessary prerequisite before final status would be addressed. Viewed from this perspective, we can hypothesize that had the KLA not resorted to violent means, the political outcome might have been the same, but with many fewer lives lost. The LDK's strategy of managing the conflict by diplomatic means combined with violence on a much smaller scale than the LPK-led KLA exercised might have been another scenario, but still one with significantly fewer losses.

Yet Rugova's political legacy can be viewed from another perspective, which may be explained in more tangible terms. Although Rugova regained power in the first general elections administered by UNMIK, the political environment in Kosovo had been somewhat taken over by the spirit of 'heroism' and militancy promoted by the LPK-led KLA and the political structures associated with it. While Rugova was alive, he navigated a dichotomy between the political culture he had cultivated over many years and the heroic, militant culture introduced by the political structures and military figures deriving from the Marxist-Leninists. After his death in 2006, Rugova's LDK split into two groups, the dominant group entering into a governing coalition with Rugova's arch-rival, ex-KLA leader Hashim Thaqi's Democratic Party, thus enabling the latter to access power within public institutions and the cultural sphere.

Thus, from a party with a national vision, which built up non-violent resistance and a state culture, the LDK was now reduced to being a party that strove to remain in power through controversial coalition governments that served group rather than national interests. This discourse led to a widespread public perception of large-scale corruption within the LDK leadership associated with Hashim Thaqi's government. This symbiotic political governance consolidated further the heroic, militant culture, which bizarrely had an effect in even the least expected ways: in front of Kosovo's Parliament building a sculpture of Rugova erected after his death resembles more a heroic, military figure than his actual image, that of a fragile or 'frail colossus',[47] which implies that even Rugova had been taken away from the real Rugova, who symbolized intellectual wisdom.

Moreover, one of his most celebrated political legacies – the cultivation of the so-called 'permanent friendship with the United States of America', and the relationship with Western democratic countries – has often become a slogan for leaders of political parties for their own political purposes. On the other hand, it is public opinion, and particularly opinion among Rugova's electorate, that extends far beyond current support for the LDK, which appears to have internalized but suppressed Rugova's political and cultural legacy much more than elites have done. In their search for a leader who adhered to Rugova's cultural and political legacy, in the last (at the time when this book going to print), February 2021 parliamentary elections support for the LDK dropped to the staggeringly low figure of less than 13 per cent, forcing the resignation of the chairman of the LDK, who had earlier himself forced a young Rugova adherent out of the party.

But there is another essential variable to Rugova's legacy that must be acknowledged. The LDK's refusal to engage in an internal violent clash with factions of the LPK during the war or Rugova's silence in the face of losing his leadership role to Hashim Thaqi at the Rambouillet Conference in February 1998 are testimony to an exceptional political maturity that Rugova and his party had cultivated over many years. This breath of tolerance in the interests of the nation seems to have been carried over into the political life of post-war Kosovo. The successful organization of elections and the smooth transition of power from one party to another remain exemplary in Kosovo, and this is arguably a legacy of Rugova's policy of non-violence and the parallel state. This confirms the claim of some scholars who find a correlation between non-violent resistance and the quality of a democracy.[48]

As for Rugova's legacy within his own party, the LDK, the situation remains somewhat daunting. While its leadership continues to retain an 'institutionalist' political philosophy, it has lost the drive and intellectual depth to promote and continue Rugova's national cultural and political tradition. Its search for a return to power seems to be lacking in political invention and conviction, but it has also been eclipsed by the current dominant left-wing government. At the time of writing, the LDK still remains in search of a return to its soul and a new vision – a post-Rugova vision.

Finally, despite the change in the conflict from non-violent to violent, Rugova's unique policy of non-violence may be a model that many nations aspiring for self-determination might adopt when waging their political battles against much more powerful adversaries. However, a prerequisite for success remains massive participation of the people and a coherent political activity.

Conclusion

This chapter has encapsulated the central thesis of this book: that it was Ibrahim Rugova's policy of non-violence that generated the idea of Kosovo's independence, created Kosovo's political identity, internationalized the Kosovo conflict and prepared the groundwork for Kosovo's independence. In doing this, I have put forward five variables that support this proposition. First, I explained how Rugova's political movement transformed the political environment in Kosovo, whereby Albanians could institutionalize their political demands. In doing this, Rugova's political party, the LDK, which drove the policy of non-violence, led to the creation of Kosovo's parallel state, and in the process it gave legitimacy to Albanians' political organization and representation while at the same time delegitimizing the Serbian presence in Kosovo, which formed my second argument. The third argument focused on internationalization. I argued that it was Rugova's political campaign and lobbying around the world that internationalized the Kosovo conflict. Before Rugova's political campaign, Kosovo was known very marginally by the international community, but as that campaign progressed, the situation changed radically. The LDK's campaign, supported by human rights organizations, the media, academics and political analysts reporting on Kosovo, led to the Kosovo issue being presented as a crisis that required international attention far beyond the human rights domain, which is how Kosovo was initially considered. However, violence as an internationalization variable also became a component, and it necessarily pushed the Kosovo conflict to the top of the international community's agenda. Nevertheless, despite the LPK, which eventually came to control the military option in Kosovo, I maintain that it was Rugova's political battle and his parallel-state structures that formed the basis on which the LPK-led KLA built and that eventually claimed the credit for the victory.

In my last, fifth argument, I concluded that, despite ongoing challenges, Rugova's political legacy remains deeply instituted within Kosovo's political life and the democratic culture in the institutions of Kosovo.

7

Conclusion: Rugova's political legacy

Twenty-five years after the international military intervention that ended the Serbian government's attempted genocide against the Albanians in Kosovo, Serbia continues to pose obstacles to solidifying lasting peace and stability in southeastern Europe. Not only does it refuse to accept the independence of Kosovo, as declared in 2008 and as recognized by 119 countries, it also continues to pursue a belligerent approach that threatens the peace and stability of the region. Mandated by the United Nations, and supported by the United States, for years, the EU has been leading negotiations between Kosovo and Serbia aimed at creating a peaceful settlement. These efforts resulted in a so-called 'Agreement on the Path to Normalization' between Kosovo and Serbia in February 2023 in Brussels, which was reconfirmed in March of the same year in Ochrid (North Macedonia) in what became known as the Ochrid Accord. Despite these efforts, in September 2023 a terrorist group likely to have been sponsored by the Serbian authorities[1] was intercepted by members of the Kosovo police. The Serbian terrorists are believed to have been engaged in a broader operation to forcibly annex Kosovo's four northern municipalities. In the ensuing firefight, a Kosovo police officer was shot dead, and the militia fled into the monastery of Banjska. Kosovo's special police units were mobilized; they neutralized the terrorist group, killing four and arresting at least three gunmen. We have yet to see whether the indictment announced by Kosovo's Special Prosecution will result in Serbia handing over those indicted to the Kosovo authorities, and what political implications this may have. What is clear from these events, however, is that Serbia's determination to engage in violence in an effort to destroy Kosovo has not dissipated. Indeed, it appears to be growing.

Despite years of constant, violent and provocative efforts in Kosovo on the part of various groups associated with or sponsored by the Serbian authorities, the vast majority of Kosovo's population and political elites have remained remarkably calm and resolute in their pursuit of Kosovo's further integration into Western and international institutions. As argued in the previous chapter, the democratic transformations in Kosovo have been commendable, and the transition of power from one party to another has been remarkably smooth. In other words, the political culture cultivated during Rugova's tenure in Kosovo politics has been enshrined in Kosovo's political life, and, as time goes by, its population seems to cherish their hard-fought political achievements more and more.

The summary below shows the path Kosovo Albanians followed under the leadership of Rugova that led to their political accomplishment – the independence of Kosovo.

The first chapter set the scene of the Kosovo crisis. Principally, it described the political circumstances that formed the preconditions for the arrival of Ibrahim Rugova into politics and his policy of non-violence. This was associated with the Serb/Yugoslav authorities' comprehensive and repressive measures against the Albanians, a campaign that had started following Albanian protests in the streets of Kosovo in 1981 calling for an upgrading of their political status. These protests were then used by Serbia as a pretext for a campaign in which the Serb intelligentsia, the Serbian Orthodox Church and the political elite colluded in order to justify the Serbs' repressive campaign against the Albanians and the removal of Kosovo's autonomy.

Having witnessed the incapacity of the Kosovo Albanians' communist leadership to defend Albanian interests, by the mid-1980s Albanian intellectuals from the Association of Writers of Kosovo (AWK) were involved in debates with their Serbian counterparts. While successful in arguing their case and proposing a dialogue to resolve contentious issues between Serbs and Albanians, the Albanian intellectuals were powerless to divert the intentions of Serbian institutions regarding Kosovo. A comprehensive mobilization of Serb institutions and the masses, including the invocation of such historical myths as the Battle of Kosovo of 1389, led to the ambushing and intimidation of Kosovo institutions, which in turn led to constitutional changes in 1989. These changes reduced Albanians' political and cultural rights significantly and placed Kosovo firmly under Serb control.

Albanian protests seeking to prevent the constitutional changes left many lying dead in the streets, while the Kosovo political leadership was silenced. It is in these precarious circumstances that the Albanian intellectuals emerged. Already engaged in debates with Serb intellectuals, and increasingly active in local and international media in his denunciations of Serb encroachments on Albanian rights, stood Ibrahim Rugova. This intellectual movement eventually led to the formation of a non-communist party – the LDK – with Rugova elected as its leader in December 1989. Owing to Rugova's symbolic capital and the organization's political orientation, the LDK quickly grew to over half a million members and successfully diverted Albanian protests from the streets into the institutionalization of their political demands. So began what became known as Ibrahim Rugova's policy of non-violence.

Considering the circumstances, Rugova's policy of non-violence seemed a shrewd, pragmatic choice that aimed to compensate Albanians for their lack of access to power by waging a political battle against Serbia, while at the same time preserving the Albanian population by preventing a potentially violent conflict with a significantly mightier Serbia. A crucial factor in its success was its internal cohesion; Rugova's approach was unique in the sense that, by successfully integrating various Albanian political factions, and sharing power with those more radical exponents within his own party, he gave his movement a hugely popular character.

Having examined the political circumstances and the background in which Rugova's policy of non-violence emerged, in Chapter 2 I developed a cultural approach, which examined the Albanian cultural and historical traditions that Rugova made use of in order to empower his political project and the policy of non-violence. Along with their less-than-proportionate access to power, compared with the Serbs, the Albanians' next biggest challenge was responding to the image and perceptions ascribed to them by Serb propaganda. These representations are noticeable from as early as the time the Serbs occupied Kosovo in 1912–13, when stereotypes and negative images about Albanians' cultural legacies, historical realities and political capabilities were used, all of which had a profound effect on the Albanian political struggle.[2] That tradition has persisted ever since, climaxing in the late 1980s and 1990s[3] (see Chapters 2 and 3), and in various forms continues to remain present even today.

The principal aim of the Albanian cultural elite was therefore to refute this narrative and shape a vastly different, positive image of their own. The policy of non-violence was a critical factor in carrying out this calling. Principally, it was Rugova who, capitalizing on his cultural and literary culture, was able to draw on Albanian traditions and give Albanian culture and tradition a radically different interpretation from the Serbs'. Principally, he interpreted Albanian culture as tolerant and secular, and he received an extraordinary response from the Albanian population, demonstrating patience and resistance. This gave the Albanian political elite the opportunity to wage a successful political battle and prove to its international interlocutors that the Albanians' cultural and political narrative was not a simple, theoretical enterprise but a political project based on cultural and historical realities, stemming from political convictions. Rugova's entire intellectual arsenal was utilized to amplify his strategy of non-violence, which in turn helped him build excellent relations with the main Western powers, such as the United States and the EU, but also the Catholic Church. Rugova's frequent visits to the Holy See and Western capitals suggested that Albanians were much more culturally compatible with the West than the Serbs themselves, and far from the image presented by Serb propaganda. This dichotomy had gained currency by the mid-1990s, particularly with the publication of Samuel Huntington's article 'The Clash of Civilizations', which placed Albanians, and particularly Kosovo, on the fault line where all three major civilizations coincided: Western Christianity, Eastern Orthodox Christianity and Islam.[4] Rugova's policy successfully marginalized this narrative.

As a cultural intellectual, Rugova was well placed to interpret the historical and cultural realities of the region, and in this context he often contested the Serbs' historical 'truth' about Kosovo. Principally, however, he was interested in building a political identity for Kosovo based on Albanians' cultural and historical past, and he did so successfully by employing a repetitive narrative that eventually gained traction among Albanian elites and the population at large. In a unique fashion, in order to build a perception among his audience that Kosovo's independence was a reality in the making, Rugova went on to invent the state infrastructure, including the design of a flag, which included unique cultural and historical elements, and a national anthem, among his vast opus of symbolic choreography.

It is this cultural and ideological background that formed the landscape in which the political struggle was waged and the development of Kosovo's 'parallel state' took place, which is the focus of the third chapter of this book. Political analysts and scholars who dealt with the parallel state of Kosovo in the 1990s often limited its role to fulfilling the social, health and educational needs of the population. However, in this book, I examine other significant functions of the parallel state that go far beyond this conventional narrative. First, I argue that Rugova's strategy of non-violence had an immediate impact in changing the political and cultural environment in Kosovo by instilling a new belief among the population and political stakeholders there that it was possible to achieve a different future for Kosovo. The Kosovo Parliament, which, under pressure from the Serb state, had voted in 1989 for a change in Kosovo's constitution, had now switched its allegiance in favour of Rugova's movement and played a crucial role in setting up the parallel-state institutions. I use the theory of legitimacy[5] to explain how the LDK and Rugova led Kosovan society in setting up parallel-state institutions while sidelining the Serb administration in Kosovo and settling the battle of legitimacy between Albanians and Serbs over the territory. The parallel state, I argue, successfully challenged Serb and Yugoslav legitimacy, which relied on the use of violence, and built its own legitimacy by successfully organizing the plebiscites that led to the declaration of Kosovo's independence and the elections that set up the parallel-state institutions. Eventually, Rugova's parallel state reduced the presence of the Serbian administration in Kosovo to that of a violent police state with no legitimacy.

Furthermore, led by the LDK and Rugova, the Albanian political parties in Kosovo formed a body, namely CCAPP, in which all political parties were represented and shared power on issues of national interest. The council, therefore, had a unifying character, whereby political representatives reached agreements before they were implemented. Moreover, the parallel state gave cohesion to the belief that not only was the independence of Kosovo possible, it was also just a matter of time before it was to be fully realized. The parallel state enabled the Albanian political elite to wage a diplomatic battle, which was another of its critical functions; however, its significance is so great that it deserved a full chapter of its own – Chapter 4.

It has been argued from the outset of this book that the internationalization of the Kosovo conflict was one of the core objectives of Rugova's policy of non-violence. Towards this end, confronting Serbia on issues concerning the 'truth' about Kosovo was crucial. While Chapter 2 in major part focused on the image and perception of Albanians that Serbs had publicly conveyed for local and international audiences, Chapter 4 centred on pulling Kosovo out of the marginalized position Serbia had confined it to, and conveying a different historical and political 'truth' about the Albanians and about Kosovo as a geographical and political term. The principal argument of this chapter is that at the beginning of Rugova's campaign in the early 1990s, Kosovo was 'terra nullius', on account of international factors, as a senior political leader of Kosovo has described.[6] Successive Serb and Yugoslav governments as a matter of public policy had managed to assign a low profile to Kosovo by presenting the Albanians as insignificant and arguing that Kosovo historically belonged to Serbia.

The aim of the Albanian political elite was to show exactly the opposite – Kosovo was incorporated within Serbia by violent means, and the Albanian population, which constituted over 90 per cent of the total population of Kosovo, were to demonstrate that they were capable of building an independent state and governing themselves while implementing the principles of democracy based on political, cultural, ethnic and religious tolerance. There are several factors on which Rugova's policy focused its campaign for the internationalization of the Kosovo conflict. First, it had to win an internal battle with the Marxist-Leninists, whose ideology had in the past not only failed to produce positive results but also damaged Kosovo's cause by displaying their communist ideology in their campaign, both in Kosovo and abroad. Having integrated many Marxist-Leninists within the LDK, Rugova was now able to wage a coherent information and diplomatic campaign, including the establishment of a highly credible information agency, the QIK, which became an integral part of the policy of non-violence. The QIK circulated daily news about Kosovo throughout the world and became the central information hub for a highly sophisticated diasporan network, which acted on behalf of Kosovo's parallel state as an information agency in Western countries.

This was supplemented by diplomatic activity led by the LDK's senior activists and Rugova himself, with their frequent visits to various Western capitals. The international media, foreign intellectuals, human rights agencies and political figures, particularly those in the United States and the EU (e.g. France, Germany and Britain), as well as the Catholic Church, were targeted. The results of this campaign were remarkable. By the mid-1990s Kosovo was no longer just a human rights issue but was fully acknowledged as a crisis that, if not dealt with promptly, might have catastrophic consequences not simply for the Kosovan population but for the whole southeast European region, and possibly wider. Recognition on the part of the international community of the magnitude of the Kosovo crisis might have been the principal reason Kosovo was not incorporated into the Dayton Accords of 1995, which ended years of fighting in Bosnia and Herzegovina between Muslims, Serbs and Croats. The mediators feared that the inclusion of Kosovo in the Dayton negotiations would have jeopardized the outcome of the accords, and therefore the Kosovo issue was postponed. However, this absence, among other factors, was perceived by some in Kosovo as showing that armed resistance was necessary in order to propel Kosovo onto the international agenda more seriously.

The dynamics that led to the transformation of the Kosovo conflict from non-violent to violent was dealt with in the fifth chapter. The analysis in this chapter began with the premise that Rugova may have been a pacifist, but his explicit goal was the freedom and independence of Kosovo from Serb domination. Therefore, his party had never completely ruled out violent confrontation with Serbia as a very last resort. Conscious of that possible scenario, in the early 1990s the LDK had undertaken contingency measures by preparing small military groups and using them as per the needs of the parallel state. With the exception of rare, small-scale actions against Serb security officers throughout the 1990s, these groups mostly remained dormant. However, post-Dayton, the situation changed. While Rugova was not prepared to drift away from his non-violent course, the Marxist-Leninist militants in his party started to agitate for armed resistance in collaboration with their old party, the LPK, which was operating predominantly from abroad. The LPK sensed that by escalating the Kosovo crisis, they might be able to intensify the international response and in the process could also take power away from Rugova.

Eventually, by the end of 1997 and into early 1998 the frequency of armed incidents increased. However, one incident, the killing of Adem Jashari and his extended family by FRY forces, stimulated massive recruitment to the armed struggle. This momentum was used by the LPK, which had by now infiltrated their own agitators into the existing guerrilla groups in order to build relationships with them[7] and eventually gain control over them. The indiscriminate response and civilian massacres by FRY forces resulted in blurred political allegiances among the recruits who joined the armed resistance, thus resulting in the LPK-led KLA establishing full control over the military insurgents.

A looming civilian humanitarian catastrophe caused by FRY forces, which drove hundreds of thousands of civilians out of their homes, propelled the Contact Group – the United States, the UK, France, Germany, Russia and Italy – into a diplomatic process that eventually had to rely on the use of force, wielded by NATO, to end the violence. Thus, the transformation of the conflict from non-violent to violent inevitably made the KLA an indispensable factor in any lasting peace settlement, which was confirmed at the Rambouillet Peace Conference organized by the Contact Group in February and March 1999, and at which the KLA's leadership replaced Rugova, until then the undisputed leader of the Albanians. The KLA's power was further underlined following the successful NATO air campaign against the FRY in which the KLA participated, thus implying that Kosovo was liberated as a result of a dual campaign led by NATO and the KLA. Despite the claim made by the LPK-led KLA that it was their actions that contributed to the freedom of Kosovo, it is argued here that it was Rugova's policy of non-violence that won the political battle against Serbia and prepared the ground for international intervention. The KLA acted merely as the catalyst for more vigorous intervention.

I consolidated this proposition in the sixth chapter, with several supporting arguments. First, I explained that fundamentally it was Rugova, through his policy of non-violence, who averted conflict with Serbia and who created the conditions for a political process that resulted in the idea of Kosovo's independence being shaped. This idea was further consolidated through the organization of the institutions of the parallel state, which gave Kosovo Albanians' political organization a legitimacy while refusing to co-operate with the FRY's institutions and delegitimizing its presence in Kosovo. This political organization facilitated Rugova's strategy of waging a campaign to create international support for Kosovo.

Here I elaborated on the strategy of internationalization, which targeted a series of relevant international factors, such as political figures, the media, human rights agencies and activists, among many others. I reaffirmed the argument that Rugova's policy of non-violence elevated the profile of Kosovo from that of an obscure region shaped by Serb propaganda into a major political conflict that required serious international attention before it erupted into violence, with consequences for the Albanian population and both regional and international stability. The reception of Rugova and other political figures in Western capitals and international organizations such as EU and UN agencies and Western leaders' statements, as well as human rights groups' reports from various international agencies about Kosovo during the 1990s, testify to the success of Rugova's strategy of internationalization.

Thus, when the conflict was transformed from non-violence to violence, the political battle that Rugova's policy had fought had already prepared the ground for Albanian guerrillas to supplement the political battle. Moreover, the existing small military groups that Rugova's parallel institutions had prepared in the early 1990s served as the nucleus of the military struggle that came to be dominated by the left-wing Marxist-Leninist organization, the LPK. The chapter concluded that even though the KLA escalated the conflict, which forced international actors to get involved more vigorously, it was Rugova's political strategy of non-violence that had waged a successful political battle both internally, by building a state infrastructure, and internationally, by lobbing international powers and thus ensuring their support for Kosovo. The groundwork for freedom and the state of Kosovo, therefore, was created by Rugova's policy.

The chapter further concluded that the triumphalist claims by the LPK-led KLA were short-lived, as Rugova returned to power with massive electoral support in the 2001 elections. This implied a lasting political legacy for Rugova and his political culture, developed over many years, which came to be manifested through a mature transition of power from one party to another and a commitment to enshrine the most advanced democratic principles within Kosovo's political life. Lastly, it was suggested that Rugova's model of a policy of non-violence could be used more generally for waging political battles against mightier adversaries, but a precondition for a successful campaign remains massive participation on the part of the populace.

Notes

Introduction

1   Depending on the source, the terms 'Kosovo' or 'Kosova' will be used
     interchangeably throughout this book. Kosova with an 'a' is used by the majority in
     Kosovo and is increasingly being adopted by international sources as well, whereas
     Kosovo with an 'o' is the legacy of Yugoslav–Serbian official usage, although it
     still enjoys widespread international usage.

2   Before the withdrawal of the Ottoman Empire from the Balkans, Albanians were
     dominant in four so-called Vilayets: Shkodër, Kosova, Yanina and Manastir. They
     comprised a territory of well over 50 per cent of Albania, recognized in 1913. The
     rest of the Albanian-inhabited territories were occupied and recognized by the
     great powers to Greece, Montenegro, Northern Macedonia and of course Kosova as
     part of the Yugoslav Kingdom, but occupied by Serbia.

3   Ivo Andrić, 'Draft on Albania', in *Gathering Clouds: The Roots of Ethnic Cleansing in
     Kosovo and Macedonia – Early Twentieth Century Documents*, 2nd edn, ed. Robert
     Elsie (London: Centre for Albanian Studies, 2015), 194–211.

4   See for example, Christina Morus, 'The SANU Memorandum: Intellectual
     Authority and the Constitution of an Exclusive Serbian "People"', *Communications
     and Critical/Cultural Studies* 4, no. 2 (June 2007): 142–65.

5   Vaso Čubrilović, 'The Expulsion of the Albanians: Memorandum (1937)', in
     Gathering Clouds: The Roots of Ethnic Cleansing in Kosovo and Macedonia – Early
     Twentieth- Century Documents, 2nd edn, ed. Robert Elsie (London: Centre for
     Albanian Studies, 2015), 148–80.

6   'The Minority Problems in the New Yugoslavia: Memorandum by Vaso Čubrilović
     (1944)', in *Gathering Clouds: The Roots of Ethnic Cleansing in Kosovo and* Macedonia –
     Early Twentieth- Century Documents, 2nd edn, ed. Robert Elsie (London: Centre for
     Albanian Studies, 2015), 211–31.

7   Noel Malcolm, 'Is the Complaint about the Serb State's Deportation Policy of
     Albanians between the Two World Wars Based on Myth?', in *The Case for Kosova:
     Passage to Independence*, ed. Anna Di Lellio (London: Anthem Press 2006), 60.

8   In Aleksandar Petrović and ĐorĐe Stefanović, 'Kosovo, 1944–1981: The Rise and
     the Fall of a Communist "Nested Homeland"', *Europe-Asia Studies* 62, no. 7 (2010):
     1073–106.

9   Fadil Kajtazi, *Ideologjija Serbe e Gjenocidit* (Prishtinë: Beqir Musliu, 2023), 301.

10   See Noel Malcolm, *Kosovo: A Short History* (London: Papermac, 1998), 268.

11   Hivzi Islami, *Rrjedha Demografike Shqiptare* (Pejë: Dukagjini, 1994), 54.

12   In Malcolm, *Kosovo*, 249.

13   See, for instance, Marko Hren, *Slovenian Peace Movement in the Context of Yugoslav Anti-War Contention: Re-discovered History of War-Prevention (1984–1992)* (Ljubljana: Samozal, 2012), Slovenian_PeaceMovement_amd_Prewar_processes20200526-64996-1a9jr8d-libre.pdf (accessed 28 February 2024).

14   The use of the term 'Yugoslav/Serbia(n)' throughout this book implies that Serbia acted on behalf of the Socialist Federal Republic of Yugoslavia's (SFRY) institutions before its dissolution in 1992, and subsequently Serbia and Montenegro declared the name of the Federal Republic of Yugoslavia (FRY), which continued until 2003.

15   In the Balkan territory, particularly in the former Yugoslavia, for different reasons, violent forms of conflict resolution had been the most common approach, at least in the last hundred or so years, including the conflicts that followed the dissolution of the SFRJ in the early 1990s. Owing to how long it lasted and its consistency, Rugova's non-violent approach marked a radically different departure from this violent discourse.

16   A section of these were adherents of the former Communist leader of Albania Enver Hoxha.

17   The term LPK-led KLA refers to the guerrilla groups associated to Lëvizja Popullore e Kosovës (LPK).

18   Municipality names, street names and cultural institution names were reviewed and renamed within a short time after KLA and the LPK personnel had occupied institutional roles immediately following the conflict.

19   There had been many high-ranking LDK activists murdered during and after the 1999 conflict; Rugova himself survived two assassination attempts, and these were often associated with the LPK-led KLA, albeit no case has been proven at trial. At the time of writing, a number of former KLA figures are being indicted by the Specialized Chambers of Kosovo in The Hague.

20   The thesis that the Yugoslav crisis had started with Kosovo and that it would conclude with Kosovo was articulated by French philosophers such as Paul Ricoeur, Edgar Morin, Claude Lefort, Andrë-Glucksmann, Alain Finkielkraut, et al., with their frequent and publicized articles. Muhamedin Kullashi, 'Kolosi i Brishtë', http://www.trepca.net/2006/02/060202_kolosi_brishte_mk.htm (accessed 13 January 2020).

21   See, for instance, Alex Bellamy, *Kosovo and International Society* (New York: Palgrave Macmillan, 2002); Ivo H. Daalder and Michael E. O' Hanlon's *Winning Ugly: NATO's War to Save Kosovo* (Washington, DC: Brookings Institution, 2000), in which the authors celebrate NATO's triumph; Stephen Badsey and Paul Latawski, eds., *Britain, NATO and the Lessons of Balkan Conflicts 1991–1999* (London: Frank Cass, 2004); Florian Bieber and Židas Daskalovski, eds., *Understanding the War in Kosovo* (London: Frank Cass, 2003).

22   Bieber and Daskalovski, eds., *Understanding the War* (chapters by Židas Daskalovski, Dejan Guzina, Lazar Nikolić), pre-military intervention-negotiation period (Wolf, Elizabeth Allen-Daphne), intervention and theories (Malazogu,

Sulyok, Blogojević, and Johnston), with the fourth and fifth part of the book focusing on the UN administration of Kosovo and the regional implications following the military conflict, with the exception of Guzina, whose account merely describes the political acts between 1990 and 1998 in his essay 'The Republic of Kosova: A State within a State'.

23 These include: Howard Clark, *Civil Resistance in Kosovo* (London: Pluto, 2000); Ruth Reitan, 'Strategic Non-violent Conflict in Kosovo', *Peace and Change* 25, no. 1 (January 2000): 70–102; Michael Salla, 'Kosovo, Non-violence and the Break-up of Yugoslavia', *Security Dialogue* 26, no. 4 (1995): 427–38; Shkëlzen Maliqi, 'Self-Understanding of the Albanians in Non-violence', in *Conflict or Dialogue: Serbian Albanian Relations and Integration of the Balkans*, ed. Dusan Janjic and Shkëlzen Maliqi (Subotica: Open University, European Centre for Conflict Resolution, 1994), 237–47; Shkëlzen Maliqi, *Separate Worlds: Reflections and Analyses 1989–1998* (Prishtinë: Dukagjini, 1998); Shkëlzen Maliqi, *Why Nonviolent Resistance in Kosovo Failed* (Prishtinë: Qendra për studime Humanistike 'Gani Bobi', 2011).

24 These include: Sabri Hamiti, *Një Memento për Rugovën* (Prishtinë: Shtëpia Botuese 55, 2008); Vehbi Miftari, *Rugova: Vizioni Nacional* (Prishtinë: AIKD, 2007) – later updated into a new title, *Rugova: Mendimi, Kultura, Politika* (Prishtinë: Shtëpia Botuese, Faik Konica, 2013); Enver Bytyqi, *Filozofia politike dhe nacionale e Ibrahim Rugovës* (The Political and National Philosophy of Rugova) (Tiranë: Shtëpia Botuese 'Koha', 2010).

Chapter 1

1 Momćilo Pavlović, 'Kosovo under Autonomy, 1974–1990', in *Confronting the Yugoslav Controversies: A Scholar's Initiative*, ed. Charles W. Ingrao and Thomas A. Emmert (West Lafayette, IN: Purdue University Press, 2009), 48–80, 60.

2 The use of the term 'Yugoslav–Serbian' suggests a frequent recurrence of policies and decisions taken at the federal level under Serbian influence yet without a broad consensus among all federal members.

3 Pavlović, 'Kosovo under Autonomy', 61.

4 Amnesty International Annual Report 1985, Yugoslavia, 299–300. 1 May 1985, Index Number: POL 10/0002/1985.

5 Amnesty International Annual Report 1986, Yugoslavia, 317–18. 1 January 1986, Index Number: POL 10/0003/1986.

6 See Muhamedin Kullashi, 'The Production of Hatred in Kosova (1981–91)', in *Kosovo/Kosova: Confrontation or Coexistence*, ed. Ger Duijizings, Shkëlzen Maliqi and Dušan Janjić (Njimegen: Peace Research Centre, University of Njimegen, 1996), 56–69, at 56.

7   Kullashi, 'The Production of Hatred in Kosova', 58.

8   Ibid., 58–60.

9   Jasna Dragović-Soso, '*The Saviours of the Nation': Serbia's Intellectual Opposition and the Revival of Nationalism* (London: Hurst, 2002), 117.

10   Pavlović, 'Kosovo under Autonomy', 22.

11   Gazmend Zajmi, 'Kosova's Constitutional Position in the Former Yugoslavia', in *Kosovo/Kosova: Confrontation or Coexistence*, ed. Ger Duijzings, Dušan Janjić and Shkëlzen Maliqi (Nijmegen: Peace Research Centre, University of Nijmegen, 1996), 95–101, at 98.

12   See Gëzim Krasniqi, 'Revisiting Nationalism in Yugoslavia: An Inside-out View of the Nationalist Movement in Kosovo', in *Debating the End of Yugoslavia*, ed. Florian Beiber, Armina Galijaš and Rory Archer (Farnham: Ashgate, 2014), 225–39, at 230.

13   The LCY defined the term 'ideo-political differentiation', which implied a formal association of an individual, and in many cases his or her entire family, with an anti-Yugoslav act, behaviour and sentiment. The 'differentiated' individuals were then suspended from membership of the LCK and from their professional positions. This mostly targeted intellectuals and young students from the University of Prishtina, who were convicted and expelled from the university (both students and academic staff alike). The participants in the 1981 demonstrations and their supporters were all differentiated.

14   Ibid., 202. Bogdanović's views on Kosovo can also be found in his book *Razgovori o Kosovu* (Discussions on Kosovo) (Beograd: Miodrag Dramatičin, 1986).

15   Dragović-Soso, '*The Saviours of the Nation*', 130.

16   Morus, 'The SANU Memorandum', 143.

17   Ibid.

18   Ibid.

19   During this period in Yugoslavia freedom of speech was severely curtailed by the infamous article 133 on the freedom of speech, sanctioning it as a verbal crime. Many Albanians and others in Yugoslavia were charged based on article 133.

20   Hoti was considered one of the most prominent young Kosovo intellectuals at the time, with a Master's degree from Zagreb University and research experience at Harvard, Washington and Belgrade. He was Kosovo's representative for foreign relations and a distinguished Prishtina University professor. In 1982, he was sentenced by a Yugoslav court and spent three and a half years in prison for his support for the 1981 protests in Kosovo. In 1983 Amnesty International declared him a prisoner of conscience. In 1994 he was sentenced again, to five years. In May 1999, Hoti was released one Sunday during NATO bombardments and was never seen again. He has since been declared 'disappeared'.

21   Discussion at the Congress of Yugoslav Writers in Novi Sad, 18–20 June 1986, in Ibrahim Rugova, *Pavarësia dhe Demokracia: intervista dhe artikuj* (Prishtinë: Faik Konica, 2005), 39–42.

22   Ibid., 42.

23　Ibid., 45.

24　The significance of the opinions and the positioning of the Serbian intellectual elite are also noted by Howard Clark, the author of *Civil Resistance in Kosovo*, who states: 'In 1997, a number of analysts believed that the elite in Serbia were ready to "lose" Kosovo. Some of those who had fanned the flames of Serbian nationalism seemed resigned to their failure to re-Serbianize Kosovo, and they looked for alternatives'. Howard Clark, 'Nonviolent Struggle in Kosovo', *War Resisters' International*, 1 January 2001, http://www.wri-irg.org/nonviolence/nvse16-en.htm.

25　*Rilindja* was the only Kosovo daily newspaper in Albanian during the existence of Yugoslavia.

26　Jusuf Buxhovi, *Kthesa Historike: Vitet e Gjermanisë dhe Epoka e LDK-s* (Prishtinë: Faik Konica, 2008), 132.

27　Buxhovi, *Kthesa Historike*, 132.

28　Ibid., 133.

29　Ibid.

30　Ibid.

31　Ibid.

32　Rugova, *Pavarësia dhe Demokracia*, 67–8.

33　Ibid., 68.

34　Ibid., 69.

35　Ibid.

36　Ibid., 70.

37　Ibid., 77–8.

38　Ibid.

39　Ibrahim Rugova interview, *Večer*, Maribor, 22 April 1989, in Rugova, *Pavarësia dhe Demokracia*, 108.

40　Buxhovi, *Kthesa Historike*, 156.

41　Ibid.

42　Slavoljub Djukić, cited in Louis Sell, *Slobodan Milošević and the Destruction of Yugoslavia* (Durham, NC: Duke University Press, 2002), 3.

43　For a detailed process of how these events unfolded, see Lenard J. Cohen, *Serpent in the Bosom: The Rise and Fall of Milošević* (Boulder, CO: Westview Press, 2002). Chapter 2 (87–139) is particularly relevant.

44　For more on the crisis frame, see Anthony Oberschall, 'The Manipulation of Ethnicity: From Ethnic Cooperation to Violence and War in Yugoslavia', *Ethnic and Racial Studies* 23, no. 6 (November 2000): 982–1001, at 990.

45　Serbeze Haxhiaj and Milica Stojanović, 'Autonomy Abolished: How Milosević Launched Kosovo's Descent into War', 23 March 2020, Balkan Transitional Justice, Bajgora Belgrade, Pristina BIRN, https://balkaninsight.com/2020/03/23/autonomy-abolished-how-milosevic-launched-kosovos-descent-into-war/ (accessed 15 January 2022).

46 Because the provinces of Kosovo and Vojvodina had obtained 'autonomous' status from Serbia, nationalists in Serbia claimed that Serbia was not a complete state.

47 *Večer* – the Slovenian newspaper of Maribor, 22 April 1989, in Rugova, *Pavarësia dhe Demokracia*, 100.

48 Rugova's interview in Večer, ibid.

49 Maliqi, 'Self-Understanding of the Albanians', 237–47, at 237–8.

50 Rugova's interview, *Der Spiegel*, 26 June 1989, in Rugova, *Pavarësia dhe Demokracia*, 10.

51 Ibid.

52 The term *Ilegalja*, or 'ilegal', denotes political activity that under the Yugoslav legal system was ruled illegal.

53 Paul Hockenos, *Homeland Calling: Exile Patriotism and Balkan Wars* (Ithaca, NY: Cornell University Press, 2003), 198.

54 Hockenos, *Homeland Calling*, 198.

55 Mehmet Kraja, *Vitet e Humbura* (Tiranë: Eurorilindja, 1995), 207.

56 Aubrey Herbert, Anglo-Albanian Society press release, March 1918 – London. Aubrey Herbert, *Albania's Greatest Friend: Aubrey Herbert and the Making of Modern Albania: Diaries and Papers 1904–1923*, ed. Bejtullah D. Destani and Jason Tomes (London: I. B. Tauris, 2011), 232.

57 Maliqi, 'Self-Understanding of Albanians', 237–47.

58 See Peter Prifti, 'Kosova's Economy: Problems and Prospects', in *Studies on Kosova*, ed. Arshi Pipa and Sami Repishti (Boulder, CO: East European Monographs, distributed by Columbia University Press, 1984), 125–65, at 126.

59 Prifti, 'Kosova's Economy', 135–7.

60 Ibid., 130.

61 See Malcolm, *Kosovo*, 318.

62 See Jens Reuter, 'Education Policy in Kosova', in *Studies on Kosova*, ed. Pipa and Repishti (Boulder, CO: East European Monographs, distributed by Columbia University Press, 1984), 259–64, at 260.

63 Prifti, 'Kosova's Economy', 142.

64 Maliqi, 'Self-Understanding of Albanians', 239.

65 Ibid.

66 Pierre Bourdieu, *Language and Symbolic Power: The Economy of Linguistic Exchanges*, ed. and intro. John B. Thompson; trans. Gino Raymond and Matthew Adamson (Cambridge: Polity in association with Basil Blackwell, 1991).

67 Ibrahim Berisha, 'Ata dhe këta themeluesit e LDK-së!': Copëza ditari personal në vitet 1989–1990'. Facebook post, 26 September 2012.

68 Ibid.

69 Ibid.

70 Buxhovi, *Kthesa Historike*, 220.

71 Berisha, 'Ata dhe këta themeluesit e LDK-së'.

72 Luljeta Pula-Beqiri, interview for TV21 Nacionale, 26 September 2022, https://nacionale.com/politike/flet-pas-dy-dekadash-pse-luljeta-pula-beqiri-u-harrua-nga-politika-e-pasluftes-video (accessed 6 December 2022).

73 Itziar Mujika Chao, 'Women's Activism in the Civil Resistance Movement in Kosovo (1989–1997): Characteristics, Development, Encounters', *Nationalities Papers* 48, no. 5 (September 2002): 843–60.

74 Lirije Kajtazi, interview with Jakup Azemi (author), 28 November 2022.

75 Discussion at the Congress of Yugoslav Writers in Novi Sad, 18–20 June 1986, in Rugova, *Pavarësia dhe Demokracia*, 39–42.

76 Rugova's non-violent approach was systematically affirmed through his weekly press releases, and the regular meetings with LDK branch leaders. This will be discussed in more detail in Chapter 4.

77 Besnik Pula, 'The Emergence of the Kosovo "Parallel State", 1988–1992', *Nationalities Papers* 32, no. 4 (2004): 487–511; Maliqi, 'Self-Understanding of Albanians'; Clark, *Civil Resistance in Kosovo*.

78 Krasniqi, 'Revisiting Nationalism', 230.

79 Clark, *Civil Resistance in Kosovo*, 56.

80 Pula, 'The Emergence', 805.

81 Maliqi, *Separate Worlds*, 30.

Chapter 2

1 Resolving Kosovo's status with a satisfactory outcome, Rugova claimed, was a major step towards resolving the whole Albanian issue in the Balkans.

2 Maria Todorova, *Imagining the Balkans* (Oxford: Oxford University Press, 1997).

3 See Chapter 1.

4 See, for example, Shkëlzen Maliqi, 'Albanians between East and West', in *Kosovo/Kosova*, ed. Ger Duijzings, Dušan Janjić and Shkëlzen Maliqi (Nijmegen: Peace Research Centre, University of Nijmegen, 1996), 115–22, at 115.

5 See Ger Duijzings, *Religion and the Politics of Identity in Kosovo* (London: Hurst, 2000), 164.

6 For example, as part of anti-Albanian nationalist propaganda, Vladan Djordjević (1844–1930), while temporarily the Serbian prime minister, framed the Albanians ('Arnauts') in a 1913 pamphlet as inferior and thus little capable of nation-building themselves: 'The Arnaut-type is meagre and small, and there is something gipsy-like, Phoenician to it. [They also remind one of] primeval men who slept in trees holding on with their tails. In later centuries, when men did not need their tails any more, it wasted away, so that there is only a trace of it left in the little coccyx of contemporary people. Only among the Albanians, it seems, men with tails

still existed in the nineteenth century.' Quoted in Stephanie Schwandner-Sievers, 'Albanians, Albanianism and the Strategic Subversion of Stereotypes', in *The Balkans and the West: Constructing the European Other, 1945–2003*, ed. Andrew Hammond (London: Routledge, 2004), 110–26, at 115–16.

7   The historian Noel Malcolm has described how some of these policies were designed and partly executed as part of the discussions among Serbian civil servants in the period between 1937 and 1939 in the 'Serbian Cultural Club' of Belgrade. Concerned that Serb colonization of Kosovo was not changing the ethnic balance beyond making it 38 per cent Serb, in these discussions it was proposed to bring in another 470,000 colonists and to expel 300,000 Albanians to Turkey. 'The most influential participant was Vaso Ćubrilović, a Bosnian Serb, who had been one of the organizers of the assassination of Archduke Franz Ferdinand in 1914.' Malcolm goes on to say: 'Another leading intellectual, the novelist Ivo Andrić, who worked in the Foreign Ministry, wrote a paper recommending the expulsion of the Muslim Albanians. The idea itself was not new: in 1926 the Yugoslav government had asked Turkey if it would be willing to take between 300,000 and 400,000 Albanians, and further negotiations on this topic had taken place during 1933–1935. Eventually, in July 1938, a formal treaty was drawn up and initialled by the two governments. Under this agreement, Turkey was to take 40,000 families of "Turks", receiving a payment from Belgrade of 500 Turkish pounds per family [...] Full statistical evidence is not available, and estimates vary, but it would be reasonable to say that between 90,000 and 150,000 Albanians and other Muslims left Kosovo between the two wars.' Malcolm, 'Is the Complaint', 59–61.

8   Dragović-Soso, *'The Saviours of the Nation'*, 115.

9   Ibid., 116.

10 Ibid., 125.

11 Ibid.

12 For a more detailed account of this, see Miranda Vickers, *Between Serb and Albanian: A History of Kosovo* (London: Hurst, 1998), 12–13. Also Tim Judah, *The Serbs, History, Myths and the Destruction of Yugoslavia* (New Haven, CT: Yale University Press, 1997).

13 Bedri Muhadri, *Kosova in the Middle Ages: XI–XV Century* (Prishtinë: The Institute of History 'Ali Hadri', 2021), 155.

14 Muhadri, *Kosova in the Middle Ages*, 155–60. For a detailed description of the process of adopting these pre-existing Albanian cultural sites by the Serbs, see particularly ibid., 155–64.

15 Dragović-Sośo, *'The Saviours of the Nation'*, 125. See also Geert van Dartel, 'A Catholic Response to the Serbian Orthodox View on Kosovo', in *Kosovo/Kosova*, ed. Duijizings, Maliqi and Janjić (Nijmegen: Peace Research Centre, University of Nijmegen, 1996), 142–9, 143.

16 Dragović-Soso, *'The Saviours of the Nation'*, 126.

17 Clark, *Civil Resistance in Kosovo*, 13.

18   Fehmi Agani, 'Diskusija' (Discussions), in *Zbornik – Kosovo – Srbija – Yugoslavija*,
     ed. Slavko Gaber and Tonči Kuzmanić (Ljubljana: Univerzitetna konferenca ZSMS,
     Knjižnica revolucionarne teorije, 1989), 131.

19   R. Petrović and M. Blagojević, *The Migration of Serbs and Montenegrins from
     Kosovo and Metohija: Results of the Survey Conducted in 1985 and 1986* (Beograd:
     Serbian Academy of Sciences and Arts, 1992), in Malcolm, *Kosovo*, 331.

20   Branko Horvat, *Kosovsko Pitanje* (Kosovo Issue) (Zagreb: Globus, 1988).

21   Horvat, *Kosovsko Pitanje*, 127.

22   Dragović-Soso, *'The Saviours of the Nation'*, 132.

23   Two such incidents that illustrate this discourse are worth mentioning. The first
     involves Djordje Martinović, a Serbian farmer from Kosovo, who, on 1 May 1985,
     had been admitted to hospital in Prishtina, where a beer bottle was removed from
     his anus. He accused two masked Albanians of attacking him in order to take his
     land. The Serbian media, such as the Belgrade magazine *NIN*, published the story,
     contributing to creating a national scandal. However, Albanian sources claimed
     that Martinović was a homosexual who had engaged in an act of self-gratification.
     The incident led to two discussions in the Yugoslav assembly: one in July 1985 and
     the second in February 1986, while the *NIN* journalist who had led the campaign
     over the incident published a 485-page book, *The Martinović Case*, which sold
     50,000 copies (in Malcolm, *Kosovo*, 338). The second incident involves the tragic
     death of six young local Kosovo Serbs killed on 14 December 1998 in a Peja (Peć,
     in the Serbian language) cafeteria called 'Panda', a crime for which twenty innocent
     Albanians were arrested and tortured. However, in an article in the Belgrade
     magazine *Danas*, on 10 October 2018, one of the victims' parents, who lost his only
     child, is quoted as saying: 'When they arrested this group [of Albanians], a friend,
     who worked in the Peć [Pejë] Ministry of Internal Affairs, told me in confidence that
     these Albanians had nothing to do with the "Panda" case.' Furthermore, the same
     article also quoted the current Serbian president, but then deputy prime minister,
     Aleksandar Vučić, as having stated that 'there was no evidence that Albanians
     had executed [the young Serbs]'. Vučić then went on to say: 'I am almost certain
     about what happened in the cafeteria "Panda", but there is no proof. I am not sure
     our authorities are proud about what they have done in that case.' Velimir Perović,
     'Masakr u "Pandi" država gura u zaborav', *Danas*, 10 October 2018, https://www.
     danas.rs/drustvo/masakr-u-pandi-drzava-gura-u-zaborav/ (accessed 3 May 2021).

24   An alliance consisting of Serbia, Montenegro, Greece and Bulgaria, whose
     populations are predominantly of Christian Orthodox belief, had already appeared
     during the Balkan Wars of 1912–13 which resulted in a significant loss of Albanian
     territory in favour of the alliance. See Vickers, *Between Serb and Albanian*, 76.

25   Maliqi, 'Albanians between East and West', 115.

26   See Samuel Huntington, 'The Clash of Civilizations?', *Foreign Affairs* 72, no. 3
     (Summer 1993): 22–49, at 30.

27 Rugova interview for Bujku, 27 September 1993, in Munish Hyseni and Fondacioni Ibrahim Rugova, *Kështu foli Rugova* (Prishtinë: Fondacioni Ibrahim Rugova, 2019), 377.

28 Ali Aliu, interview with Jakup Azemi (author), 28 April 2017.

29 Famously known to have compiled the Albanian codex, namely the 'Canon' (*Kanun*).

30 Ibrahim Rugova, *Qështja e Kosovës* (Prishtinë: Faik Konica, 2005), 134.

31 The closest term to *pleqërimi* is perhaps a form of conciliation or arbitration, which was conducted by senior elderly men recognized for their intelligence and impartiality when resolving disputes.

32 Gjeçovi was a nineteenth-century Albanian Catholic priest.

33 Rugova, *Qështja e Kosovës*, 135.

34 Buxhovi, *Vitet e Gjermanisë*, 195.

35 For an overview of the concepts of ethnic and civic nationalisms, see Stephen Shulman, 'Challenging the Civic/Ethnic and West/East Dichotomies in the Study of Nationalism', *Comparative Political Studies* 35, no. 5 (2002): 554–85.

36 In Presidenca e Kosovës, *Presidenti Rugova*, ed. Muhamet Hamiti, Skënder Hyseni, Sabedin Haliti, Adil Pireva, Vehbi Miftari and Xhavit Beqiri (Prishtinë: Presidenca e Kosovës, 2007), 55.

37 Michel Roux in Duijzings, *Religion and the Politics of Identity*, 5.

38 In Miftari, *Rugova*, 37.

39 Ibid.

40 See, for instance, Rexhep Qosja, in Dukagjin Gorani, 'Orientalist Ethnonationalism: From Irredentism to Independentism: Discourse Analysis of the Albanian Ethnonationalist Narrative about the National Rebirth (1870–1930) and Kosovo Independence (1980–2000)' (unpublished doctoral thesis, University of Cardiff, 2011), http://orca.cf.ac.uk/24085/1/2012goranigphd.pdf.pdf (accessed 15 September 2016), 176.

41 Gjergj Fishta. *Lahuta e Malcis*. Prepared by Nazmi Rrahmani. (Prishtinë: Faik Konica, 2000). See also Gorani, 'Orientalist Ethnonationalism', 183.

42 Mehmet Rukiqi, *Shtypi për Rugovën* (Prishtinë: ShB. Faik Konica, Kolegjiumi i FRLDK, 2009), Vol. I, 18.

43 Sabri Hamiti, in Presidenca e Kosovës, *Presidenti Rugova*, 25.

44 Naim Frashëri (1846–1900) was one of the most celebrated intellectuals of the Albanian renaissance, whereas Gjergj Fishta (1871–1940) was an Albanian Franciscan friar and nationalist writer, among the most celebrated of nationalist writers, particularly known for his epic poem *Lahuta e Malcis* (Highland Lute).

45 Sabri Hamiti, in Presidenca e Kosovës, *Presidenti Rugova*, 25. Rugova's work on Bogdani will be discussed later in this chapter.

46 Marie-Fançois Allain and Xavier Galmiche, *La question du Kosovo / Ibrahim Rugova*, Entretiens realisés par Marie-Francoise Allain et Xavier Galmiche (Paris: Fayard, 1994), translated by Ibrahim Rugova as *Qështja e Kosovës*.

47　Rugova Interview, *Der Spiegel*, Hamburg, 26 June 1989, in Rugova, *Pavarësia dhe Demokracia*, 9–10.

48　Ibid., 10.

49　Anna Di Lellio, *The Battle of Kosovo 1389: An Albanian Epic* (London: I. B. Tauris, 2009), 4.

50　See Ibrahim Rugova, *Vepra e Bogdanit* (Prishtinë: Rilindja, 1982).

51　Rugova, *Vepra e Bogdanit*, 34.

52　Ibid., 35.

53　Miftari, *Rugova*, 20.

54　Ibrahim Rugova, *Refuzimi Estetik* (Prishtinë: Hejza, 1987), 9.

55　Rugova, *Refuzimi Estetik*, 21.

56　Ibid., 23.

57　Ibid., 24.

58　Hamiti, *Një Memento për Rugovën*, 54.

59　Don Lush Gjergji, 'Filozofia dhe politika sipas Dr Ibrahim Rugovës' (Philosophy and Politics of Dr Ibrahim Rugova), 21 January 2013, *Zemra Shqiptare*, https:// dardaniapress.com/filozofia-dhe-politika-sipas-dr-ibrahim-rugoves/ (accessed 8 March 2017).

60　Ibid.

61　Presidenca e Kosovës, *Presidenti Rugova*, 103.

62　Ibid.

63　Di Lellio, *Battle of Kosovo*, 11.

64　The agreement meant the reinstatement of higher education in Kosovo that had been abolished after the 1989 revocation of the Kosovo autonomy of 1974. However, due to Miloseviç's reluctance it was never implemented.

65　Engjëll Sedaj, *The Holy See and the Crisis in Kosovo* (Città del Vaticano: L' Osservatore Romano, 2002), 43–7.

66　In Adnan Merovci, *Në hap me Rugovën* (Prishtinë: Amerkos, 2012), 160–1.

67　In Presidenca e Kosovës, *Presidenti Rugova*, 55–6.

68　Deklarata Politike e Këshillit Koordinues të Partive Politike Shqiptare në Jugosllavi (A Political Statement of the Coordination Body of Albanian Political Parties in Yugoslavia).

69　Nyja Sqiptare, in Rukiqi, *Shtypi për Rugovën*, 17.

70　In 2002, an Albanian author came to the conclusion that there was no public support among either part of Albanians for a unified Albanian state. The cry for a greater Albania he simply called a myth – Paulin Kola, *The Myth of Greater Albania* (London: Hurst, 2002).

71　'After every war we all are less', Rugova's statement, in Presidenca e Kosovës, *Presidenti Rugova*, 23.

72　Ibid., 71.

73　Rugova, *Qështja e Kosovës*, 215.

74　See Kullashi, 'Kolosi i Brishtë'.

75 Presidenca e Kosovës, *Presidenti Rugova*, 185–6.

76 Dardania was an Illyrian province of the Roman Empire believed to have existed between the second and first centuries BC.

77 Presidenca e Kosovës, *Presidenti Rugova*, 165–6.

78 Ibid., 166.

79 Ibid.

80 Ibid., 166.

81 There has been major dissatisfaction among the mass of the population with the new flag that the international community imposed on Kosovo following its declaration of independence in 2008, and that, in stark contrast to Rugova's Dardanian flag, does not contain cultural symbols.

82 Dr Rugova, 'Kurë ka ra kushtrimi n' Kosovë' ma kujton Simfoninë e Nëntë të Bethovenit. Excerpts from an initerview published in 'Bota Sot', 27 November 2002. In *Priseidenca e Kosovës*, 168–9.

83 Ibid.

84 Llapi is a geographical description of a region consisting of the town of Podujevë and villages in the north of Kosovo all the way down to Prishtina. Rugova, on the other hand, comprises the town of Peja and the villages that lie along the border with Montenegro and close to Albania.

85 The modern game of golf is said to have originated in fifteenth-century Scotland. However, historians such as Rudolf Brasch trace the origins of this sport back to the Roman game of *paganica*, in which participants used a bent stick to hit a stuffed leather ball. See Rudolf Brasch, *How Did Sports Begin?: A Look at the Origins of Man at Play* (London: Longman, 1972).

86 Rugova, *Qështja e Kosovës*, 207.

87 Presidenca e Kosovës, *Presidenti Rugova*, 109.

88 Ibid., 108.

Chapter 3

1 A day before the vote took place, 22 March, the leadership of the LCK called on lawmakers to back the constitutional changes. The following day, the provincial parliament building was besieged, and the assembly was surrounded by tanks and police. In Haxhiaj and Stojanović, 'Autonomy Abolished'.

2 David Beetham, *The Legitimation of Power*, 2nd edn (Basingstoke: Palgrave Macmillan, 2013), 16.

3 Beetham, *The Legitimation of Power*, 16.

4 Ibid., 17.

5 Ibid., 18.

6 Ibid.

7 Ibid., 19.

8   Ibid.

9   According to the Yugoslav Constitution of 1974, Serbia was unable to change even
     its own constitution in parts that affected the provinces of Kosovo and Vojvodina
     without the consent of the provincial assembles.

10   This involved a series of acts, including 'revoking gains made by Albanians since
     1996; one official language (Serbo-Croatian); street names changed; Albanian statues
     and monuments taken down, and figures from Serbian history (or mythology)
     erected in their place; shops ordered to have Cyrillic; the reinstatement of "Kosovo
     and Metohija" as the territory's official name; reversion to the derogatory *šiptar* to
     refer to Albanians', cited by Clark, *Civil Resistance in Kosovo*, 71.

11   Nekibe Kelmendi, cited ibid.

12   This period marked the beginning of a silent exodus of Kosovo Albanians, which in
     a short time reached the tens of thousands.

13   Since the issue of constitutional amendments became a public matter in
     1988–9, Albanian political and intellectual elites drew attention to the potential
     consequences that the proposed changes might have for Kosovo. Debate intensified,
     and public protests and demonstrations emerged that had profound effects on the
     unification of the Albanian population.

14   In Hockenos, *Homeland Calling*, 184.

15   Edita Tahiri, interview with Jakup Azemi (author), 26 March 2018.

16   Dr Milazim Krasniqi, interview with Jakup Azemi (author), 22 March 2017.

17   Ilaz Ramajli, interview with Jakup Azemi (author), 24 March 2017. He was the
     deputy chairman of Parliament, who later replaced the chairman when Parliament
     declared the constitution. Ramajli was eventually nominated a representative of
     Kosovo in Albania during the parallel state.

18   Blood feud, as a traditional form of maintaining social order, had persisted among
     Albanians, and the Yugoslav system did not do enough to root it out in the territory
     of Kosovo. At that time there were thousands of families involved in this cyclical
     violence of vengeance.

19   See Muhamet Pirraku, *Lëvizja Gjithëpopullore Shqiptare për faljen e gjaqeve:
     1990–1992* (Prishtinë: Instituti Albanologjik, 1998), 396.

20   Ibrahim Rugova interview for *Eurorilindja*, 26 August 1990, in Rukiqi, *Shtypi për
     Rugovën*, 43.

21   Ramajli, interview.

22   Merovci, *Në hap me Rugovën*, 61.

23   Ibid., 61–6.

24   Ramajli, interview.

25   Jusuf Zejnullahu interview, *Fjala e Lirë* (2014–15), www.fjala.info/arkiv/fjala4,
     Fondi i Republikës së Kosovës ishte projekt i qeverisë së Kosovës, interview
     conducted by Xhafer Leci.

26   Ramajli, interview.

27   Krasniqi, interview.

28   Buxhovi, *Kthesa Historike*, 287.

29   Rexhep Ismaili, Hivzi Islami, Esat Stavileci and Ilaz Ramajli, *Akte të Kuvendit të Republikës së Kosovës 2 Korrik 1990–2 Maj 1991* (Prishtinë: Akademia e Shkencave dhe e Arteve të Kosovës (ASHAK), 2005).

30   In my interview with Ramajli, he praises the LDK's chairman, Kaçanik Rizah Shoshi, in particular as having played a prominent role in this organization.

31   Ismaili et al., *Akte të Kuvendit të Republikës së Kosovës*, 12.

32   Ibid., 47.

33   Author's interview with Ramush Tahiri (27 May 2017), who was the general secretary and co-founder of the Demo Christian party and their representative in the *Coordinating Council of Political Parties.*

34   Babken Babajanian, *Social Protection and Its Contribution to Social Cohesion and State-Building* (Bonn: Deutsche Gesellschaft für internationale Zusammenarbeit (GIZ) GmbH, June 2012), https://cdn.odi.org/media/documents/7759.pdf (accessed 20 June 2020).

35   For how the LDK covered the informational aspects, see Chapter 5.

36   It needs to be clarified, though, that in order to avoid giving the Serbian authorities a pretext for firing more employees, the LDK did not support the strike. Professor Ali Aliu confirms that after a debate on this matter, the LDK decided not to support the strike, a decision that the head of the BSPK, Hajrullah Gorani, ignored. Aliu, supplementary interview.

37   Skënder Zogaj, interviews with Jakup Azemi (author), 28 April 2018 and supplementary interview on 6 July 2020.

38   Ibrahim Berisha, in his speech on the twenty-fifth anniversary of the humanitarian organization Mother Teresa, in '25 vite shërbim të Shoqatës Humanitare Bamirëse "Nënë Tereza" për popullin e Kosovës', Biblioteka Kombetare në Prishtinë, 4 September 2015, http://shqiptarja.com/news.php?IDNotizia=313334 (accessed 22 September 2021).

39   Zogaj, interviews.

40   See Zijadin Gashi, *Mbijetesa dhe Pavarësia e Shkollave Fillore Shqipe në Komunën e Prishtinës 1990–1999* (Prishtinë: Shtëpia Botuese, 2014), 55.

41   Denisa Kosotovicova, *Kosovo: The Politics of Identity and Space* (London: Routledge, 2005), 76.

42   Several international experts and institutions that supported the Albanian claim are quoted in Gashi's *Mbijetesa dhe Pavarësia*, 55–6.

43   Ibid., 61.

44   Ibid., 63.

45   Ibid., 64–5.

46   Rexhep Gjergji, interview with Jakup Azemi (author), 6 September 2018; supplementary interview on 13 November 2020.

47   In one instance, Zkënder Zogaj reports that in 1993 a Kosovar Albanian émigré in the Czech Republic, Sylë Gërguri, donated 100,000 German Marks to him as financial aid for schools. Zogaj, interview.

48   Rugova, *Qështja e Kosovës*, 132–3.

49   Rugova was frequently criticized, most notably by Demaçi and Qosja, for having too much control; they pointed to his leading roles as the president of Kosovo, chairman of the LDK, head of the Coordinating Council and chairman of the Writers' Association, disregarding the fact that he, arguably, did not necessarily fight to control these institutions.

50   Kraja, *Vitet e Humbura*, 203–4.

51   Aliu, interview; supplementary interview, 28 March 2019. Also, in a meeting that Rugova and the LDK hosted for a number of these former prisoners in September 1991, his careful handling of some criticisms and ideas that several of these visitors raised was clearly noted. Following this meeting, many of them joined the LDK. Transcripts of the meeting can be found in Merovci, *Në hap me Rugovën*, 112–27.

52   It should be noted that before founding the UNIKOMB, Hoti was head of the LDK branch in Rahovec, a Kosovo municipality.

53   Qosja preferred to qualify himself as an 'independent intellectual' to maintain his intellectual 'impartiality' and influence.

54   Kraja, *Vitet e Humbura*, 220.

55   Ibid., 207.

56   Ibid.

57   Krasniqi, interview.

58   Edita Tahiri, interview.

59   Rexhep Gjergji, interview.

60   Qualification made by Gjergji, ibid.

61   Edita Tahiri, interview.

62   Rugova's statement in Merovci, *Në hap me Rugovën*, 179.

63   Kraja, *Vitet e Humbura*, 219.

64   This is a self-designated qualification by Rexhep Qosja.

65   Rexhep Qosja's interview for the Albanian portal Portalb *Dritare Realitet*i, 25 December 2013, at https://portalb.mk/22686-rexhep-qosja-rugova-tradhtar-shkoi-tek-milloshevici/ (accessed 19 November 2022). In the same interview, even fourteen years after Rugova's death and the independence of Kosovo, Qosja had not lost his passion for criticizing Rugova. Most of his anti-Rugova slogans were recapitulated, including his calling Rugova a 'traitor' and accusing him of 'treachery, before and during the war of 1999'.

66   Kraja, *Vitet e Humbura*, 224.

67   Merovci, *Në hap me Rugovën*, 61–6.

68   Kraja, *Vitet e Humbura*, 225.

69   One such publication that the Forum sponsored was a volume edited by Masar
     Stavileci, Agim Vinca, Abdyl Kadolli and Zymer Neziri, *Çështja Kombëtare dhe
     Vetëdija Kritike* (The National Question and Critical Awareness) (Prishtinë: Forumi
     i Intelektualëve Shqiptarë (FISH), 1998).

70   Hydajet Hyseni, a senior LDK member with an LPK background, but a close ally
     of Demaçi, in an unpublished article he has shared with me, portrays Demaçi as
     a campaigner for an active non-violence movement, accusing Rugova of a passive
     non-violence movement.

71   For more about Demaçi's idea of Ballkania, see Chapter 6.

72   Kraja, *Vitet e Humbura*, 219.

73   Ever since, the term 'institutionalism' has been somewhat associated with the
     LDK, which has maintained its significance even in the current political climate
     in Kosovo, and it is invoked by LDK personnel with such slogans as 'We are an
     institutionalist party' to denote resolving major political issues institutionally rather
     than through protests.

74   Ramush Tahiri, interview.

75   Rugova, *Qështja e Kosovës*, 110.

76   Formohet Këshilli Koordinues i Partive Politike Shqiptare të Kosovës (nga arkivi i
     QIK-ut te dates, 22 korrik 1991).

77   Hivzi Islami, leader of the Agrarian Party of Kosovo during the parallel-state years,
     'E vërteta rreth "Fronti i Jugut"' (The Truth about the 'Southern Front'), 20 January
     2018, https://presheva.com/e-verteta-rreth-fronti-i-jugut/?fbclid=IwAR1PdRL
     4hgHVFogVKn9TksU3lboIEooz-Ie6sW1SnfAdLbp01lxeWADa4Do (accessed
     2 February 2022).

78   Ibid.

79   Ibid.

80   Zogaj, interviews.

81   A political declaration for three options for the resolution of Albanian issue, in
     Presidenca e Kosovës, *Presidenti Rugova*, 50–2.

82   Ismaili et al., *Akte të Kuvendit të Republikës së Kosovës*, 111.

83   Of particular importance is the act of the Constitutional Law for the execution of
     the amendment of the Republic of Kosovo. Ibid., 117.

84   Raphaël Pouyé, '"Shadow States"? State Building and National Invention under
     External Constraint in Kosovo and East Timor (1974–2002)', 13 February 2005,
     available at SSRN, https://ssrn.com/abstract=2290906 or http://dx.doi.org/10.2139/
     ssrn.2290906 (accessed 25 January 2021).

85   Human Rights Watch was among those who documented the abuse of
     human rights in Kosovo. See Helsinki Watch, *Yugoslavia: Human Rights Abuses in
     Kosovo 1990–1992* (New York: Helsinki Watch, a Division of Human Rights Watch,
     October 1992).

86   Within a short time after the announcement of the government, the police went
     to Bukoshi's house, only to find out that he had left the country. Bujar Bukoshi,
     interview with Jakup Azemi (author), 24 November 2017.

87   Zogaj, interview. Also confirmed by Edita Tahiri, interview.

88   Rugova's speech at the second meeting of the Central Council of the LDK, 19 May
     1991. In Merovci, *Në hap me Rugovën*, 76.

89   Beetham, *The Legitimation of Power*, 18.

90   Ibid.

91   Ibid., 19.

92   Clark, *Civil Resistance in Kosovo*, 85.

93   Jože Pirjevec, in Luca De Poli, *Ibrahim Rugova: Rrugtimi në Kujtesën e tij mes
     Kosovës dhe Italisë*, Translated from Italian by Elvi Sidheri (Prishtinë: Fondacioni
     Ibrahim Rugova, 2017), 53.

94   Fehmi Agani's published letter in Ismaili et al., *Akte të Kuvendit të Republikës së
     Kosovës*, 151.

95   Rugova's long-term bodyguard and companion Adnan Merovci reports that a heavy
     jar was thrown from the balcony of a Serb family in the building where Rugova
     lived and nearly hit him when he was returning from voting. Merovci, *Në hap me
     Rugovën*, 137.

96   Geert-Hinrich Ahern, *Diplomacy on the Edge: Containment of Ethnic Conflict and
     the Minorities Working Group of the Conference on Yugoslavia* (Washington, DC:
     Woodrow Wilson Centre Press, 2007), 331.

97   Quoted in QIK, *Informatori* no. 21, Prishtinë (18 September 1992).

98   The Congress of the US House of Representatives, Washington, DC 201515-3219,
     26 June 1992. Courtesy of Muhamet Hamiti, a former political advisor to Ibrahim
     Rugova.

99   Ramush Tahiri, interview.

100 Edita Tahiri, interview.

Chapter 4

1   See Maliqi, 'Albanians between East and West', 115.

2   See, for example, Kullashi, 'The Production of Hatred in Kosova (1981–91)', 56–69.
     On the other hand, in a monograph edited by Arshi Pipa and Sami Repishti, *Studies
     on Kosova* (Boulder, CO: East European Monographs, 1984), several area specialists
     have documented the many aspects of the disadvantaged conditions of Albanians
     during those years (I also treated this subject in Chapter 1).

3   Alain Ducellier, 'Is It True That Albanians Invaded Kosova?', in *The Case for
     Kosova*, ed. Di Lellio (London: Anthem Press, 2006), 28–36. The term 'Arnaut' is

used derogatively and refers to the Ottoman description of rebel Albanians – my emphasis.

4   See Noel Malcolm, 'Is It True That Albanians in Kosova Are Not Albanians, but Descendants from Albanianized Serbs?', in *The Case for Kosovo: Passage to Independence*, ed. Di Lellio (London: Anthem Press, 2006), 19–22.

5   See Kullasi, 'The Production of Hatred in Kosova (1981–1991)', 56–69.

6   See Marc Weller, *The Crisis in Kosovo: 1989–1999* (Cambridge: Documents and Analysis, 1999), 75.

7   For a detailed account of the Marxist-Leninist and Enverist organizations, see Sabile Keçmezi-Basha, *Organizatat dhe grupet ilegale në Kosovë 1981–1989, sipas aktgjykimeve të gjykatave ish-jugosllave* (Prishtinë: Instituti I Historisë, 2003), 170.

8   Hockenos, *Homeland Calling*, 198.

9   Three prominent Kosovo Albanian activists, the brothers Jusuf and Bardhosh Gërvalla, and Kadri Zeka, were assassinated in Germany in 1982, but the killers were never indicted. Also, Enver Hadri, another prominent activist in Belgium, who had reportedly managed to establish contacts in European Community institutions, was also assassinated, in 1992 in Brussels, and the perpetrators, believed to be linked to the Yugoslav secret services, were never indicted.

10   Extracts from a number of these interviews during 1988–9 are found in Merovci, *Në hap me Rugovën*, 34–5.

11   Rugova's interview, *Der Spiegel*, 26 June 1989, in Presidenca e Kosovës, *Presidenti Rugova*, 44–7.

12   Zogaj, supplementary interview.

13   Ibid.

14   Merovci, *Në hap me Rugovën*, 160–1.

15   QIK, *Informatori* no. 223, Prishtinë, 25 September 1992.

16   Interview with Bajram Mjeku, 31 October 2017.

17   These Serbian measures followed in response to Kosovo's Parliament having declared independence on 2 July 1990 and the massive publicity that the Kosovo media gave this event.

18   Examining hundreds of *Informatori* issues, it became evident that this publication had indeed covered in so much detail everything that was going on in and around Kosovo.

19   Safet Zejnullahu, *Lajmi në kohë lufte e krize* (Prishtinë: UBT, 2017), 35.

20   Zejnullahu, *Lajmi në kohë lufte e krize*, 34.

21   Ibid.

22   In Muhamet Hamiti and Safet Zejnullahu, eds., *Enver Maloku: Gjuha e Stuhisë* (Prishtinë: Faik Konica, 2002), 404.

23   In Merovci, *Në hap me Rugovën*, 168.

24 See Weller, *Crisis in Kosovo*, 74.

25 QIK, *Informatori* no. 256, Prishtinë, 28 October 1992.

26 Excerpts from the article can be found in QIK, *Informatori* no. 220, Prishtinë, 22 September 1992.

27 Elez Biberaj, *Kosova: The Balkan Powder Keg* (London: Research Institute for the Study of Conflict and Terrorism, 1993), 22.

28 Biberaj, *Kosova*, 22.

29 Hafiz Gagica, interview with Jakup Azemi (author), 6 August 2019.

30 Shaip Latifi, interview with Jakup Azemi (author), 6 July 2020. In fact, according to Latifi, the government's '3 per cent fund' originated with the fund they established in 1990, which, on 4 December 1991, Latif's LDK branch in Switzerland handed over to the government in exile.

31 Ibid.

32 Xhafer Shatri, interview with Jakup Azemi (author), 13 June 2020.

33 Komiteti i Kosovës për Informimit të Opinionit Botëror (KKIOB – Kosovo Committee for Information of the World) in 1987 published information and memoranda in foreign languages and circulated them to the media and to Western governments.

34 Shatri, interview.

35 In Merovci, *Në hap me Rugovën*, 90.

36 Buxhovi, *Kthesa Historike*, 237.

37 Edita Tahiri, interview.

38 Bukoshi, interview.

39 The PPK was led by Bajram Kosoumi, who had been convicted for participating in the 1981 demonstrations.

40 Gagica, interview.

41 Ibid.

42 Ibid.

43 Ibid.

44 Ibid.

45 Fan Noli had also for a short time become prime minister of Albania, before King Zog resumed the throne.

46 For a detailed account of Vatra's activities and President Wilson's role in securing Albanian independence, see Mal Berisha, 'Roli i Federatës Pan-Shqiptare Vatra në mbrojtjen e kufijve dhe pavarësinë e Shqipërisë para dhe gjatë Konferencës së Paqës në Paris, 1919', 30 October 1999, http://malberisha.com/wp-content/uploads/2014/03/ROLI-I-FEDERATES-PAN-SHQIPTARE-VATRA.pdf (accessed 18 June 2021).

47 '300,000 Albanians Pour into Streets to Welcome Baker', *New York Times*, 23 June 1991.

48 An article published by Dielli, of the Pan-Albanian Federation of America, reported that although some individual Albanians might have emigrated earlier, a group of seventeen from Korça, having emigrated in 1894, created the first nucleus of Albanians in the United States. Uran Butka, 'Emigrimi i Shqiptarëve në SHBA', *Gazeta Dielli*, 6 January 2014, https://gazetadielli.com/emigrimi-ne-shba/ (accessed 14 April 2021).

49 In David L. Phillips, *Liberating Kosovo: Coercive Diplomacy and US Intervention* (Cambridge, MA: MIT Press, 2012), 32.

50 For an extensive compilation of Albanian activities in the United States, see Sergio Bitici, *Kosovo, Path to Freedom: The Role of The Albanian Kosovar Youth in the Free World in the Liberation of Kosovo* (Bronx, NY: VATRA Pan-Albanian Federation of America, 2012).

51 Ibid., 89.

52 Sami Repishti, interview with Jakup Azemi (author), 8 June 2021; 13 June 2021; 14 June 2021.

53 Repishti, interview.

54 Ibid.

55 See the Albanian-American Civic League Archive, https://www.aacl.com/our-25-year-history (accessed 14 April 2021).

56 Repishti, interviews.

57 In Phillips, *Liberating Kosovo*, 34.

58 Alush Gashi, interview with Jakup Azemi (author), 7 August 2019. Also, a detailed account of the invitation and the Albanian delegation is provided by Jususf Buxhovi, himself a participant, in *Kthesa Historike*, 254.

59 Rugova's interview for the Kosovo magazine *Fjala*, 15 May 1990, in Hyseni and Fondacioni Ibrahim Rugova, *Kështu foli Rugova*, 26.

60 Ibid.

61 Repishti, interviews.

62 Ibid.

63 Ibid.

64 Ibid.

65 In Buxhovi, *Kthesa Historike*, 265.

66 Ibid.

67 Repishti, interviews.

68 Presidenca e Kosovës, *Presidenti Rugova*, 182.

69 Recorded speech, courtesy of the Albanian American Civic League Archive.

70 Multiple interviewed sources have confirmed that an Albanian from southern Serbia, namely Xhimi Xhema, was instrumental in enlightening Senator Dole as to the situation in Kosovo and the plight of the Albanian population in Yugoslavia, and the two subsequently maintained a close relationship. See also Philips, *Liberating Kosovo*, 2012, 35–9.

71   Gashi, interview.

72   Buxhovi, *Kthesa Historike*, 273.

73   Ibid.

74   Ibid.

75   Ibid., 274.

76   Ibid.

77   Ibid.

78   Ibid., 275.

79   Phillips, *Liberating Kosovo*, 36.

80   Gashi, interview.

81   Ibid.

82   Ibid.

83   Ibid.

84   One of these episodes is discussed by Phillips, *Liberating Kosovo*, 54. When Kosovo
     Albanians were struggling to push Kosovo onto the UN agenda, it was Bob Dole
     who had intervened to the US representative in Geneva (UN), J. Kenneth Blackwell,
     who then endorsed the Kosovo delegation's campaign, which subsequently
     enjoyed a much more positive response from the rest of the international
     delegations.

85   Bob Dole, interview for the Albanian US-based newspaper *Illyria*, in QIK,
     Informatori no. 223, Prishtinë, 25 September 1992.

86   Harry Bajraktari, 'The Albanian Nation Will Be Forever Grateful to the Honourable
     Congressman Engel', 21 July 2020, http://illyriapress.com/the-albanian-nation-will-
     be-forever-grateful-to-the-honorable-congressman-engel/ (accessed 24 June 2021).

87   Ibid.

88   Ibid.

89   Zogaj, interviews.

90   In De Poli, *Ibrahim Rugova*, 60.

91   Ibrahim Rugova, interview for *Flaka e Vëllaznimit*, 26 and 29 August 1990, in
     Hyseni and Fondacioni Ibrahim Rugova, *Kështu foli Rugova*, 68.

92   See Helsinki Watch, *Yugoslavia*.

93   Rugova, interview for *Flaka e Vëllaznimit*, in Hyseni and Fondacioni Ibrahim
     Rugova, *Kështu foli Rugova*, 68.

94   Latifi, interview.

95   Ibid.

96   Ibid.

97   Malcolm's *Kosovo* represents a milestone in this context. Elsie and Roux also were
     among those rare authors in the 1990s who represented a departure from the
     traditional literature, which viewed Kosovo through the Serbian lens.

98   See for instance Richard McAllister, 'French Perceptions', in *Kosovo: Perceptions
     of War and Its Aftermath*, ed. Mary Buckley and Sally Cummings (New York and
     London: Continuum, 2001) 92–105, at 92.

99 'L.D.K. DHE IBRAHIM RUGOVA', article by Musa Jupolli, courtesy of Jupolli.

100 MËRGATA, article by Musa Jupolli, courtesy of Jupolli.

101 His article 'Différenciés, les Albanais du Kosovo' appeared in November 1989, at a time when the Yugoslav authorities were taking harsh measures against Albanian intellectuals.

102 Kullashi, 'Kolosi i Brishtë'.

103 McAllister, 'French Perceptions', 92.

104 Allain and Galmiche, *La question du Kosovo / Ibrahim Rugova*.

105 Ismail Kadare, hailed as the most prominent living Albanian author, sought political asylum in France in October 1990 to protest against the lack of reforms by the Albanian communist regime, and became a prominent voice for Kosovo.

106 Kullashi, 'Kolosi i Brishtë'.

107 Ibid.

108 Don Lush Gjergji, interview with Jakup Azemi (author), 21 April 2017.

109 Don Lush Gjergji, interview.

110 Ibid.

111 De Poli, *Ibrahim Rugova*, 95.

112 Ibid., 92.

113 Extract from a letter by Bill Ryerson, first American ambassador to Albania (1991–4), to Sami Repishti, 5 September 2001. Courtesy of Sami Repishti.

114 Edita Tahiri, interview.

Chapter 5

1 Rugova constantly called for the international community to intervene in Kosovo as some form of international protectorate in a transitional phase before final political status – independence was to be reached.

2 Peter Russell, 'The Exclusion of Kosovo from the Dayton Negotiations', *Journal of Genocide Research* 11, no. 4 (2009): 487–511, at 494.

3 Ibid., 495.

4 Warren Zimmermann, quoted in Russell, 'Exclusion', 496.

5 See Enver Hasani, 'The "Outer Wall" of Sanctions and the Kosovo Issue', *Perceptions: Journal of International Affairs* 3, no. 3 (September–November 1998): 1–11.

6 Adem Demaçi, quoted in Hydajet Hyseni's unpublished article that the author shared with me.

7 Edita Tahiri, interview.

8 Rexhep Gjergji, interview.

9 Bedri Islami, 'Pse u prishën Berisha e Rugova', article published in the Albanian publication *Dita*, online version of 25 March 2015, http://www.gazetadita.al/25-mars-2015/ (accessed 23 December 2020).

10	Statement by Demaçi, in Shkëlzen Gashi, *Adem Demaçi: An Un-authorised Biography* (Prishtinë: Rrokullia, 2010), 119.

11	Gashi, *Adem Demaçi*, 125.

12	Authors such as Henry H. Perritt, in *Kosovo Liberation Army: The Inside Story of an Insurgency* (Champaign: University of Illinois Press, 2008.), James Pettifer in *The Kosova Liberation Army: Underground War to Balkan Insurgency, 1948–2001* (London: Hurst, 2012) and Tim Judah, *Kosovo: War and Revenge* (New Haven, CT: Yale University Press, 2000) are among the most cited sources on the emergence and the conduct of the insurgency by the KLA. They all overlook the fact that when the first three small armed groups started insurgency activities in Kosovo in the early to mid-1990s, they were not associated with the LPK, nor did they call themselves the KLA. In particular Pettifer's narrative on the origins of the KLA is misleading. While he correctly associates it with Adem Jashari, it was senior figures within the LDK who negotiated the deal with Tirana that allowed the LDK to organize volunteers and have them trained in Albania.

13	Rexhep Gjergji, interview.

14	Rexhep Gjergji, supplementary interview.

15	Ibid.

16	Xhevat Meha, 'Vazhdimësia e Turpit me Luftën e Prekazit të Vitit 1991', 8 January 2018, *Kosova Sot*, online newspaper, https://www.kosova-sot.info/opinione/239774/vazhdimesia-e-turpit-me-luften-e-prekazit-te-vitit-1991/ (accessed 10 February 2021).

17	Rexhep Gjergji (Gjergji, interview) is among numerous LDK sources that claim such a meeting took place.

18	Aliu, interview.

19	Ibid.

20	Ibid.

21	Hafiz Gagica, '"Tri dekada më pare": An Account of Military Training of the Kosovo Parallel State in Albania', article with extracts from Gagica's diaries (Facebook post, 24 October 2021). Courtesy of Hafiz Gagica.

22	Ismet Abdullahu, as one of the co-ordinators of the volunteers, states that there were no divisions along political lines and LPK volunteers were also included. Ismet Abdullahu, interview with author (Jakup Azemi), 15 January 2024.

23	Rexhep Gjergji, interview.

24	Ibid. Months later Gjergji met Çeku in Skopje to get instructions as where to collect those arms in case the war started.

25	Ismet Ibishi, interview with Jakup Azemi (author), 25 September 2024.

26	Ibid.

27	Rexhep Gjergji, interview.

28   Ibid.

29   Anton Kolaj, interview with Jakup Azemi (author), 28 March 2024.

30   For an account on the movements and the activity of ex-Albanian military officers in the Yugoslav Army, see Nikë Gjeloshi, *Ministria e Mbrojtjes e Republikës së Kosovës, 1991–1995* (Zagreb: Unija Albanaca u Republiku Harvatsku, 2017).

31   Kolaj, interview.

32   Ibid.

33   Ibid.

34   Rexhep Gjergji, interview.

35   Ibid.

36   Rrustem Mustafa, interview with Jakup Azemi (author), 14 January 2021.

37   Anton Kolaj told me: 'Having known him personally from the time we worked as teachers in the same secondary school in our municipality, Klinë, I approached Azemi Syla [a senior figure in the LPRK/LPK] and invited him to participate with their [the LPK's] recruits. However, after a few days his answer was: "We don't have any personnel, therefore we can't contribute". Kolaj, interview.

38   Sabri Kiçmari, interview with Jakup Azemi (author), 27 November 2020. However, no details have been provided as to what this organization looked like.

39   Gani Geci, *Lufta pa Maska: 1991–1999* (Prishtinë: Bota Sot, 2001).

40   Rexhep Gergji and Zogaj, interviews.

41   Rexhep Gjergji, interview.

42   Fatmir Sejdiu interview and video documenting his speech, 28 November 2020, at https://www.syri.net/syri_kosova/politike-lajme/191581/video-e-rralleose-momenti-i-daljes-publike-te-uck-se-ne-varrimin-e-halil-gecit/.

43   20 vjet nga dalja publike e UÇK-së / Daut Haradinaj, Mujë Krasniqi dhe Rexhep Selimi /VIDEO, lajmi.net, at: https://lajmi.net/20-vjet-nga-dalja-publike-e-uck-se-daut-haradinaj-muje-krasniqi-dhe-rexhep-selimi-video-2

44   Kosovo Report, *Independent International Report on Kosovo* (Oxford: Oxford University Press, 2000), 68.

45   Armend Bekaj, 'The KLA and the Kosovo War: From Intra-State Conflict to Independent Country', Berghof Transition Series/Liberation Movements and Transition to Politics, 1 September 2010, https://berghof-foundation.org/library/the-kla-and-the-kosovo-war-from-intra-state-conflict-to-independent-country, 22 (accessed 10 February 2021).

46   Meha, 'Vazhdimësia e Turpit me Luftën e Prekazit të Vitit 1991'.

47   Kosovo Report, *Independent International Report*, 68.

48   Bekaj, 'The KLA and the Kosovo War', 20.

49   Perritt, *Kosovo Liberation Army*, 99.

50   Referring to LPK-led KLA activists and fighters so as to denote their affiliation to the left of Albanian politics and more specifically to Prime Minister Fatos Nano.

51 Geci, *Lufta pa Maska*, online version, https://www.ballikombetar.info/lufta-pa-mas
    ka/?fbclid=IwAR1NSmmGANTHljZDLcVOsLX_5d6uCfZxkxpeWWnaJY90g9Do
    nsjq6_tvS88 (accessed 15 September 2021).

52 Gani Geci, interview on T7 (Kosovo TV channel, 14 March 2019), https://www.
    youtube.com/watch?v=9u-xZW9wisg (accessed 15 September 2021).

53 Ibid.

54 Geci, *Lufta pa Maska*, 85. Communiqué 59 typically adopts language that stirs up
    families against each other. Ibid., 110.

55 Ibid., 110.

56 15 Nëntor 1998, Bota Sot, Reagim i Komandës së UÇK-së në Llaushë dhe ZO të
    Drenicës ndaj Komunikatës nr. 59 të SHP të UÇK-së, in Geci, *Lufta pa Maska*. The
    communiqué has since been withdrawn, and Hashim Thaqi reportedly apologized
    to Geci.

57 Ibrahim Kelmendi, interview with Jakup Azemi (author), 21 January 2021.

58 Geci, *Lufta pa Maska*, 52.

59 In Perritt, *Kosovo Liberation Army*, 47.

60 At the time of writing, four former LPK–KLA leaders, including Hashim Thaqi,
    former president and founder of the Democratic Party, the head of the Democratic
    Party and the chair of Parliament, Kadri Veseli and the KLA spokesperson Jakup
    Krasniqi, as well as Rexhep Selimi, are being indicted by the Kosovo Specialist
    Chambers at The Hague under a mandate and jurisdiction over crimes against
    humanity, war crimes and other crimes under Kosovo law that were commenced
    or committed in Kosovo between 1 January 1998 and 31 December 2000 by or
    against citizens of Kosovo or the Federal Republic of Yugoslavia. Kosovo Specialist
    Chambers & Specialist Prosecutor's Office, https://www.scp-ks.org/en.

61 Rifat Haxhiaj, interview with Jakup Azemi (author), 17 November 2020.

62 Ibid.

63 Ibid.

64 Ibid.

65 Kiçmari, interview. Ramush Haradinaj was a prominent fighter and war
    commander, and led a military group in Deçan, western Kosovo. After the war he
    formed Alenca for Ardhmërinë e Kosovës (AAK) and became prime minister
    twice, as well as being indicted by the Hague Tribunal, but he was acquitted of all
    charges. He lost two brothers during the fighting.

66 Ahmet Krasniqi, interview for the FARK military magazine *Revistë Ushtarake:
    Organ i Minsitrisë së Mbrojtjes të Republikës së Kosovës* no. 1 (September 1998).
    Courtesy of Rifat Haxhiaj.

67 Haxhiaj, interview and supplementary interview.

68 Ibid.

69 Fatos Klosi interview, 24 April 2015, on Kosovo TV programme *Komiteti*, https://
    www.youtube.com/watch?v=mZfZG8S1fmc (accessed 15 September 2021).

70   Aliu, interview.

71   Rexhep Gjergji, interview and supplementary interview.

72   Christopher Jarvis, 1999, 'The Rise and Fall of Pyramid Schemes in Albania', *International Monetary Fund Staff Papers* 37, no. 1 (March 2000): 1–29, https://www.imf.org/external/pubs/ft/fandd/2000/03/jarvis.htm (accessed 21 February 2021).

73   For several days in a row QIK reported reactions from Kosovo's political spectrum, including Rugova himself, who called upon the Albanian leadership to respect the will of the people of Kosovo and conform with the Albanian Parliament, which, in 1991, had recognized the independence of Kosovo. QIK, *Informatori* no. 1881, Prishtinë, 7 November 1997. Rugova's advisor for information, Xhemaj Mustafa, was much harsher, stating: 'Declarations, in particular those of Nano and Milošević, represent a major failure of the policy of Fatos Nano on the issue of Kosovo', QIK, *Informatori* no. 1879, Prishtinë, 5 November 1997.

74   Hockenos, *Homeland Calling*, 193.

75   Klosi interview, *Komiteti*.

76   In his publication *Ditari i një Ministri të Jashtëm: 1997–1999* (The Diary of a Foreign Minister) (Tirana: Toena, 2009), Paskal Milo did not hide the Nano government's frosty relationship with Rugova, who repeatedly refused to visit Tirana and meet his Albanian counterparts as a response to Albania's positioning on the Kosovo conflict and the internal affairs of Kosovo Albanians.

77   Haxhiaj, interview.

78   Haxhiaj, supplementary interview.

79   Even twenty years after his execution, Ahmet Krasniqi is a talking point in Kosovo, with open public requests in the media for an investigation by the Albanian authorities.

80   Anton Quni, 'Debat Plus Me Ermal Pandurin, Tema: Kush e vrau Ahmet Krasniqin?' 25 September 2018, https://www.youtube.com/watch?v=fhuXcYt89KQ&t=823s (accessed 16 September 2021).

81   Ibid.

82   Ibid.

83   Weller, *Crisis in Kosovo*, 287.

84   William G. O'Neill, *Kosovo: An Unfinished Peace* (London: Lynne Rienner, 2002), quoted in Bekaj, 'The KLA and the Kosovo War', 21.

85   Bekaj, 'The KLA and the Kosovo War', 21.

86   Milazim Krasniqi, *Sekretet që nuk i mori me vete Ibrahim Rugova* (Prishtinë: PEN Qendra e Kosovës, 2017).

87   Reportedly, there were two groups within the LDK, one around Professor Agani, consisting of senior LDK founders, who generally supported Rugova, and the (Hydajet) Hyseni Group, Hyseni being a senior LPK figure, with other Marxist-Leninist members balancing the former. Both Agani and Hyseni were Rugova's vice-presidents.

88　Krasniqi, *Sekretet që nuk i mori me vete Ibrahim Rugova*, 79.

89　Merovci, *Në hap me Rugovën*, 252.

90　Ibid., 260.

91　Contact Group Statement on Kosovo, 9 March 1998, http://www.ohr.int/ohr_archive/statement-of-kosovo-moscow-09031998/ (accessed 1 October 2021).

92　Now the Republic of North Macedonia.

93　Blerim Shala, *Libri i Fitores* (Prishtinë: KOHA, 2012), I, 40.

94　'You have asked for my services. Here I am, and I am telling you that it is good to meet with Milošević. You will come out as winners because you will have demonstrated to the West that you are prepared to swallow a lot only to be able to stop the war. Then, soon afterwards, you will be extended an offer for a visit to our President Clinton, who will be eager to show how committed to Kosovo he is'; Shala describes Holbrook's insistence that Rugova meet Milošević. Ibid., 66.

95　QIK, *Informatori* no. 2073 G, 29 May 1998.

96　Weller, *Crisis in Kosovo*, 348.

97　In April 1998 Milošević, then president of the FRY, called a referendum in Serbia in which the proposition for Kosovo to be treated as an internal Serbian issue was supported. FRY press release, 'Serbian government proposes calling of a referendum', 2 April 1998.

98　Shala, *Libri i Fitores*, I, 74.

99　Perritt, *Kosovo Liberation Army*, 105.

100　Shala, *Libri i Fitores*, I, 107.

101　Ibid., 129.

102　Blerim Shala, interview with Jakup Azemi (author), 23 August 2021. See also Daalder and O'Hanlon, *Winning Ugly*, 39.

103　Shala, interview.

104　Weller, *Crisis in Kosovo*, 190.

105　Ibid., 347.

106　Perritt, *Kosovo Liberation Army*, 165.

107　Weller, *Crisis in Kosovo*, 289.

108　North Atlantic Council (NAC) Statement, 30 April 1998, in Weller, *The Crisis in Kosovo*, 272.

109　Remarks by the US president, 8 October 1998, ibid.

110　Shala, *Libri i Fitores*, I, 162.

111　Ibid., 165. See also Shala, interview.

112　In Weller, *Crisis in Kosovo*, 272.

113　Shala, *Libri i Fitores*, I, 120.

114　Ibid., 124.

115　Lawrence Freedman, 'Victims and Victors: Reflections on the Kosovo War', *Review of International Studies* 26, no. 3 (July 2000): 335–58, at 342.

116　Freedman, 'Victims and Victors', 342.

117 CRS Report for Congress, 'Kosovo Conflict Chronology: September 1998 – March 1999', 6 April 1999.

118 Frontline Interviews. Ambassador Walker, https://www.pbs.org/wgbh/pages/ frontline/shows/kosovo/interviews/walker.html>.

119 In Weller, *Crisis in Kosovo*, 290.

120 Bill Clinton statement upon receiving Rugova with a Kosovar delegation to the White House on 29 May 1998. In Shala, *Libri i Fitores*, I, 79.

121 Shala, *Libri i Fitores*, II, 41.

122 For a detailed account of the role of international actors in forming the Albanian political delegation at the Rambouillet Conference, see Tobias Wille, 'Representation and Agency in Diplomacy: How Kosovo Came to Agree to the Rambouillet Accords', *Journal of International Relations and Development* 22, no. 4 (December 2019): 808–31.

123 Skender Hyseni, interview with Jakup Azemi (author), 06 August 2021.

124 Ibid.

125 Christopher R. Hill, *Outpost: A Diplomat at Work* (New York: Simon & Schuster, 2014), 156.

126 Marc Weller, 'The Rambouillet Conference on Kosovo', *International Affairs (Royal Institute of International Affairs 1944–)* 75, no. 2 (April 1999): 211–51, at 225.

127 Hill, *Outpost*, 150. For a more detailed analysis of how negotiations unfolded concerning Yugoslav sovereignty, Serbian control over Kosovo and the Rugova government's position on self-determination for Kosovo, see 'The Summons to the Conference and Renewed Threat of Force' in Weller, *Crisis in Kosovo*, 392.

128 Weller, *Crisis in Kosovo*, 410.

129 James Rubin Press Briefing on the Kosovo Peace Talks, Rambouillet, France, 21 February 1999, in ibid., 451.

130 Ibid., 452.

131 Wille, 'Representation and Agency in Diplomacy', 825.

132 Weller, 'Rambouillet Conference on Kosovo', 232.

133 Weller, *Crisis in Kosovo*, 405.

134 Statement by the Kosovo delegation, 23 February 1999, printed in ibid., 471.

135 Hill, *Outpost*, 155.

136 Interim Agreement for Peace and Self-Government in Kosovo (Rambouillet Accords), https://peacemaker.un.org/sites/peacemaker.un.org/files/990123_ RambouilletAccord.pdf.

137 Hill, *Outpost*, 156.

138 Among speculation about Milošević's reasons for not signing the Rambouillet Accords is the view that 'he expected only a short bombing campaign, after which NATO would offer him a better deal', or as Sell, *Slobodan Milosevic*, 301 argues in

his biography of the Serb leader, 'Milosevic thought that he could outlast NATO in a duel of wills.' See Wille, 'Representation and Agency in Diplomacy', 827.

139	Rugova's testimony at The Hague Tribunal against Milošević, in Adnan Merovci, *Pengu* (The Hostage) (Prishtinë: Amerkos, 2020), 46.

140	Joint Statement, the copy of the letter, in ibid., 63.

141	Ibid., 79.

142	Various reactions from individuals, mostly those closer to the KLA and the Albanian left in Tirana, followed. See in ibid., 70.

143	Copy of Rugova's statement, in ibid., 189.

144	Ibid.

145	Ibid., 238.

146	Ibid., 240. See also Milo, *Ditari*, 197.

147	Merovci, *Pengu*, 240. See also Milo, *Ditari*, 217.

148	At the meeting the death of his 'right-hand' man, Professor Fehmi Agani, along with the names of many Albanian intellectuals who had been murdered during the campaign, were commemorated. In Merovci, *Pengu*, 262.

149	Municipality names, street names and cultural institution names were reviewed and renamed within a short time after KLA and LPK personnel occupied institutional roles immediately after the conflict.

150	There had been many LDK activists murdered during and after the 1999 conflict; Rugova himself survived two assassination attempts. At the time of writing, a number of former KLA exponents are being indicted by the Specialized Chambers of Kosovo at The Hague.

Chapter 6

1	Rugova, *Qështja e Kosovës*, 134. Original title: Allain and Galmiche, *La question du Kosovo / Ibrahim Rugova*.

2	See Beetham, *The Legitimation of Power*.

3	Ismaili et al., *Akte të Kuvendit të Republikës së Kosovës*, 114.

4	Merovci, *Në hap me Rugovën*, 135.

5	Rexhep Gjergji, interview.

6	The role of images and perceptions in international politics has been well presented over the last several decades by many authors and specialists, with classic scholars of international politics such as Robert Jervis, in his seminal book *Perception and Misperception in International Politics* (Princeton, NJ: Princeton University Press, 1976), and K. E. Boulding, 'National Images and International Systems', *The Journal of Conflict Resolution* 3, no. 2 (1959): 120–31.

7	For a discussion of this Serb propaganda, see for instance Maliqi, 'Albanians between East and West', 115–22. For a similar account, see also Warren

Zimmermann, *Origins of a Catastrophe: Yugoslavia and Its Destroyers* (New York: Times Books, 1999).

8 See Blerim Reka, *Kosova në documentet e Kongresit Amerikan (1986–1995)* (Prishtinë: Ndërmarrja Botuese, 1995), 87.

9 Phillips, *Liberating Kosovo*, xv.

10 For the series of Rugova's visits to the United States throughout the 1990s, see the article by Beqir Sina, 'Takime historike në SHBA të presidentit Rugova: Ai i bëri shqiptarët mik të mëdhenjë me Amerikën' (Historical Meetings by President Ibrahim Rugova in the United States: He Made the Albanians Great Friends of the United States), *Gazeta Nacional*, 21 January 2024, https://gazeta-nacional.com/beqir-sina-new-york-takime-historike-ne-shba-s-te-presidentit-rugova-ai-i-beri-shqiptaret-mik-te-medhenje-me-ameriken/ (accessed 28 January 2024).

11 Steven Erlanger, 'Clinton Meets Delegation from Kosovo Seeking Talks', *New York Times*, 30 May 1998, https://www.nytimes.com/1998/05/30/world/clinton-meets-delegation-from-kosovo-seeking-talks.html (accessed 18 March 2024).

12 General K. Wesley Clark, *Waging Modern War: Bosnia, Kosovo, and the Future of Combat* (New York: PublicAffairs Books, 2002), 134.

13 Daalder and O'Hanlon, *Winning Ugly*, 12.

14 For a relatively detailed account as to how Operation Horseshoe was discovered, see Daalder and O'Hanlon, *Winning Ugly*, 58.

15 Peter Baumont and Patrick Wintour, 'Milošević and Operation Horseshoe', *Guardian*, 18 July 1999, https://www.theguardian.com/world/1999/jul/18/balkans8 (accessed 24 March 2024). See also James Gow, 'The War in Kosovo, 1998–1999', in *Confronting the Yugoslav Controversies: A Scholars' Initiative*, ed. Charles Ingrao and Thomas A. Emmert (West Lafayette, IN: Purdue University Press, 2012), 305–44, at 311, https://docs.lib.purdue.edu/purduepress_ebooks/28/ (accessed 24 March 2024).

16 See Muhamedin Kullashi, *Qështja e Kosovës në Hapësirën Publike të Francës* (Prishtinë: Akademia e Shkencave dhe e Arteve, 2021).

17 Kullashi, 'Kolosi i Brishtë'.

18 Article by Robyn Wright, 'US, Allies Get Ready for Force in Kosovo Crisis', *Los Angeles Times*, 14 June 1998, https://www.latimes.com/archives/la-xpm-1998-jun-14-mn-59972-story.html (accessed 22 March 2024).

19 For the discussions and dynamics within the Contact Group where the United States, the UK, Russia, France, Germany and Italy debated the Kosovo crisis prior to NATO's intervention in 1999, see Madeleine Albright, *Madam Secretary: A Memoir* (London: Pan Books, 2004).

20 Prime Minister Tony Blair, speech before the Kosovo Parliament, 9 July 2010. Source, https://www.youtube.com/watch?v=TIlBTaKCFKU&t=90s.

21   Stefan Troebst, *Conflict in Kosovo: Failure of Prevention? An Analytical Documentation, 1992–1998* (Flensburg: European Centre for Minority Issues, 1998), 62.

22   Steve Terrett, *The Dissolution of Yugoslavia and the Badinter Arbitration Commission* (London: Routledge, 2000), 79.

23   See Weller, *Crisis in Kosovo*, 76.

24   QIK, *Informatori* no. 257, Prishtinë, 29 October 1992.

25   Troebst, *Conflict in Kosovo* 36.

26   Phillips, *Liberating Kosovo*, 50.

27   Ibid., 54.

28   Tadeusz Mazowiecki, 'Report about Human Rights in the Territory of the Former Yugoslavia', Special Rapporteur of the Commission on Human Rights, 10 February 1993, in Phillips, *Liberating Kosovo*, 55.

29   For a detailed compilation of the UN resolutions on Kosovo, see Weller, *Crisis in Kosovo*.

30   'One day, a man by the name of Murat Ajeti came to see me and asked me: "If what I am doing [committing actions against the Serb police] might damage your [the LDK's] cause?" "On the contrary, you are helping us a lot, I told him"' – Rexhep Gjergji, interview.

31   Mentor Agani, interview with the author (Jakup Azemi), 29 April 2017.

32   Agani, interview.

33   Ibid.

34   See, for instance, Komunikatë no. 13, in which the responsibility for a dozen actions in Kosovo was claimed by the LPK-led KLA, in Gafurr Elshani, *Ushtria Çlirimtare e Kosovës: Dokumente dhe Artikuj*, 'Komunikatë nr. 13', Botim i dytë (Aarau: Zëri i Kosovës, 1998), 5000 Aarau/CH, 32. It should be added that Komunikatë nr. 13 (communiqué n. 13) does not mention Ushtria Çlirimtare e Kosovës (the Kosovo Liberation Army) but says 'Komanda Qendrore' (the Central Command), which implies that it was an LPK entity, but in fact these actions were committed by groups that were not part of the LPK-led KLA.

35   Hill, *Outpost*, 144.

36   Bukoshi, interview.

37   Kolaj, interview.

38   Following the incident, several Albanians were arrested and tortured. However, the parents of the murdered Serb children were told by credible Serb sources that the Albanians had nothing to do with the incident. For a detail account, see Perović, 'Masakr u "Pandi" država gura u zaborav'.

39   See Ibrahim Rugova's ten objectives, QIK, *Informatori* ditor no. 348, Prishtinë, 16 February 1993.

40   Albright, *Madam Secretary*, 388.

41 In March 2004 unexpected riots burst in Kosovo following the death of three Albanian children chased by Serbs in the north of Kosovo, which sparked histeric reaction from Albanians, expressing among others their dissatisfaction with the UNMIK administration.

42 Such a view is, for instance, promoted by Henry Perritt, *The Road to Independence for Kosovo* (Cambridge: Cambridge University Press, 2010).

43 The Dayton Accords of 1995, in relation to Kosovo, only left the so-called 'outer wall' of sanctions on the FRY, but were largely insignificant in forcing Serbia into a substantial political dialogue.

44 Following NATO's intervention in 1999, the United Nations went on to establish a UN administration, known as the UN Mission in Kosovo (UNMIK), which was responsible for preparing the region for a long-term political settlement.

45 'Our proposal for an (international) protectorate is simply a political method to reach independence', Rugova reaffirmed while responding to media following a diplomatic tour of Europe that included meeting the French foreign minister Alain Juppé in Paris. QIK, *Informatori* no. 632, Prishtinë, 15 January 1994.

46 'Dr.Ibrahim Rugova propozon Planin për Paqe prej Dhjetë Pikash' (Dr Ibrahim Rugova unveils his Working Peace Plan of Ten Objectives), QIK, *Informatori* ditor no. 348, Prishtinë, 16 February 1993.

47 The term attributed to Rugova by the French authors Jean Yves Carlen, Steve Duchêne and Joël Ehrhart, *Ibrahim Rugova: Le frêle colosse du Kosovo* (Paris: Desclée de Brouwer, 1999).

48 Felix S. Bethke and Jonathan Pinckney, in their article 'Non-violent Resistance and the Quality of Democracy', quoting multiple sources, provide strong evidence that initiating a democratic transition through non-violent resistance substantially improves democratic quality – in *Conflict Management and Peace Science* 38, no. 5 (September 2021): 503–23.

Chapter 7

1 After almost a year of investigations, on 11 September 2024 Kosovo's Special Prosecution announced that it had filed an indictment charging forty-five Serbs who had participated in the September 2023 attack. The leading suspect, a businessman and political activist called Milan Radoičić, is known to be a close political ally of Serbian president Alexandar Vučić. 'We filed an indictment today against forty-five suspects […] There is a well-grounded suspicion that they have committed crimes related to terrorism, specifically crimes against Kosovo's constitution, order and security, financing of terrorism, and money-laundering',

Blerim Isufaj, head of the Special Prosecution, stated in a press conference on 11 September 2024. Report by Xhorxhina Bami and Milica Stojanović, 'Kosovo Indicts 45 for Deadly Attack by Armed Serb Group in Banjska', *BalkanInsight*, 11 September 2024, at: https://balkaninsight.com/2024/09/11/kosovo-indicts-45-for-deadly-attack-by-armed-serb-group-in-banjska/ (accessed 12 September 2024).

2   As early as in 1913, Vladan Djordjević (1844–1930), while temporarily the Serbian prime minister, framed Albanians ('Arnauts') in a 1913 pamphlet as inferior and thus incapable of nation-building themselves, and invoking a series of derogatory terms to describe Albanians. See Stephanie Schwandner-Sievers, 'Albanians, Albanianism and the Strategic Subversion of Stereotypes', in *The Balkans and the West: Constructing the European Other, 1945–2003*, ed. Andrew Hammond (London: Routledge, 2006), 115–16.

3   In similar vein is Dimitrije Bogdanović's *Knjiga o Kosovo* (Book on Kosovo) (Beograd: Srpska akademija nauka i umetnosti, 1985), in which he even contested Albanian origins and their existence in the region, while arguing the opposite for the Serbs. In reality, no credible historian has contested the Albanians' ethnic origins and their presence in the Balkans for at least many centuries before the arrival of Slavs in the region.

4   See Huntington, 'The Clash of Civilizations?', 22–49, at 30.

5   See Beetham, *The Legitimation of Power*.

6   Edita Tahiri, interview.

7   Kiçmari, interview.

Bibliography

Books

Ahern, Geert-Hinrich. *Diplomacy on the Edge: Containment of Ethnic Conflict and the Minorities Working Group of the Conference on Yugoslavia*. Washington, DC: Woodrow Wilson Centre Press, 2007.

Albright, Madeleine. *Madam Secretary: A Memoir*. London: Pan Books, 2004.

Allain, Marie-Fançois and Xavier Galmiche. *La question du Kosovo/Ibrahim Rugova*. Entretiens réalisés par Marie-Françoise Allain et Xavier Galmiche. Paris: Fayard, 1994. Translated by Ibrahim Rugova as *Qështja e Kosovës*, Prishtinë: Faik Konica, 2005.

Avdyli, Brahim Ibish. *Çështja Kombëtare dhe Vetëdija Kritike* (The National Question and Critical Awareness). Prishtinë: Forumi i Intelektualëve Shqiptarë FISH, 1998.

Babken, Babajanian. *Social Protection and Its Contribution to Social Cohesion and State-Building*. Bonn: Deutsche Gesellschaft für internationale Zusammenarbeit (GIZ) GmbH, June 2012. https://cdn.odi.org/media/documents/7759.pdf (accessed 20 June 2020).

Badsey, Stephen and Paul Latawski, eds. *Britain, NATO and the Lessons of Balkan Conflicts 1991–1999*. London: Frank Cass, 2004.

Beetham, David. *The Legitimation of Power*. 2nd edn. Basingstoke: Palgrave Macmillan, 2013.

Bellamy, Alex. *Kosovo and International Society*. New York: Palgrave Macmillan, 2002.

Biberaj, Elez. *Kosova: The Balkan Powder Keg*. London: Research Institute for the Study of Conflict and Terrorism, 1993.

Bieber, Florian and Židas Daskalovski, eds. *Understanding the War in Kosovo*. London: Frank Cass, 2003.

Bitici, Sergio. *Kosovo, Path to Freedom: The Role of the Albanian Kosovar Youth in the Free World in the Liberation of Kosovo*. Bronx, NY: VATRA Pan-Albanian Federation of America, 2012.

Bogdanović, Dimitrije. *Knjiga o Kosovo* (Book on Kosovo). Beograd: Srpska akademija nauka i umetnosti, 1985.

Bogdanović, Dimitrije. *Razgovori o Kosovu* (Discussions on Kosovo). Beograd: Miodrag Dramatičin, 1986.

Bourdieu, Pierre. *Language and Symbolic Power: The Economy of Linguistic Exchanges*. Edited and introduced by John B. Thompson; translated by Gino Raymond and Matthew Adamson. Cambridge: Polity in association with Basil Blackwell, 1991.

Brasch, Rudolf. *How Did Sports Begin?: A Look at the Origins of Man at Play*. London: Longman, 1972.

Brinkmann, Svend. *Qualitative Interviewing: Conversational Knowledge through Research Interviews*. Oxford: Oxford University Press, 2022.

Brinkmann, Svend and Steinar Kvale, eds. *InterViews: Learning the Craft of Qualitative Research Interviewing*. 3rd edn. Thousand Oaks, CA: Sage, 2015.

Buckley, Mary and Sally Cummings, eds. *Kosovo: Perceptions of War and Its Aftermath*. New York: Continuum, 2001.

Burr, Vivien. *An Introduction to Social Constructionism*. London: Sage, 1995.

Buxhovi, Jusuf. *Kthesa Historike: Vitet e Gjermanise dhe Epoka e LDK-s*. Prishtinë: Faik Konica, 2008.

Bytyqi, Enver. *Filozofia politike dhe nacionale e Ibrahim Rugovës* (The Political and National Philosophy of Rugova). Tiranë: Shtëpia Botuese 'Koha', 2010.

Carlen, Y. Jean, Steve Duchêne and Joël Ehrhart. *Ibrahim Rugova: Le frêle colosse du Kosovo*. Paris: Desclée de Brouwer, 1999.

Clark, Howard. *Civil Resistance in Kosovo*. London: Pluto, 2000.

Clark, K. Wesley (General). *Waging Modern War: Bosnia, Kosovo, and the Future of Combat*. New York: PublicAffairs Books, 2002.

Cohen, Lenard J. *Serpent in the Bosom: The Rise and Fall of Milosevic*. Boulder, CO: Westview Press, 2002.

Daalder, Ivo H. and Michael E. O'hanlon. *Winning Ugly: NATO's War to Save Kosovo*. Washington, DC: Brookings Institution, 2000.

De Poli, Luca. *Ibrahim Rugova: Rrugtimi në Kujtesën e tij mes Kosovës dhe Italisë*. Translated from Italian by Elvi Sidheri. Prishtinë: Fondacioni Ibrahim Rugova, 2017.

Di Lellio, Anna. *The Battle of Kosovo 1389: An Albanian Epic*. London: I. B. Tauris, 2009.

Dragović-Soso, Jasna. '*The Saviours of the Nation': Serbia's Intellectual Opposition and the Revival of Nationalism*. London: Hurst, 2002.

Duijzings, Ger. *Religion and the Politics of Identity in Kosovo*. London: Hurst, 2000.

Elshani, Gafurr. *Ushtria Çlirimitare e Kosovës: Dokumente dhe Artikuj*. 'Komunikatë nr. 13.' Botim i dytë. Aarau: Zëri i Kosovës, 1998.

Fairclough, Norman. *Discourse and Social Change*. Cambridge: Polity, 1992.

Fishta, Gjergj. *Lahuta e Malcis*. Prepared by Nazmi Rrahmani. Prishtinë: Faik Konica, 2000.

Foucault, Michel. *The Archaeology of Knowledge*. Translated by A. M. Sheridan Smith. London: Routledge, 2002, c1972.

Gashi, Shkëlzen. *Adem Demaçi: An Un-authorised Biography*. Prishtinë: Rrokullia, 2010.

Gashi, Zijadin. *Mbijetesa dhe Pavarësia e Shkollave Fillore Shqipe në Komunën e Prishtinës 1990–1999*. Prishtinë: Shtëpia Botuese, 2014.

Geci, Gani. *Lufta pa Maska: 1991–1999*. Prishtinë: Bota Sot, 2001.

Gjeloshi, Nikë. *Ministria e Mbrojtjes e Republikës së Kosovës, 1991–1995*. Zagreb: Unija Albanaca u Republiku Harvatsku, 2017.

Hamiti, Muhamet and Safet Zejnullahu, eds. *Enver Maloku: Gjuha e Stuhisë*. Prishtinë: Faik Konica, 2002.

Hamiti, Sabri. *Një Memento për Rugovën*. Prishtinë: Shtëpia Botuese 55, 2008.

Herbert, Aubrey. *Albania's Greatest Friend: Aubrey Herbert and the Making of Modern Albania: Diaries and Papers 1904–1923*, edited by Bejtullah D. Destani and Jason Tomes. London: I. B.Tauris, 2011.

Hill, Christopher R. *Outpost: A Diplomat at Work*. New York: Simon & Schuster, 2014.

Hockenos, Paul. *Homeland Calling: Exile Patriotism and Balkan Wars*. Ithaca, NY: Cornell University Press, 2003.

Horvat, Branko. *Kosovsko Pitanje* (Kosovo Issue). Zagreb: Globus, 1988.

Hren, Marko. *Slovenian Peace Movement in the Context of Yugoslav Anti-War Contention: Re-discovered History of War-Prevention (1984–1992)*. Ljubljana: Samozal, 2012. Slovenian_PeaceMovement_and_Prewar_processes20200526-64996-1a9jr8d-libre.pdf (accessed 28 February 2024).

Hyseni, Munish and Fondacioni Ibrahim Rugova. *Kështu foli Rugova*. Prishtinë: Fondacioni Ibrahim Rugova, 2019.

Islami, Hivzi. *Rrjedha Demografike Shqiptare*. Pejë: Dukagjini, 1994.

Islami, Hivzi. *Studime Demografike: 100 vjet të zhvillimit demografik të Kosovës*. Prishtinë: Akademia e Shkencave dhe e Arteve e Kosovës, 2005.

Ismaili, Rexhep, Hivzi Islami, Esat Stavileci and Ilaz Ramajli. *Akte të Kuvendit të Republikës së Kosovës 2 Korrik 1990 – 2 Maj 1991*. Prishtinë: Akademia e Shkencave dhe e Arteve të Kosovës (ASHAK), 2005.

Jervis, Robert. *Perception and Misperception in International Politics*. Princeton, NJ: Princeton University Press, 1976.

Jørgensen, Marianne and Loiuse J. Philips. *Discourse Analysis as Theory and Method*. London: Sage, 2002.

Judah, Tim. *The Serbs, History, Myths and the Destruction of Yugoslavia*. New Haven, CT: Yale University Press, 1997.

Judah, Tim. *Kosovo: War and Revenge*. New Haven, CT: Yale University Press, 2000.

Kajtazi, Fadil. *Ideologjija Serbe e Gjenocidit*. Prishtinë: Beqir Musliu, 2023.

Keçmezi-Basha, Sabile. *Organizatat dhe grupet ilegale në Kosovë 1981–1989, sipas aktgjykimeve të gjykatave ish-jugosllave*. Prishtinë: Instituti I Historisë, 2003.

Kola, Paulin. *The Myth of Greater Albania*. London: Hurst, 2002.

Kosotovicova, Denisa. *Kosovo: The Politics of Identity and Space*. London: Routledge, 2005.

Kosovo Report. *Independent International Report on Kosovo* (group of 12 authors). Oxford: Oxford University Press, 2000.

Kraja, Mehmet. *Vitet e Humbura*. Tiranë: Eurorilindja, 1995.

Krasniqi, Milazim. *Sekretet që nuk i mori me vete Ibrahim Rugova*. Prishtinë: PEN Qendra e Kosovës, 2017.

Kullashi, Muhamedin. *Qështja e Kosovës në Hapësirën Publike të Francës*. Prishtinë: Akademia e Shkencave dhe e Arteve, 2021.

Malcolm, Noel. *Kosovo: A Short History*. London: Papermac, 1998.

Maliqi, Shkelzen. *Separate Worlds: Reflections and Analyses 1989–1998*. Prishtinë: Dukagjini, 1998.

Maliqi, Shkëlzen. *Why Nonviolent Resistance in Kosovo Failed*. Prishtinë: Qendra për studime Humanistike 'Gani Bobi', 2011.

Merovci, Adnan. *Në hap me Rugovën*. Prishtinë: Amerkos, 2012.

Merovci, Adnan. *Pengu* (The Hostage). Prishtinë: Amerkos, 2020.

Miftari, Vehbi. *Rugova: Vizioni Nacional*. Prishtinë: AIKD, 2007.

Miftari, Vehbi. *Rugova: Mendimi, Kultura, Politika*. Prishtinë: Shtëpia Botuese, Faik Konica, 2013.

Milo, Paskal. *Ditari i një Ministri të Jashtëm: 1997–1999* (The Diary of a Foreign Minister). Tirana: Toena, 2009.

Muhadri, Bedri. *Kosova in the Middle Ages: XI–XV Century*. Prishtinë: The Institute of History 'Ali Hadri', 2021.

O'Neill, William G. *Kosovo: An Unfinished Peace*. London: Lynne Rienner, 2002.

Perritt, Henry H. *Kosovo Liberation Army: The Inside Story of an Insurgency*. Champaign: University of Illinois Press, 2008.

Perritt, Henry H. *The Road to Independence for Kosovo*. Cambridge: Cambridge University Press, 2010.

Petrović, Ruža and Marina Blagojević. *The Migration of Serbs and Montenegrins from Kosovo and Metohija: Results of the Survey Conducted in 1985 and 1986*. Beograd: Serbian Academy of Sciences and Arts, 1992.

Pettifer, James. *The Kosova Liberation Army: Underground War to Balkan Insurgency, 1948–2001*. London: Hurst, 2012.

Phillips, David L. *Liberating Kosovo: Coercive Diplomacy and US Intervention*. Cambridge, MA: MIT Press, 2012.

Pirjevec, Jože. *Le guerre jugoslave 1991–1999*. Torino: Giulio Einaudi Editore, 2001.

Pirraku, Muhamet. *Lëvizja Gjithëpopullore Shqiptare për faljen e gjaqeve: 1990–1992*. Prishtinë: Instituti Albanologjik, 1998.

Presidenca e Kosovës. *Presidenti Rugova*, edited by Muhamet Hamiti, Skënder Hyseni, Sabedin Haliti, Adil Pireva, Vehbi Miftari and Xhavit Beqiri. Prishtinë: Presidenca e Kosovës, 2007.

Prijevec, Jože. *Le guerre jugoslave 1991 – 1999*. Torino: Giulio Einaudi Editore, 2001.

Prorok, Christiane. *Ibrahim Rugova's Leadership: Eine Analyse der Politik des kosovarischen Präsidenten*. Frankfurt am Main: Peter Lang, 2004.

Reka, Blerim. *Kosova në documentet e Kongresit Amerikan (1986–1995)*. Prishtinë: Ndërmarrja Botuese, 1995.

Roux, Michel. 1992. *Les Albanais en Yugoslavie: Minorité nationale territoire et développement*. Paris: Éditiones de la Maison des Sciences de l' Homme. S.R., 1979.

Rugova, Ibrahim. *Vepra e Bogdanit*. Prishtinë: Rilindja, 1982.

Rugova, Ibrahim. *Refuzimi Estetik*. Prishtinë: Hejza, 1987.

Rugova, Ibrahim. *Pavarësia dhe Demokracia: intervista dhe artikuj*. Prishtinë: Faik Konica, 2005.

Rukiqi, Mehmet. *Shtypi për Rugovën*. Vol. I. Prishtinë: ShB. Faik Konica, Kolegjiumi i FRLDK, 2009.

Schwandner-Sievers, S. and Duijzings Ger. *War within a War: Historical and Cultural-Anthropological Background Report*. Expert witness report commissioned by the International Criminal Tribunal for the former Yugoslavia (ICTY), The Hague, 31 May 2004. No. P201 IT-03-66-T.

Sedaj, Engjëll. *The Holy See and the Crisis in Kosovo*. Città del Vaticano: L' Observatore Romano, 2002.

Sell, Louis. *Slobodan Milosevic and the Destruction of Yugoslavia*. Durham, NC: Duke University Press, 2002.

Shala, Blerim. *Libri i Fitores*. Vol. I. Prishtinë: KOHA, 2012a.

Shala, Blerim. *Libri i Fitores*. Vol. II. Prishtinë: KOHA, 2012b.

Sharp, Gene. *Social Power and Political Freedom*. Boston, MA: Porter Sargent, 1980.

Stavileci, Masar, Agim Vinca, Abdyl Kadolli and Zymer Neziti, eds. *Çështja Kombëtare dhe Vetëdija Kritike* (The National Question and Critical Awareness). Prishtinë: Forumi i Intelektualëve Shqiptarë (FISH), 1998.

Terrett, Steve. *The Dissolution of Yugoslavia and the Badinter Arbitration Commission*. London: Routledge, 2000.

Todorova, Maria. *Imagining the Balkans*. Oxford: Oxford University Press, 1997.

Troebst, Stefan. *Conflict in Kosovo: Failure of Prevention? An Analytical Documentation, 1992–1998*. Flensburg: European Centre for Minority Issues, 1998.

Vickers, Miranda. *Between Serb and Albanian: A History of Kosovo*. London: Hurst, 1998.

Weller, Marc. *The Crisis in Kosovo: 1989–1999*. Cambridge: Documents and Analysis, 1999.

Zejnullahu, Safet. *Lajmi në kohë lufte e krize*. Prishtinë: UBT, 2017.

Zimmermann, Warren. *Origins of a Catastrophe: Yugoslavia and Its Destroyers*. New York: Times Books, 1999.

Chapters in books

Agani, Fehmi. 'Diskusija' (Discussions). In *Zbornik – Kosovo – Srbija – Yugoslavija*, edited by Slavko Gaber and Tonči Kuzmanić, 126–32. Ljubljana: Univerzitetna konferenca ZSMS, Knjižnica revolucionarne teorije, 1989.

Andrić, Ivo. 'Draft on Albania'. In *Gathering Clouds: The Roots of Ethnic Cleansing in Kosovo and Macedonia – Early Twentieth Century Documents*, 2nd edn, edited by Robert Elsie, 194–211. London: Centre for Albanian Studies, 2015.

Badsey, Stephen. 'Media Interaction in the Kosovo Conflict'. In *Britain, NATO and the Lessons of Balkan Conflicts 1991–1999*, edited by Stephen Badsey and Paul Latawski, 79–98. London: Frank Cass, 2004.

Čubrilović, Vaso. 'The Expulsion of the Albanians: Memorandum (1937)'. In *Gathering Clouds: The Roots of Ethnic Cleansing in Kosovo and Macedonia – Early Twentieth-Century Documents*, 2nd edn, edited by Robert Elsie, 148–80. London: Centre for Albanian Studies, 2015a.

Čubrilović, Vaso. 'The Minority Problems in the New Yugoslavia: Memorandum (1944)'. In *Gathering Clouds: The Roots of Ethnic Cleansing in Kosovo and Macedonia – Early Twentieth-Century Documents*, 2nd edn, edited by Robert Elsie, 211–31. London: Centre for Albanian Studies, 2015b.

Ducellier, Alain. 'Is It True That Albanians Invaded Kosova?' In *The Case for Kosova: Passage to Independence*, edited by Anna Di Lellio, 27–36. London: Anthem Press, 2006.

Galtung, Johan. 'Principles of Nonviolent Action: The Great Chain of Nonviolence Hypothesis'. In *Nonviolence and Israel/Palestine*, edited by John Galtung, 13–34. Honolulu, HI: University of Hawaii Institute of Peace, 1989.

Gow, James. 'The War in Kosovo, 1998–1999'. In *Confronting the Yugoslav Controversies: A Scholars' Initiative*, edited by Charles Ingrao and Thomas A. Emmert, 305–44. West Lafayette, IN: Purdue University Press, 2012, https://docs.lib.purdue.edu/purduepress_ebooks/28/ (accessed 24 March 2024).

Guzina, Dejan. 'Kosovo or Kosova – Could It Be Both? The Case of Interlocking Serbian and Albanian Nationalisms'. In *Understanding the War in Kosovo*, edited by Florian Bieber and Židas Daskalovski, 31–52. London: Frank Cass, 2003.

Krasniqi, Gëzim. 'Revisiting Nationalism in Yugoslavia: An Inside-out View of the Nationalist Movement in Kosovo'. In *Debating the End of Yugoslavia*, edited by Florian Bieber, Armina Galija and Rory Archer, 225–39. Farnham: Ashgate, 2014.

Kullashi, Muhamedin. 'The Production of Hatred in Kosova (1981–91)'. In *Kosovo/Kosova: Confrontation or Coexistence*, edited by Ger Duijzings, Dušan Janjić and Shkëlzen Maliqi, 56–69. Nijmegen: Peace Research Centre, University of Nijmegen, 1996.

Latawski, Paul. 'NATO's Military Action over Kosovo: The Conceptual Landscape after the Battle'. In *Britain, NATO and the Lessons of Balkan Conflicts 1991–1999*, edited by Stephen Badsey and Paul Latawski, 121–38. London: Frank Cass, 2004.

Malcolm, Noel. 'Myths of Albanian National Identity: Some Key Elements, as Expressed in the Works of Albanian Writers in America in the Early Twentieth Century'. In *Albanian Identities: Myths and History*, edited by Stephanie Schwandner-Sievers and Bernd J. Fischer, 70–87. London: Hurst, 2002.

Malcolm, Noel. 'Is It True That Albanians in Kosova Are Not Albanians, but Descendants from Albanianized Serbs?' In *The Case for Kosova: Passage to Independence*, edited by Anna Di Lellio, 19–22. London: Anthem Press, 2006a.

Malcolm, Noel. 'Is the Complaint about the Serb State's Deportation Policy of Albanians between the Two World Wars Based on Myth?' In *The Case for Kosova: Passage to Independence*, edited by Anna Di Lellio, 59–61. London: Anthem Press, 2006b.

Maliqi, Shkëlzen. 'Self-Understanding of Albanians in Non-violence'. In *Conflict or Dialogue: Serbian Albanian Relations and Integration of the Balkans*, edited by Dušan Janjić and Shkëlzen Maliqi, 237–47. Subotica: Open University, European Civic Centre for Conflict Research, 1994.

Maliqi, Shkëlzen. 'Albanians between East and West'. In *Kosovo/ Kosova*, edited by Ger Duijzings, Dušan Janjić and Shkëlzen Maliqi, 115–22. Nijmegen: Peace Research Centre, University of Nijmegen, 1996.

McAllister, Richard. 'French Perceptions'. In *Kosovo: Perceptions of War and Its Aftermath*, edited by Mary Buckley and Sally Cummings, 92–105. New York and London: Continuum, 2001.

Pavlović, Momćilo. 'Kosovo under Autonomy, 1974–1990'. In *Confronting the Yugoslav Controversies: A Scholar's Initiative*, edited by Charles W. Ingrao and Thomas A. Emmert, 44–81. West Lafayette, IN: Purdue University Press, 2009.

Prifti, Peter. 'Kosova's Economy: Problems and Prospects'. In *Studies on Kosova*, edited by Arshi Pipa and Sami Repishti, 125–65. Boulder, CO: East European Monographs, distributed by Columbia University Press, 1984.

Reuter, Jens. 'Education Policy in Kosova'. In *Studies on Kosova*, edited by Arshi Pipa and Sami Repishti, 259–64. Boulder, CO: East European Monographs, distributed by Columbia University Press, 1984.

Roberts, S. J. L. 'Media Operations: Lessons from Kosovo'. In *Britain, NATO and the Lessons of Balkan Conflicts 1991–1999*, edited by Stephen Badsey and Paul Latawski, 67–78. London: Frank Cass, 2004.

Schmider, Klaus. 'The Wehrmacht's Yugoslav Quagmire: Myth or Reality?' In *Britain, NATO and the Lessons of Balkan Conflicts 1991–1999*, edited by Stephen Badsey and Paul Latawski, 14–24. London: Frank Cass, 2004.

Schwandner-Sievers, Stephanie. 'Albanians, Albanianism and the Strategic Subversion of Stereotypes'. In *The Balkans and the West: Constructing the European Other, 1945–2003*, edited by Andrew Hammond, 110–26. London: Routledge, 2004.

Trew, Simon. 'Yugoslav Quagmires: The Image of the Past and the Fear of Intervention'. In *Britain, NATO and the Lessons of Balkan Conflicts 1991–1999*, edited by Stephen Badsey and Paul Latawski, 3–13. London: Frank Cass, 2004.

Van Dartel, Gert. 'A Catholic Response to the Serbian Orthodox View on Kosovo'. In *Kosovo/Kosova*, edited by Duijzings, Janjić and Maliqi, 142–9. Nijmegen: Peace Research Centre, University of Nijmegen, 1996.

Zajmi, Gazmend. 'Kosova's Constitutional Position in the Former Yugoslavia'. In *Kosovo/Kosova: Confrontation or Coexistence*, edited by Ger Duijzings, Dušan Janjić and Shkëlzen Maliqi, 95–101. Nijmegen: Peace Research Centre, University of Nijmegen, 1996.

Journals

Bethke, S. Felix and Pinckney Jonathan. 'Non-violent Resistance and the Quality of Democracy'. *Conflict Management and Peace Science* 38, no. 5 (September 2001): 503–23.

Boulding, E. K. 'National Images and International Systems'. *The Journal of Conflict Resolution* 3, no. 2 (1959): 120–31.

Chao, Mujika Itziar. 'Women's Activism in the Civil Resistance Movement in Kosovo (1989–1997): Characteristics, Development, Encounters'. *Nationalities Papers* 48, no. 5 (September 2002): 843–60.

Freedman, Lawrence. 'Victims and Victors: Reflections on the Kosovo War'. *Review of International Studies* 26, no. 3 (July 2000): 335–8.

Hasani, Enver. 'The "Outer Wall" of Sanctions and the Kosovo Issue'. *Perceptions: Journal of International Affairs* 3, no. 3 (September–November 1998): 1–11.

Huntington, Samuel. 'The Clash of Civilizations?' *Foreign Affairs* 72, no. 3 (Summer 1993): 22–49.

Jarvis, Christopher. 1999. 'The Rise and Fall of the Pyramid Schemes in Albania'. *International Monetary Fund Staff Papers* 37, no. 1 (March 2000): 1–29.

Morus, Christina. 'The SANU Memorandum: Intellectual Authority and the Constitution of an Exclusive Serbian "People"'. *Communications and Critical/Cultural Studies* 4, no. 2 (2007): 142–65.

Oberschall, Anthony. 'The Manipulation of Ethnicity: From Ethnic Cooperation to Violence and War in Yugoslavia'. *Ethnic and Racial Studies* 23, no. 6 (November 2000): 982–1001.

Petrović, Aleksandar and ÐorÐe Stefanović. 'Kosovo, 1944–1981: The Rise and the Fall of a Communist "Nested Homeland"'. *Europe-Asia Studies* 62, no. 7 (2010): 1073–106.

Pula, Besnik. 'The Emergence of the Kosovo "Parallel State", 1988–1992'. *Nationalities Papers* 32, no. 4 (2004): 797–826.

Reitan, Ruth. 'Strategic Non-violent Conflict in Kosovo'. *Peace and Change* 25, no. 1 (2000): 70–102.

Russell, Peter. 'The Exclusion of Kosovo from the Dayton Negotiations'. *Journal of Genocide Research* 11, no. 4 (2009): 487–511.

Salla, Michael. 'Kosovo, Non-violence and the Break-up of Yugoslavia'. *Security Dialogue* 26, no. 4 (1995): 427–38.

Scotland, James. 'Exploring the Philosophical Underpinnings of Research: Relating Ontology and Epistemology to the Methodology and Methods of the Scientific, Interpretive, and Critical Research Paradigms'. *English Language Teaching* 5, no. 9 (2012): 9–16.

Shulman, Stephen. 'Challenging the Civic/Ethnic and West/East Dichotomies in the Study of Nationalism'. *Comparative Political Studies* 35, no. 5 (2002): 554–85.

Temple, Bogusia. 'Watch Your Tongue: Issues in Translation and Cross-Cultural Research'. *Sociology* 31, no. 3 (1997): 607–18.

Walker, William, G. 'OSCE Verification Experiences in Kosovo: November 1998–June 1999'. *The International Journal of Human Rights* 4, nos. 3–4 (2000): 127–42.

Weller, Marc. 'The Rambouillet Conference on Kosovo'. *International Affairs (Royal Institute of International Affairs 1944–)* 75, no. 2 (April 1999): 211–51.

Wille, Tobias. 'Representation and Agency in Diplomacy: How Kosovo Came to Agree to the Rambouillet Accords'. *Journal of International Relations and Development* 22, no. 4 (December 2019): 808–31.

Internet sources

'20 vjet nga dalja publike e UÇK-së / Daut Haradinaj, Mujë Krasniqi dhe Rexhep Selimi /VIDEO (lajmi.net editorial), 28 November 2017, https://lajmi.net/20-vjet-nga-dalja-publike-e-uck-se-daut-haradinaj-muje-krasniqi-dhe-rexhep-selimi-video-2 (accessed 8 August 2021).

Albanian-American Civic League Archive. https://www.aacl.com/our-25-year-history (accessed 14 April 2021).

Bajraktari, Harry. 'The Albanian Nation Will Be Forever Grateful to the Honourable Congressman Engel'. 21 July 2020, http://illyriapress.com/the-albanian-nation-will-be-forever-grateful-to-the-honorable-congressman-engel/ (accessed 24 June 2021).

Bami, Xhorxhina and Milica Stojanović. 'Kosovo Indicts 45 for Deadly Attack by Armed Serb Group in Banjska'. *BalkanInsight*, 11 September 2024 at, https://balkaninsight.com/2024/09/11/kosovo-indicts-45-for-deadly-attack-by-armed-serb-group-in-banjska/ (accessed 12 September 2024).

Baumont, Peter and Patrick Wintour. 'Milošević and Operation Horseshoe'. *Guardian*, 18 July 1999, https://www.theguardian.com/world/1999/jul/18/balkans8 (accessed 24 March 2024).

Bekaj, Armend. 'The KLA and the Kosovo War: From Intra-State Conflict to Independent Country'. Berghof Transition Series/Liberation Movements and Transition to Politics, 1 September 2010, https://berghof-foundation.org/library/the-kla-and-the-kosovo-war-from-intra-state-conflict-to-independent-country (accessed 10 February 2021).

Berisha, Ibrahim. 'Ata dhe këta themeluesit e LDK-së!': Copëza ditari personal në vitet 1989–1990'. Facebook post, 26 September 2012.

Berisha, Ibrahim (speech). '25 vite shërbim të Shoqatës Humanitare Bamirëse "Nënë Tereza" për popullin e Kosovës'. 3 November 2015, Biblioteka Kombetare në Prishtinë, 2015, http://shqiptarja.com/news.php?IDNotizia=313334 (accessed 22 September 2021).

Berisha, Mal. 'Roli i Federatës Pan-Shqiptare Vatra në mbrojtjen e kufijve dhe pavarësinë e Shqipërisë para dhe gjatë Konferencës së Paqës në Paris, 1919'. New York, 30 October 1999, http://malberisha.com/wp-content/uploads/2014/03/ROLI-I-FEDERATES-PAN-SHQIPTARE-VATRA.pdf (accessed 18 June 2021).

Blair, Tony, British Prime Minister. Speech at the special session of the Kosovo Parliament on 9 July 2010, 'I premtova Rugovës, do ta ndihmoj popullin e Kosovës … ' (I promised Rugova, I will help the Kosovo people), https://www.youtube.com/watch?v=TIlBTaKCFKU&t=90s (accessed 15 June 2020).

Brunborg, Helge. 'Report on the Size and Ethnic Composition of the Population of Kosovo'. 14 August 2002, https://www.icty.org/x/file/About/OTP/War_Demographics/en/milosevic_kosovo_020814.pdf (accessed 25 November 2022).

Butka, Uran. 'Emigrimi i Shqiptarëve në SHBA'. *Gazeta Dielli*, 6 January 2014, https://gazetadielli.com/emigrimi-ne-shba/ (accessed 14 April 2021).

Clark, Howard. 'Nonviolent Struggle in Kosovo'. *War Resisters' International*, 1 January 2001, http://www.wri-irg.org/nonviolence/nvse16-en.htm (accessed 25 September 2016).

Contact Group Statement on Kosovo. 9 March 1998, http://www.ohr.int/ohr_archive/statement-of-kosovo-moscow-09031998/ (accessed 1 October 2021).

Erlanger, Steven. 'Clinton Meets Delegation from Kosovo Seeking Talks'. *New York Times*, 30 May 1998, https://www.nytimes.com/1998/05/30/world/clinton-meets-delegation-from-kosovo-seeking-talks.html (accessed 18 March 2024).

Fazliu, Eraldin. 'Two Decades on, the Question Persists: "Where Is Ukshin Hoti?"'. 16 May 1999, Prishtina Insight, https://prishtinainsight.com/two-decades-on-the-question-persists-where-is-ukshin-hoti/ (accessed 16 May 2019).

Gagica, Hafiz. '"Tri dekada më pare": An Account of Military Training of the Kosovo Parallel State in Albania'. Article with extracts from Gagica's diaries (Facebook post, 24 October 2021).

Gjergji, Don Lush. 'Filozofia dhe politika sipas Dr Ibrahim Rugovës' (Philosophy and Politics of Ibrahim Rugova), 21 January 2013, *Zemra Shqiptare*, http://www.zemrashqiptare.net/news/30703/don-lush-gjergji-dr-ibrahim-rugova-ne-vleresimin-tim.html (accessed 8 March 2017).

Haxhiaj, Serbeze and Milica Stojanović. 'Autonomy Abolished: How Milosević Launched Kosovo's Descent into War'. 23 March 2020, Balkan Transitional Justice, Bajgora Belgrade, Pristina BIRN, https://balkaninsight.com/2020/03/23/autonomy-abolished-how-milosevic-launched-kosovos-descent-into-war/ (accessed 15 January 2022).

Islami, Bedri. 'Pse u prishën Berisha e Rugova'. Article in the Albanian publication *Dita*, online version of 25 March 2015, http://www.gazetadita.al/25-mars-2015/ (accessed 23 December 2020).

Islami, Hivzi. 'E vërteta rreth "Fronti i jugut"' (The Truth about the 'South Front'), 20 January 2018, https://presheva.com/e-verteta-rreth-fronti-i-jugut/?fbclid=IwAR1P dRL4hgHVFogVKn9TksU3lboIEooz-Ie6sW1SnfAdLbp01lxeWADa4Do (accessed 2 February 2022).

Klosi, Fatos interview, 24 April 2015, Kosovo TV programme *Komiteti*, https://www.youtube.com/watch?v=mZfZG8S1fmc (accessed 15 September 2021).

Kullashi, Muhamedin. 'Kolosi i Brishtë'. http://www.trepca.net/2006/02/060202_kolosi_brishte_mk.htm (accessed 13 January 2020).

Lantos, Tom. Speech recorded on the floor of the House of Representatives, 1 June 1990, Albanian American Civic League archive, https://www.youtube.com/watch?v=RvX3BUdmD4E (accessed 21 August 2021).

Meha, Xhevat. 'Vazhdimësia e Turpit me Luftën e Prekazit të Vitit 1991'. 8 January 2018, *Kosova Sot*, online newspaper, https://www.kosova-sot.info/opinione/239774/vazhdimesia-e-turpit-me-luften-e-prekazit-te-vitit-1991/ (accessed 10 February 2021).

Perović, Velimir. 'Masakr u "Pandi" država gura u zaborav'. *Danas*, 10 October 2018, https://www.danas.rs/drustvo/masakr-u-pandi-drzava-gura-u-zaborav/ (accessed 3 May 2021).

Pouyé, Raphaël. '"Shadow States"? State Building and National Invention under External Constraint in Kosovo and East Timor (1974–2002)'. 13 February 2005, available at SSRN, https://ssrn.com/abstract=2290906 or http://dx.doi.org/10.2139/ssrn.2290906 (accessed 25 January 2021).

Pula-Beqiri, Luljeta. Interview for the TV21 Nacionale, 26 September 2022, https://nacionale.com/politike/flet-pas-dy-dekadash-pse-luljeta-pula-beqiri-u-harrua-nga-politika-e-pasluftes-video (accessed 6 December 2022).

Qosja, Rexhep. Interview for the Albanian portal Portalb Dritare Realiteti, 25 December 2013, https://portalb.mk/22686-rexhep-qosja-rugova-tradhtar-shkoi-tek-milloshevici/ (accessed 19 November 2022).

Quni, Anton. 'Debat Plus Me Ermal Pandurin, Tema: Kush e vrau Ahmet Krasniqin?' 25 September 2018, https://www.youtube.com/watch?v=fhuXcYt89KQ&t=823s (accessed 16 September 2021).

Sejdiu, Fatmir. Interview and video documenting his speech, 28 November 2020, https://www.syri.net/syri_kosova/politike-lajme/191581/video-e-rralleose-momenti-i-daljes-publike-te-uck-se-ne-varrimin-e-halil-gecit/ (accessed 8 August 2021).

Sina, Beqir. 'Takime historike në SHBA të presidentit Rugova: Ai i bëri shqiptarët mik të mëdhenjë me Amerikën' (Historical Meetings by President Ibrahim Rugova in the United States: He Made the Albanians Great Friends of the United States), *Gazeta Nacional*, 21 January 2024, https://gazeta-nacional.com/beqir-sina-new-york-takime-historike-ne-shba-s-te-presidentit-rugova-ai-i-beri-shqiptaret-mik-te-medhenje-me-ameriken/ (accessed 28 January 2024).

Wright, Robyn. 'US, Allies Get Ready for Force in Kosovo Crisis'. *Los Angeles Times*, 14 June 1998, https://www.latimes.com/archives/la-xpm-1998-jun-14-mn-59972-story.html (accessed 22 March 2024).

Theses

Gorani, Dukagjin. 'Orientalist Ethnonationalism: From Irredentism to Independentism: Discourse Analysis of the Albanian Ethnonationalist Narrative about the National Rebirth (1870–1930) and Kosovo Independence (1980–2000)' (unpublished doctoral thesis, University of Cardiff, 2011), http://orca.cf.ac.uk/24085/1/2012goranigphd.pdf.pdf (accessed 15 September 2016).

Interviews

Abdullahu, Ismet. Interview with Jakup Azemi (author), 15 January 2024.

Agani, Mentor. Interview with Jakup Azemi (author), 29 April 2017.

Aliu, Ali. Interview with Jakup Azemi (author), 28 April 2017; supplementary interview on 28 March 2019.

Bukoshi, Bujar. Interview with Jakup Azemi (author), 24 November 2017.

Gagica, Hafiz. Interview with Jakup Azemi (author), 6 August 2019.

Gashi, Alush. Interview with Jakup Azemi (author), 7 August 2019.

Gjergji, Don Lush. Interview with Jakup Azemi (author), 21 April 2017.

Gjergji, Rexhep. Interview with Jakup Azemi (author), 6 September 2018; supplementary interview on 13 November 2020.

Hamiti, Muhamet. Interview with Jakup Azemi (author), 15 June 2017.

Haxhiaj, Rifat. Interview with Jakup Azemi (author), 17 November 2020; supplementary interview on 4 March 2021.

Hyseni, Skender. Interview with Jakup Azemi (author), 06 August 2021.

Ibishi, Ismet. Interview with Jakup Azemi (author), 25 September 2024.

Kajtazi, Lirije. Interview with Jakup Azemi (author), 28 November 2022.

Kelmendi, Ibrahim. Interview with Jakup Azemi (author), 21 January 2021.

Kiçmari, Sabri. Interview with Jakup Azemi (author), 27 November 2020.

Kolaj, Anton. Interview with Jakup Azemi (author), 28 March 2024.

Krasniqi, Milazim. Interview with Jakup Azemi (author), 22 March 2017.

Latifi, Shaip. Interview with Jakup Azemi (author), 6 July 2020.

Mjeku, Bajram. Interview with Jakup Azemi (author), 31 October 2017.

Mustafa, Rrustem. Interview with Jakup Azemi (author), 14 January 2021.

Ramajli, Ilaz. Interview with Jakup Azemi (author), Prishtinë, 24 March 2017.

Repishti, Sami. Interviews with Jakup Azemi (author), 8 June 2021; 13 June 2021; 14 June 2021.

Shala, Blerim. Interview with Jakup Azemi (author), 23 August 2021.

Shatri, Xhafer. Interview with Jakup Azemi (author), 13 June 2020.

Tahiri, Edita. Interview with Jakup Azemi (author), 26 March 2018.

Tahiri, Ramush. Interview with Jakup Azemi (author), 27 May 2017.

Zejnullahu, Jusuf. Interview. *Fjala e Lirë* (2014–15), www.fjala.info/arkiv/fjala4, Fondi i Republikës së Kosovës ishte projekt i qeverisë së Kosovës, interview conducted by Xhafer Leci.

Zogaj, Skënder. Interview with Jakup Azemi (author), 28 April 2018 and supplementary interview on 6 July 2020.

Newspapers

Baumont, Peter and Patrick Wintour. 'Milošević and Operation Horseshoe'. *Guardian*, 18 July 1999, https://www.theguardian.com/world/1999/jul/18/balkans8 (accessed 24 March 2024).

Dr Rugova, 'Kurë ka ra kushtrimi n' Kosovë' ma kujton Simfoninë e Nëntë të Bethovenit. Excerpts from an initerview published in 'Bota Sot', 27 November 2002. In *Priseidenca e Kosovës*, 168–9.

'300,000 Albanians Pour into Streets to Welcome Baker'. *New York Times*, 23 June 1991.

Archived sources

Amnesty International Annual Report 1985, Yugoslavia, 299–300, 1 May 1985, Index Number: POL 10/0002/1985.

Amnesty International Annual Report 1986, Yugoslavia, 317–18, 1 January 1986, Index Number: POL 10/0003/1986.

CRS Report for Congress, 'Kosovo Conflict Chronology: September 1998 – March 1999'. 6 April 1999.

Helsinki Watch, *Yugoslavia: Crisis in Kosovo: A Report from Helsinki Watch and the International Helsinki Federation for Human Rights* (New York: Helsinki Watch, a Division of Human Rights Watch, March 1990).

Helsinki Watch, *Yugoslavia: Human Rights Abuses in Kosovo 1990–1992* (New York: Helsinki Watch, a Division of Human Rights Watch, October 1992).

Interim Agreement for Peace and Self-Government in Kosovo (Rambouillet Accords), https://peacemaker.un.org/sites/peacemaker.un.org/files/990123_RambouilletAccord.pdf (accessed 27 July 2021).

The archive of Qendra e Informimit të Kosovës (QIK), Informatori

Informatori no. 21, Prishtinë (18 September 1992).

Informatori no. 220, Prishtinë (22 September 1992).

Informatori no. 223, Prishtinë (25 September 1992).

Informatori no. 256 Prishtinë (28 October 1992).

Informatori no. 257, Prishtinë (29 October 1992).

Informatori ditor no. 348, Prishtinë (16 February 1993).

Informatori no. 632, Prishtinë (15 January 1994).

Informatori no. 1879, Prishtinë (5 November 1997).

Informatori no. 1881, Prishtinë (7 November 1997).

Informatori no. 2073 G, Prishtinë (29 May 1998).

Index